WAR AND CHIVALRY

WAR AND CHIVALRY

Warfare and Aristocratic Culture in England, France and Burgundy
at the End of the Middle Ages

Malcolm Vale

The University of Georgia Press
Athens, Georgia

The University of Georgia Press
Athens, Georgia 30602

Printed in Great Britain

Library of Congress Cataloging in Publication Data
Vale, M.G.A. (Malcolm Graham Allan).
    War and chivalry.
    Bibliography: p.
    Includes index.
    1. Military art and science—England—History.
    2. Military art and science—France—History.
    3. Military art and science—France—Burgundy—History.
    4. Chivalry.   5. Great Britain—History,
Military—Medieval period, 1066–1485.
    6. France—History, Military—1328–1589.
    7. Burgundy (France)—History, Military.
    I. Title.
U43.G7V34   1981   355′.00942   81-3046
ISBN 0-8203-0571-5   AACR2

Photoset in Great Britain by
Specialised Offset Services Limited, Liverpool
and printed by
Page Bros. (Norwich) Ltd., Norwich

Contents

Acknowledgments

To the Bibliothèque Nationale, Paris, for plates 1, 2, 5, 6, 7; the Bibliothèque Royale, Brussels, for plate 4; the Bodleian Library, Oxford, for plates 8, 9, 11, 12, 27, 28 and end-papers; the Musées Royaux des Beaux-Arts de Belgique for plate 13; the Metropolitan Museum of Art, New York, for plate 10; the Wallace Collection, London, for plates 14, 16, 17, 18, 19, 20, 24, 25; the Musée de l'Armée, Paris, for plates 15, 21, 22, 23; the British Library, London, for plate 29; the Ashmolean Museum, Oxford, for plate 26.

Illustrations

Abbreviations

AB	*Annales de Bourgogne*
ADN	Archives Départmentales du Département du Nord
AHG	*Archives Historiques du Département de la Gironde*
AM	*Annales du Midi*
AMB	*Archives Municipales de Bordeaux*
AML	Archives Municipales de Lille
AOGV	Archiv des Ordens vom Goldenen Vliesse
BEC	*Bibliothèque de l'Ecole des Chartes*
BHR	*Bibliothèque d'Humanisme et de la Renaissance*
BIHR	*Bulletin of the Institute of Historical Research*
BL	British Library
BN	Bibliothèque Nationale, Paris
BR	Bibliothèque Royale, Brussels
EETS	*Early English Text Society*
EHR	*English Historical Review*
JWCI	*Journal of the Warburg and Courtauld Institutes*
MA	*Le Moyen Age*
PCEEBM	*Publications du Centre Européen des Etudes Burgundo-Medianes*
PRO	Public Record Office
RH	*Revue Historique*
RIHM	*Revue Internationale d'Histoire Militaire*
RS	*Rolls Series*
SHF	*Société de l'Histoire de France*

Preface

I have incurred many debts whilst working upon this book. My gratitude may first of all be expressed for the generosity with which the British Academy granted me an award without which research in French and Belgian archives and libraries would have been impossible. I am also glad to take this opportunity of thanking the History Department at the University of York for assistance with research expenses and for the sabbatical term which gave me time to write; and the Institut d'Histoire at the Université de Bordeaux III for inviting me to deliver papers there which formed the themes of two chapters. I am much indebted to Liverpool University Press for kind permission to adapt and reproduce material which previously appeared in my essay 'New Techniques and Old Ideals: the Impact of Artillery on War and Chivalry at the end of the Hundred Years War' in *War, Literature and Politics in the late Middle Ages* (1976), ed. C.T. Allmand. The staffs of those archives and libraries listed in my Bibliography of Primary Sources have all made my work very much less difficult than it might have been. I am especially indebted to the staff of the British Library, the Bodleian Library, the J.B. Morell Library (University of York) and the Brotherton Library (University of Leeds) for sustained help on a regular basis.

It is an especial pleasure to record my indebtedness to all those who have answered my questions, made helpful suggestions and generously brought material to my notice. Among then, I am particularly conscious of what is owed to Dr C.T. Allmand, Mr C.A.J. Armstrong, Mr Claude Blair, the late Dr L.M.J. Delaissé, Mr David Harding, Dr M.C.E. Jones, Dr M.H. Keen, Mr P.S. Lewis, Dr M.E. Mallett, Mr Christopher Page, and Dr A.R. Williams. The members of the History Department and the Centre for Medieval Studies at the University of York between 1970 and 1978 provided valuable reactions to some of the ideas which I have tried to develop here.

Since the book went to press, Professor Philippe Contamine has published a volume in the *Nouvelle Clio* series, entitled *La Guerre au Moyen Age* (Paris, 1980). It unfortunately appeared at too late a stage for his views to be taken into account. Although our approaches are necessarily different, his general conclusion (p. 485) that 'entre la guerre médiévale et celle des Temps modernes, pas de solution de continuité, mais au contraire un passage progressif, de lentes mutations, tant au niveau de la pratique qu'à celui des mentalités' is broadly shared by this book.

St John's College, Oxford   M.V.

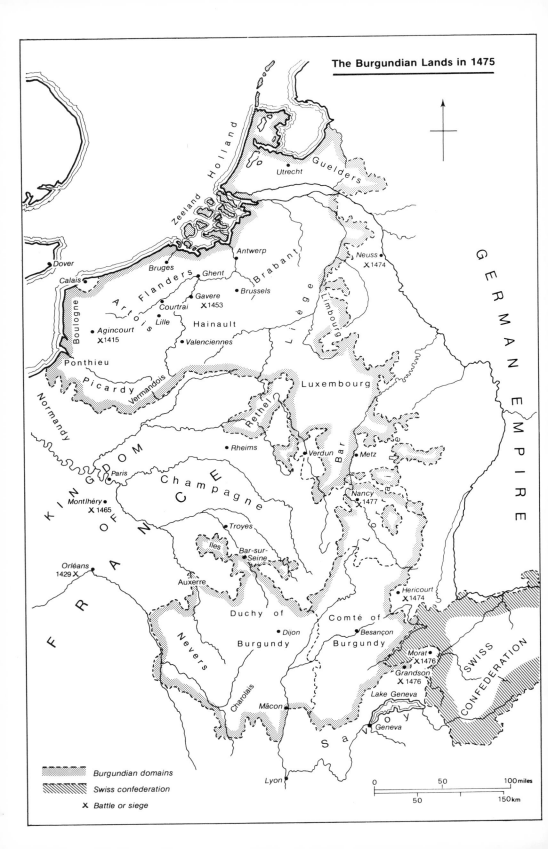

The Burgundian Lands in 1475

Holland

Zeeland

Guelders

Utrecht

Dover

Bruges

Antwerp

Neuss
X 1474

Calais

Ghent

Brabant

Flanders

Brussels

Boulogne

Artois

Gavere
X 1453

Courtrai

Lille

Hainault

Liège

Limbourg

Agincourt
X 1415

Valenciennes

GERMAN EMPIRE

Ponthieu

Picardy

Vermandois

Luxembourg

Normandy

Rethel

Rheims

Verdun

Bar

Metz

KINGDOM OF FRANCE

Paris

Champagne

Montlhéry
X 1465

Nancy
X 1477

Troyes

Iles

Bar-sur-Seine

Orléans
1429 X

Auxerre

Hericourt
X 1474

Nevers

Duchy of

Burgundy

Dijon

Comté of

Besançon

Burgundy

SWISS

Morat
X 1476

Grandson
X 1476

CONFEDERATION

Charolais

Mâcon

Savoy

Lake Geneva

Geneva

Lyon

Burgundian domains

Swiss confederation

X Battle or siege

0   50   100 miles

0   50   150 km

Introduction: the views of Johan Huizinga

The cult of chivalry in the Middle Ages is not a subject that lends itself easily to analysis. It is a vague and imprecise topic, which lacks strict boundaries and overlaps the territories of the political, military and cultural historian. Ideas are always among the most nebulous agents in the historical process, and their exact influence upon the practical conduct of affairs is notoriously difficult to assess. There is too much that can never be known about the motives which have led men to wage war, and to adopt (or to reject) certain codes of behaviour towards both their comrades and their enemies. Yet there can be no doubt that the ideal qualities of chivalry – honour, loyalty, courage, generosity – have fulfilled a fundamental human need, felt especially among warrior élites whose social function has been to fight. Chivalry was often no more, and no less, than the sentiment of honour in its medieval guise. That sentiment has been confined neither to the Middle Ages, nor to Western Europe, and is found in Ancient, Asiatic, African and Oriental civilisations. Among warrior classes, it possesses a universal and, perhaps, an eternal validity.

My purpose in this book is limited, however, to a consideration of some aspects of the relationship between the chivalric ideals of honour and virtue and their expression in war, politics and ceremony during the fifteenth century. It was in the course of warfare that those ideals were most frequently displayed, disregarded or put to the test. Warfare was endemic in the fifteenth century, and the effective ending of the Hundred Years War in 1453 gave no real or prolonged respite from armed conflicts to England, France or the Burgundian lands. At this time of wars between and within states, elevated ideas of a Crusade against the infidel Turks stood little chance of realisation. This relative lack of crusading zeal among the chivalrous classes, whose task it was to defend Western Christendom, has led historians to see fifteenth-century chivalry as the decadent and degenerate offspring of a pure and rigorous code. The classic expression of such a view is to be found in the works of the great Dutch historian Johan Huizinga (1872-1945). To understand his ideas it is essential to attempt to place them in the context of his own intellectual development. Only then can their originality, and the influences which contributed to their inception, be fully appreciated.

Huizinga's masterpiece, *The Waning of the Middle Ages* (1919), formulated an orthodoxy which has gradually found its way into virtually every area of the study of the fourteenth and fifteenth centuries.[1] The seven editions of the book which appeared between 1919 and 1950, and its translation into eight languages, have ensured the widest possible diffusion of his ideas.[2] He commented modestly in an autobiographical essay that 'the scope of my bibliography is unlikely to be awe-inspiring',[3] but such reticence must be set against the eight volumes of *Collected Works* and the profound influence which *The Waning of the Middle Ages* has exerted over other minds. Huizinga's arguments were taken further by R.L. Kilgour's *The Decline of Chivalry as shown in the French Literature of the Late Middle Ages* (1937) and A.B. Ferguson's *The Indian Summer of English Chivalry: Studies in the Decline and Transformation of Chivalric Idealism* (1960), in which his premises are unhesitatingly accepted. Their echoes can still be heard, transmitted to a wider audience, in general textbooks or exhibition catalogues[4] which describe the Burgundian court of the fifteenth century in terms of its 'sumptuous tournaments and pageants, the gorgeous trappings of an obsolete chivalry, in which the nobility and the wealthy delighted'.[5] *The Waning of the Middle Ages* still casts its spell.

The origins of Huizinga's analysis of the significance of chivalry in fourteenth- and fifteenth-century culture are not hard to find. They are suggested in his own account of his development as a historian which he wrote, but did not publish, towards the end of his life.[6] His view of chivalry forms merely one aspect of a more general thesis about later medieval civilisation. Its genesis is therefore worth investigating. Huizinga's movement away from the

1. Unless otherwise stated, references are to the English edition: J. Huizinga, *The Waning of the Middle Ages*, trans. F. Hopman (Harmondsworth 1965). See also 'La valeur politique et militaire des idées de chevalerie à la fin du Moyen Age', *Revue d'histoire diplomatique*, xxv (1921), pp. 126-38, repr. J. Huizinga, *Verzamelde Werken*, iii (Haarlem 1953), pp. 519-30, trans. 'The political and military significance of chivalric ideas in the late Middle Ages', *Men and Ideas*, ed. J.S. Holmes, H. van Marle (London 1960), pp. 196-206; 'La physionomie morale de Philippe le Bon', *Annales de Bourgogne*, iv (1932), pp. 101-39, repr. *Verzamelde Werken*, ii (Haarlem 1948) pp. 216-37; and *Homo Ludens* (London, 1949, repr. 1970), with introduction by G. Steiner.

2. For a discussion of the reception and influence of *The Waning of the Middle Ages* see F.W.N. Hugenholtz, 'The fame of a masterwork', *Johan Huizinga, 1872-1945: Papers delivered to the Johan Huizinga conference, Groningen, 11-15 Dec. 1972*, ed. W.R.H. Koops, E.H. Kossmann, G. van der Plaat (The Hague 1973), pp. 91-103.

3. J. Huizinga, 'My path to history', *Dutch Civilisation in the Seventeenth Century and Other Essays*, ed. P. Geyl, F.W.N. Hugenholtz (London 1968), pp. 244-76 (first published posthumously in 1947).

4. *William Caxton: an exhibition to commemorate the quincentenary of the introduction of printing into England*, (British Library, London 1976), p. 23. See also R.L. Kilgour, *The Decline of Chivalry as shown in the French literature of the late Middle Ages* (Cambridge, Mass., 1937); A.B. Ferguson, *The Indian summer of English chivalry* (Durham, North Carolina 1960). I am indebted to Dr M.H. Keen for allowing me to see a copy of his paper, 'Huizinga, Kilgour and the decline of chivalry' which criticises these views and offers some convincing alternative hypotheses. This has since been published in *Medievalia et Humanistica*, vii (1977), pp. 1-20.

5. Cf. e.g. for the dukes of Burgundy and 'their gluttonous, chivalric magnificence' and a description of 1350-1450 as 'that period of contraction and reaction, of deadening clericalism and vain social revolt', H.R. Trevor-Roper, *The Rise of Christian Europe* (London 1965), pp. 32, 180-1.

6. *Supra*, n. 3.

philological and anthropological studies of Indian and Oriental culture in which he had been trained towards medieval history was, he tells us, 'fed mainly on artistic notions and greatly reinforced by the Bruges exhibition of Old Dutch paintings in the summer of 1902'.[7] Here were gathered together more than four hundred Flemish paintings from the fifteenth and sixteenth centuries in the Hôtel Gruthuyse at Bruges, and Professor Pieter Geyl later maintained that this was the decisive moment in Huizinga's career: 'Life styled in art – that touched him in his inmost being.'[8] What fascinated him most about later medieval culture was its unity. His Hegelian background led him, perhaps unconsciously, to see the 'forms of life, thought and art' as expressions of a 'spirit' which 'unites all the cultural products of an age and makes them homogeneous'.[9] Late Gothic styles in the arts, a prolix and outworn scholasticism, an outworn, though still influential, cult of chivalry, and a superabundance of images in religious life and thought – all emanated from the same 'spirit', a spirit which Huizinga considered 'decadent'. Images, in both religious and secular thought, had become confused with reality and the chasm between illusion (or delusion) and the actual nature of the world became consequently wider.[10] During a walk which he took in the countryside round Groningen, probably in 1907, he was struck by the thought that 'the late Middle Ages were not so much the prelude to the future [that is, the Renaissance] as an epoch of fading and decay'.[11] The Bruges exhibition of 1902 had stimulated him to look afresh at that period and here was the genesis of his view, not merely of chivalry, but of Franco-Burgundian culture as a whole. This view, he wrote in the Preface to *The Waning of the Middle Ages*, was formed 'whilst endeavouring to arrive at a genuine understanding of the art of the brothers Van Eyck and their contemporaries ... to grasp its meaning by seeing it in connexion with the entire life of their times'.[12] His Hegelianism gave him a sketch-map of this uncertain terrain. If he could explain the stylistically homogeneous, highly realistic and detailed painting of the age by what he knew of the other aspects of his chosen period, his task would be accomplished. A Hegelian *Zeitgeist* haunts his masterpiece – a 'spirit of the age' which constantly refers back to the medieval past, not to the Renaissance individualism which he knew from the work of his predecessor, Jakob Burckhardt.[13]

For Huizinga, the cult of chivalry in the later Middle Ages evoked responses

---

7. 'My path to history', pp. 266-7. For the scope and composition of the exhibition see *Exposition des primitifs flamands et d'art ancien: Bruges, 1ère section; Tableaux*, ed. W.H.J. Weale (Bruges 1902).

8. P. Geyl, 'Huizinga as accuser of his age', *Encounters in History* (2nd ed., London 1967), p. 207.

9. J. Huizinga, 'The task of cultural history', *Men and Ideas*, p. 76. For a discussion of Huizinga's Hegelianism see E.H. Gombrich, *In Search of Cultural History* (Oxford 1969), pp. 29-32.

10. *The Waning of the Middle Ages*, pp. 147-8, 206-11, 251-2.

11. 'My path to history', pp. 272-3.

12. *The Waning of the Middle Ages*, p. 7.

13. H.R. Guggisberg, 'Burckhardt und Huizinga', *Johan Huizinga, 1872-1945*, pp. 155-74.

of an aesthetic and emotional kind. His 'first contact with history', he wrote, took place during his boyhood when he witnessed a pageant re-enacting the triumphal entry of Edzard, count of Holland, into Groningen in 1506.[14] The banners, plumes and gleaming armour made a profound impression upon him, and this early experience lay, it seems, at the root of many of his later ideas. The visual stimulus given by such episodes, and by the Bruges exhibition, to a fertile historical imagination led him to entitle his inaugural lecture of November 1905 'The Aesthetic Element in Historical Thought'. In this remarkable address he spoke of the value of visualisation to the historian. He must 'conjure up living pictures in the private theatre of the mind'.[15] His picture of medieval chivalry was, on the face of it, an essentially Romantic one. In *The Waning of the Middle Ages* he observed that 'Romanticism was inclined to identify the Middle Ages with the age of chivalry. It saw there mostly helmets with nodding plumes'[16] – just as he himself had seen them in the procession at Groningen in 1878. 'However paradoxical this may sound today,' he continued, 'to a certain extent it was right in doing so.'[17] He began from the premise that chivalry was a beneficial force in European history because it offered a touchstone of virtue to those who practised it. In 1831, Sir Walter Scott had written:

> The spirit of chivalry had in it this point of excellence, that, however overstrained and fantastic many of its doctrines may appear to us, they were founded on generosity and self-denial, of which, if the earth were deprived, it would be difficult to conceive the existence of virtue among the human race ...[18]

Chivalry was therefore an ideal, to which men might aspire, but never attain, because what Scott called the 'extravagant and exclusive principles of honour and virtue' were 'cast in a mould of perfection too lofty for the practice of fallible beings'.[19] Huizinga took up this view and concluded:

> Chivalry would never have been the ideal of life during several centuries if it had not contained high social values. Its strength lay in the very exaggeration of its generous and fantastic views. The soul of the Middle Ages, ferocious and passionate, could only be led by placing far too high the ideal towards which its aspirations should tend. Thus acted the Church, thus also feudal thought ... That reality has constantly given the lie to these high illusions of a pure and noble social

14. 'My path to history', pp. 244-5. For a discussion of the episode see E.H. Gombrich, 'Huizinga's *Homo Ludens*', *Johan Huizinga, 1872-1945*, p. 137.

15. 'The aesthetic element in historical thought', *Dutch Civilisation*, p. 237. The influence of Symbolist thought and of the intellectual movements of the 1890s is evident here and in the statement that the historian's task is to 'help the reader's imagination to conjure up a vision that goes far beyond the precise meaning of the written words' (ibid., p. 230).

16. The passage is considerably altered in the English translation: see *The Waning of the Middle Ages*, p. 54; Gombrich, op. cit., p. 139 and n. 8.

17. Ibid., p. 139.

18. Sir Walter Scott, *Quentin Durward*, 2 vols (Edinburgh 1831), p. iv.

19. Ibid., p. viii.

life, who would deny? But where would we be, if our thoughts had never trans-
cended the exact limits of the feasible?[20]

Yet, for Huizinga, the gulf between such idealism and the brutal facts of war,
politics and social life had never been greater than during the fourteenth and
fifteenth centuries. Chivalry, like other aspects of the age, had reached its
autumnal phase, and was in decline. As a guide to social behaviour and as an
ethical code it had outlived its value, and even in warfare 'tactics had long since
given up all thought of conforming to its rules'.[21] A sceptic might retort: had
they ever done so? Yet the implied contrast between idealism and reality is an
essential part of Huizinga's thesis, because that thesis was built upon a dialectic
of Hegelian origins.

In a lecture given in 1921, Huizinga commented on the lack of attention given
to chivalry by the historians of his time. 'Combing the records,' he said 'in
which chivalry is, indeed, little mentioned, they have succeeded in presenting a
picture of the Middle Ages in which economic and social points of view are so
dominant that one tends at times to forget, that, next to religion, chivalry was
the strongest of the ideas that filled the minds and hearts of those men of
another age.'[22] Until very recently, historians, as opposed to students of
literature, have done little to change this state of affairs.[23] Current vogues in
historical research have led to the preponderance of 'economic and social points
of view' to a degree of which Huizinga scarcely dreamt in 1921. Studies of the
later medieval nobility have, on the whole, confined themselves to analysis of
the political behaviour, economic position and social structure of their chosen
subjects without reference to ideas of chivalry.[24] Recent work on later medieval
war has, with some notable exceptions, dealt primarily with military
organisation, and with the more concrete manifestations of social and economic
distress occasioned by warfare.[25] The presentation of evidence for the
devastation, dislocation and material damage caused by war has merely served
to reinforce the historian's scepticism – if not cynicism – about the function of
chivalry in the later Middle Ages. This, it might be argued, is to misunder-

20. *The Waning of the Middle Ages*, p. 103.
21. Ibid., p. 100. This statement was somewhat qualified in his lecture of 1921 on 'The political
and military significance of chivalric ideas': see *Men and Ideas*, pp. 202-3.
22. Ibid., p. 197; also *The Waning of the Middle Ages*, p. 54.
23. For a recent attempt to stress the importance of chivalrous ideas as an influence on the
military and social behaviour of later medieval nobles see J. Barnie, *War in Medieval Society: Social
Values and the Hundred Years War, 1337-99* (London 1974), ch. 3, pp. 56-96.
24. Among the most distinguished examples are R. Boutruche, *La Crise d'une Société: Seigneurs et
Paysans du Bordelais pendant la Guerre de Cent Ans* (2nd ed., Strasbourg 1963); K.B. McFarlane, *The
Nobility of Later Medieval England* (Oxford 1973); P. Contamine (ed.), *La Noblesse au Moyen Age* (Paris
1976).
25. See e.g. H.J. Hewitt, *The Organisation of War under Edward III, 1338-62* (Manchester 1966); P.
Contamine, *Guerre, Etat et Société à la Fin du Moyen Age: Etudes sur les Armées des Rois de France, 1337-1494*
(Paris-The Hague 1972); M.E. Mallett, *Mercenaries and their Masters: Warfare in Renaissance Italy*
(London 1974).

stand the nature of war and chivalry. Much has been written about the horrors
of war, about the laudable attempts of peace-makers and the writers of 'war-
criticism' to prevent and resolve conflicts and about the miseries inflicted by
those who fought wars upon those who tilled the soil and provided that peasant
surplus which, through taxation, enabled wars to be fought.[26] The underdogs
and the rebels command the historian's sympathy. Yet this sympathy, if his
picture is not to be a distorted one, must be less exclusive: without some understanding of the behaviour of the 'chivalrous' classes, for whom war was a
profession, even a vocation, there is always a risk that the later Middle Ages
may be judged by twentieth-century standards.

Although from a totally different viewpoint, recent studies of later medieval
society – of popular revolts, popular heresy, criminality and the effects of
warfare and disease – have done little to modify Huizinga's conclusions about
the poor and disagreeable quality of life during the period. In his vivid and
intentionally dramatic description of the violent contrasts and extremes to
which later medieval men were subject, he wrote:

> Bad government, exactions, the cupidity and violence of the great, wars and
> brigandage, scarcity, misery and pestilence – to this is contemporary history
> nearly reduced in the eyes of the people. The feeling of general insecurity which
> was caused by the chronic form wars were apt to take, by the constant menace of
> the dangerous classes, by the mistrust of justice, was further aggravated by the
> obsession of the coming end of the world, and by the fear of hell, of sorcerers, and
> of devils ...[27]

Beside such pictures of dislocation and distress, the Romantic view of the
Middle Ages as the age of chivalry would appear to cut a sorry figure. Even in
warfare, where one might expect chivalric ideals to have exercised some
moderating influence on mens' violent instincts, M.H. Keen has recently
concluded that:

> chivalry, with its idealisation of the freelance fighting man, could not be a force
> effective in limiting the horrors of war: by prompting men to seek wars and
> praising those who did so, its tendency, for all its idealism and because of it, was
> rather to help make those horrors endemic.[28]

---

26. See E. Miller, *War in the North* (Hull 1960); R. Boutruche, 'La dévastation des campagnes
pendant la Guerre de Cent Ans et la reconstruction agricole de la France', *Mélanges 1945: III. Etudes
historiques* (Paris 1947), pp. 127-63; C.T. Allmand, 'The aftermath of war in fifteenth-century
France', *History*, lxi (1976), pp. 344-67; G. Bois, *Crise du Féodalisme* (Paris 1976) esp. pp. 251-308;
J.J.N. Palmer, *England, France and Christendom, 1377-99* (London 1972); Barnie, op. cit., esp. pp. 117-
38; R.H. Hilton, 'Y eut-il une crise générale de la féodalité?', *Annales*, (1951), pp. 23-30 and *The
English Peasantry in the Later Middle Ages* (Oxford 1975).
27. *The Waning of the Middle Ages*, p. 28.
28. M.H. Keen, 'Chivalry, nobility and the man-at-arms', *War, Literature and Politics in the Late
Middle Ages*, ed. C.T. Allmand (Liverpool 1976), p. 45.

Plate 1. St Maurice, from a Latin *Life of St Maurice* (1453). Paris, Bibliothèque de l'Arsenal, MS 940, fo. 34v.

One of the central tenets of Huizinga's thesis has thus come under attack.

Huizinga was concerned throughout his published work with the problems of control over the more violent impulses in human nature, whether in the fifteenth or the twentieth century. Understandably, that concern became all the greater towards the end of his life. Whether human conflict took the form of open warfare regulated by conventions, as in the later Middle Ages, or 'the systematic undermining of the social order through class struggle and class antagonism',[29] as in his own time, the difficulties of containing and restraining overt and latent violence disturbed him deeply. In the later Middle Ages, he wrote, 'all emotions required a rigid system of conventional forms, for without them passion and ferocity would have made havoc of life'.[30] By 1938 his stress on the importance of 'limiting rules' was firmly applied to the conduct and practice of war: 'fighting, as a cultural function, always presupposes limiting rules, and requires, to a certain extent anyway, the recognition of its play-quality'.[31] War, to possess any 'cultural function', had to be waged between opponents who regarded each other 'as equals or antagonists with equal rights'.[32] This was the condition, he argued, of medieval warfare. The kind of conventions taught in military academies since the eighteenth century were inculcated, in the later Middle Ages, by a chivalrous education and training. The laws of war – to Huizinga, the precursors of the law of nations – attempted to enforce those conventions, and, as far as possible, to moderate and restrict the excesses to which war gave rise. Chivalry thus played a vital part in the development of international law, with its rules about the treatment of prisoners, the granting of safe-conducts and immunities, the conduct of battles and sieges, and the limitation of military engagements to time and place. Beside the formal codes and ordinances of war, moreover, lay the dynamic force contained in the notion of honour. This, wrote Huizinga, was a social force 'likely to abate or even to overcome natural instincts'.[33] Inculcated by a noble education, the sentiment of honour – and fear of dishonour – could act as a check upon the unbridled release of violence in warfare, a process which has been called 'essentially chaotic and instinctive'.[34] The positive contribution of chivalry to civilisation was set out by Huizinga in *Homo Ludens*, when he observed:

> Even if it were no more than a fiction, these fancies of war as a noble game of
> honour and virtue have still played an important part in developing civilisation,

29. J. Huizinga, *In the Shadow of Tomorrow* (London 1936), p. 17.

30. *The Waning of the Middle Ages*, p. 48.

31. *Homo Ludens*, p. 110.

32. Ibid., pp. 110-11. War against heretics and heathens (presumably including Crusades) had, for Huizinga, no 'play-quality' nor 'cultural function' and could only be restrained by a mutual agreement by both sides 'for the sake of their own honour' (ibid., p. 111).

33. 'La physionomie morale de Philippe le Bon', p. 27.

34. J. Keegan, *The Face of Battle* (London 1976), p. 20.

for it is from them that the idea of chivalry sprang and hence, ultimately, of international law.[35]

How far such ideas of honour and virtue had any impact on the actual conduct of war remains to be more fully investigated. It has, however, been concluded that in one respect 'Huizinga was right: the chivalrous conceptions of honour and loyalty of an age when the idea of nationality was not fully understood prepared the way for the notion of a law of nations.'[36] This book will examine some of the ways in which these conceptions were expressed, whether in theory or practice, in the thick of battle, or in the political behaviour of the nobility. Huizinga was aware that changes were taking place in the conduct of war during the fifteenth century, and that concurrent changes might be expected in attitudes towards war and chivalry. 'The feudal knight,' he wrote, 'is merging into the soldier of modern times; the universal and religious ideal is becoming national and military.'[37] The issues raised here have not been developed. In the course of the fifteenth century the establishment of standing armies and the rise of the Swiss, as well as the increasing sophistication of artillery, had marked effects on the conduct and organisation of war. If chivalry could further rather than restrain the distress and disorder caused by war, then, it has been argued, one remedy lay in 'a new concept of the rôle of the man-at-arms and indeed of nobility ... as the state's servant, not called to seek wars by birth and vocation, but licensed to fight them by his sovereign'.[38] It remains to be seen how far this process had gone by the end of the fifteenth century and how far it was able to solve the problems which had allegedly defeated chivalry.

Huizinga's analysis of the place of chivalry in later medieval politics, culture and society has also been called into question. If 'the ultimate vindication of honour lies in physical violence'[39] then one cannot argue (as Huizinga did) that chivalry promoted moderation. Wars, as well as duels and judicial combats, could be fought over the ostensible issue of honour, and, as Huizinga himself pointed out 'when blood flows, honour is satisfied'.[40] There is therefore an inherent contradiction in this aspect of his thesis. On the one hand, chivalry is seen as a means whereby limiting rules were imposed on later medieval warfare;

35. *Homo Ludens*, p. 117.
36. M.H. Keen, *The Laws of War in the Late Middle Ages* (London 1965), p. 247. The precise extent to which ideas of chivalry contributed to the development of 'laws of war', in the modern sense, rather than to the medieval 'law of arms' has recently been questioned: N.A.R. Wright, '*The Tree of Battles* of Honoré Bouvet [Bonet] and the Laws of War', *War, Literature and Politics*, pp. 12-31, esp. pp. 20-3. Huizinga himself was sceptical of the value of any legal system of regulating the conduct of warfare: 'If a little clemency was slowly introduced into political and military practices, it was as a result rather of the sentiment of honour than of legal and moral convictions.' *Men and Ideas*, p. 205. It is with the notion of honour and its expression that I shall be largely concerned.
37. *The Waning of the Middle Ages*, p. 73.
38. Keen, 'Chivalry, nobility and the man-at-arms', p. 45.
39. J. Pitt-Rivers, 'Honour and social status', *Honour and Shame: the Values of Mediterranean Society*, ed. J.G. Peristiany (London 1965), p. 29.
40. *Homo Ludens*, p. 116.

on the other, it permitted and justified the exercise of violence in the prosecution and avenging of essentially private quarrels. Such feuds could lead to wars between both nobles and sovereign princes, and the difficulty of drawing a line between a private quarrel and a public war was an acute one.[41]

There is one other aspect of chivalry which, to Huizinga, possessed some value at the end of the Middle Ages. His vivid picture of the harsh realities of life was intended to impress upon the reader the necessity of finding a means of escape from such misery. For the later medieval nobility that means lay in 'the way of dream and illusion'.[42] Chivalry was not only an ethic, a code of behaviour and an institution, it was a 'collective dream'.[43] His thesis of the 'play-element of culture' came into its own in this notion. Life was not only styled in art, but in literature. Hence the chronicles, in which literary methods, preoccupations and techniques are used to relate factual events, were rehabilitated by Huizinga in the face of considerable opposition from the historians of his time.[44] The value of documentary sources to the exclusion of others had, he believed, been overestimated. 'For the history of civilisation,' he wrote, 'every delusion or opinion of an epoch has the value of an important fact.'[45] It was in the chivalric chronicles that those delusions and opinions were to be found and his exploitation of Froissart, Monstrelet, Olivier de la Marche and Chastellain was a logical extension of this view. 'In the fifteenth century,' he continued 'chivalry was still, after religion, the strongest of all the ethical conceptions which dominated the mind and the heart.'[46] The shortcomings of later medieval religious life have often been set out;[47] the extent to which the chivalrous classes – nobles and knights – fell short of the mark remains to be considered. If standards of behaviour in war were changing as war changed, then the rôle of chivalry itself must be reassessed.

Much of Huizinga's treatment of war and chivalry derived its evidence and inspiration from the writings of the chroniclers and from such theoretical literature as Honoré Bovet's *Arbre des Batailles* and Christine de Pisan's *Livre des Fais d'Armes et de Chevalerie*. How far such works corresponded to reality in the fourteenth and fifteenth centuries has been the subject of recent debate.[48] In this

41. Keen, *The Laws of War*, pp. 63-81.

42. Gombrich, op. cit., p. 139; also *The Waning of the Middle Ages*, p. 81.

43. Gombrich, op. cit., p. 139. For the 'play-element' in medieval culture see (most recently) D.A. Bullough, 'Games people played: drama and ritual as propaganda in medieval Europe', *TRHS* 5th ser., xxiv (1974), pp. 92-122.

44. Hugenholtz, 'The fame of a masterwork', pp. 96-7.

45. *The Waning of the Middle Ages*, p. 55. The passage argues for something close to the *histoire des mentalités* practised (with a very different methodology) by the *Annales* school of French historians. The affinities between Huizinga's ideas and those of Lucien Febvre and Marc Bloch have been noted by Hugenholtz, art. cit., pp. 102-3 and A.G. Jongkees, 'Une génération d'historiens devant le phénomène bourguignon', *Johan Huizinga 1872-1945*, pp. 98-9.

46. *The Waning of the Middle Ages*, p. 55.

47. See e.g. M. Aston, *The Fifteenth Century: the Prospect of Europe* (London 1968), pp. 149-73.

48. Wright, art. cit., pp. 29-31.

Plate 2. Honoré Bovet's *Arbre des Batailles*, from a manuscript commissioned by Artur de Richemont, constable of France, in 1450. The illumination shows Charles VII of France flanked by his son, the Dauphin Louis, on the left, and by Richemont, the constable, on the right. Paris, Bibliothèque de l'Arsenal, MS 2695, fo. 6v.

book my concern is with the practice rather than the theory of war. The prescriptive literature of the period is often of little help in determining the practical reality of war. Here such sources as eye-witness accounts of battles, news-letters, account books and other financial records, and that increasingly common *genre*, the military memoir, have to be consulted. These were almost entirely neglected by Huizinga. Similarly, the more formal records of secular orders of chivalry, such as the *Toison d'Or* and the *Croissant*, were not exploited by him to any great extent. It is here that much of the influence of chivalrous ideas on war and politics is to be found. Fundamental questions, such as the precise function of the tournament, the effects of technical innovations on the conduct of war and attitudes towards it, and the degree to which changes in the nature and organisation of war were reflected in its external apparatus and insignia are still largely unanswered.[49] Institutional studies of military organisation too often tend to produce static pictures, in which armies are recruited, organised, paid, fed, disciplined and sociologically analysed – where, in short, they do everything but fight. It has been said that 'war ... is the institutional military historian's irritant'.[50] It upsets his neat categories and wreaks havoc upon his generalisations. This is not an institutional study and little will be found in it about the social origins of captains, the machinery of payment and provisioning, or the relations between soldiers and civilians. Its concern is with the relationship between ideas and behaviour among an élite for whom war was not only a profession but a justification for their social position and privileges.

49. For the latter, see Appendix XIII: 'Cris de guerre, drapeaux, uniformes', in Contamine, *Guerre, Etat et Société*, pp. 667-76.
    50. Keegan, op. cit., p. 29.

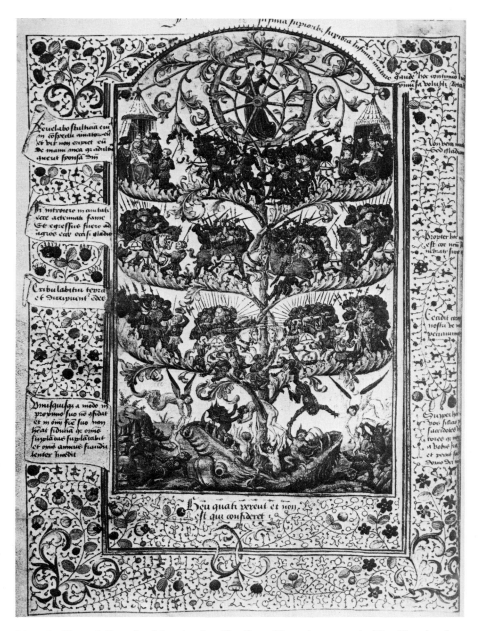

Plate 3. Honoré Bovet's *Arbre des Batailles* (late fifteenth century). The illumination shows the warring powers of Christendom. Chantilly, Musée Condé, MS Lat. 1561.

CHAPTER ONE

The Literature of Honour and Virtue

In ancient times ... when Rome ruled almost all the world, there were at Rome two temples: one called the temple of honour, and the other the temple of virtue; but the temple of honour was built and set up in such a way that no one could enter it who had not first passed through the temple of virtue. By reason of which, you should know and understand that no one, of whatever rank he may be, can attain honour without virtue.[1]

The fifteenth-century author of *L'Instruction d'un Jeune Prince* was in no doubt as to the relationship between the supreme chivalrous qualities of honour and virtue. Without virtue, honour was unattainable. To be honoured, a noble-man's conduct should be virtuous; whatever his rank and claim to social precedence, the yardstick of honour was behaviour rather than birth. His use of classical example reinforced this point, and drew the reader's attention to a contemporary debate about nobility of birth and nobility of virtue.[2] It is against this background that the didactic literature produced largely for the court of Burgundy in the fifteenth century may be viewed. That literature was soon to find its way to England in manuscript copies and through translations commissioned by William Caxton and others for English readers. As a result of the Anglo-Burgundian alliance which followed the marriage of Margaret of York and Charles the Bold of Burgundy in 1468, cultural contacts between England and the Burgundian lands increased. Edward IV's exile in the Low Countries (1470-1) strengthened these bonds, and his host, Louis de Bruges, lord of La Gruthuyse, came to act as Edward's cultural adviser. He was rewarded for his manifold services with the earldom of Winchester in 1472.[3]

---

1. Ghillebert de Lannoy, *Oeuvres*, ed. C.T. Potvin (Louvain 1878), p. 416. 'Et, ad ce propoz, l'en treuve que anciennement, ou temps que Rome seignourissoit presque sur tout le monde, avoit à Rome deux temples, l'un nommé le temple d'onneur et l'autre le temple de vertu; mais le temple d'onneur estoit ediffié et assis en telle manière que nul n'y povoit entrer que premiers ne passast par le temple de vertu. Pour quoy l'en doit sçavoir et entendre que nul, de quelque estat qu'il soit, sans vertu ne poeut parvenir à honneur.'

2. See C.C. Willard, 'The concept of true nobility at the Burgundian court', *Studies in the Renaissance*, xiv (1967), pp. 33-48.

3. J. Monfrin, 'Les traducteurs et leur public en France au Moyen Age', *L'Humanisme médiéval dans les littératures romanes du xiie au xive siècle* (Paris 1964), pp. 248-9; C.A.J. Armstrong, 'The court of Burgundy', *Courts of Europe, 1400-1700* ed. A.G. Dickens (London 1977), pp. 55-75; W. St. John Hope, 'On a grant of arms under the great seal of Edward IV to Louis de Bruges, seigneur de la Gruthuyse and earl of Winchester, 1472', *Archaeologia*, lvi (1898), pp. 27-38.

The courts of England and Burgundy therefore to some extent possessed a common literary culture, in which didactic works were especially popular. Ideas derived from Greek and Roman history merged with medieval precedents to form a corpus of writing concerned essentially with questions of individual reputation. Warfare was one area in which renown could be achieved: the fifteenth-century nobility were presented with certain notions of their rôle in both war and peace intended to influence the way in which they behaved. A literate nobility was thought to be open to persuasion – what they read was therefore designed to determine what they did.

Advice on what a nobleman should read was forthcoming from many quarters in the fifteenth century – from the Church, from private tutors and from a young noble's parents. In his *Enseignements Paternels* (*c.*1440), Ghillebert de Lannoy, noble by birth, counsellor of Philip the Good, and member of the Order of the Golden Fleece, summed up in a paragraph the value of literacy to those who sought honour.[4] He told his son:

> ... you should know that one should do nothing against honour, for life, death or money. Furthermore, truly believe that it is better to die honourably than to live censured and dishonoured in this mortal world. As for myself, my very dear son, I would prefer you to die gloriously in an honourable battle, with banner unfurled, than to return cravenly from it. Read Valerius Maximus, Tullius, Lucan, Orosius, Sallust, Justin and other *hystoriographes*, and you will find marvellous, honourable and innumerable examples of how our predecessors loved honour and the public weal, how they exposed themselves to death for the good of the land, and also of how they preserved their reputation with the discipline of *chevalerie*, and did not fear to put their own children to death when they sinned against their laws. And from this they gained great honour, and achieved so much by their good sense and noble conduct that it is of eternal memory. For stronger reasons, we who are Christians should wish even more to do honourable and virtuous deeds, and preserve ourselves from vile reproaches, than those Romans who believed that the soul died with the body.[5]

The pursuit of honour is here allied to the defence of the public weal, and severe rules of conduct derived from Roman history are applied to the present.

4. See J.H. Hexter, 'The education of the aristocracy in the Renaissance', *Reappraisals in History* (London 1961), p. 64.

5. Lannoy, op. cit., pp. 456-7: '... doiz sçavoir ... que on ne doit, pour mort, pour vie, pour chevance ne autrement, faire chose contre honneur. Et pourtant, saches tout de vray qu'il vault mieulx honnourablement mourir que vivre à reproche et à deshonneur en ce mortel monde. Quant est à moy, mon très chier filz, j'ameroie mieulx ta glorieuse mort en une honnourable bataille, à banière desployée, que tu te retournasses vilainement d'icelle. Regarde Vallerianus Maximus, Tulle, Lucain, Orose, Saluste, Justin et autres hystoriographes, et tu trouveras merveilles de telz exemples honnourables et sans nombre et comment nos devanciers amèrent honneur et le bien publicque, et aussy comment ilz se exposoient à mort pour le bien du pays, et aussy comment pour garder leur los avec discipline de chevalerie, et ne craignoient point de faire morir leurs enfans quant ilz transgressoient à l'encontre de leurs loix. Et de ce ilz acquéroient grant honneur, et firent tant par leur sens et bonne conduite qu'il en est mémoire perpétuele. Et par plus fortes raisons, nous quy sommes crestiens, devons plus désirer à faire choses honnourables et vertueuses et nous garder de vilaines reproches que eulx rommains qui cuidoient que l'âme morust ainsy comme le corps.'

Lannoy's choice of authorities is striking. His list includes no medieval writer, either of didactic treatises or romances. The sources of his historical exemplars of noble conduct – that is, of virtue – are drawn exclusively from antiquity. He had previously advised his son to read 'books of Roman histories or other chronicles of the deeds of the ancients' so that he should then behave honourably in all his worldly affairs.[6] The Romans had practised 'the discipline of *chevalerie*' and an anonymous treatise on the virtues echoed Lannoy by observing that the 'discipline of *chevalerie*, fiercely held and guarded, gave to the Roman empire the monarchy of the world'.[7] He who wished to gain honourable dominion and lordship should emulate the Romans. As honour was unattainable without virtue, so discipline was essential to chivalry. The deeds of the Romans exemplified that discipline, whatever discrepancies there were between their conduct of war and politics and that prevailing in the mid-fifteenth century. By that time, a wider range of classical learning was available to nobles than that contained in such earlier miscellanies as *Li Fais des Romains*.[8] It was available in French translations, and an examination of the contents of their libraries may demonstrate the extent to which such learning had penetrated their ranks.

In his essay 'The education of the aristocracy in the Renaissance', J.H. Hexter remarked: 'That we should find the earliest impetus towards education – clerkly bookish education – for the aristocracy among the nobles of Burgundy ... may come to us as a surprise. Historians have tended to see only archaism in the Burgundian revival.'[9] Previous work had tended to single out the recasting and elaborating of Carolingian epics and Arthurian prose romance as the major literary achievement of the court of Burgundy under Philip the Good (1419-67). This notion still informs recent work on the subject and Y. Lacaze can write that 'literary production under Charles the Bold (1467-77) was based more on ... didactic treatises than on the *mises en prose* of the preceding reign'.[10] Yet the movement towards translation of both classical

6. Ibid., p. 456: 'aulcuns livres des histoires rommaines ou aultres croniques des fais des anciens'.

7. BN, MS n.a. fr. 10,017, fo. 48v, 'discipline de chevalerie, aigrement tenue et gardee, enfanta a l'empire de Romme la monarchie du monde.'

8. See J. Monfrin, 'Le goût des lettres antiques à la cour de Bourgogne au xve siècle', *Bulletin de la Société Nationale des Antiquaires de France*, (1967), pp. 286-7; Y. Lacaze, 'Le rôle des traditions dans la genèse d'un sentiment national au xve siècle: la Bourgogne de Philippe le Bon', *BEC*, cxxix (1971), pp. 358-64. For *Li Fait des Romains*, a late thirteenth-century compilation, see L. Flutre, *Li Fait des Romains dans les littératures française et italienne du xiiie au xve siècle*, (Paris 1932); B. Guenée, 'La culture historique des nobles: le succès des *Faits des Romains* (xiie-xve siécles)', *La Noblesse au Moyen Age*, pp. 261-88.

9. Hexter, art. cit., p. 61.

10. Lacaze, art. cit., p. 364, n. 7. A decline of interest in Arthurian, but not Carolingian, romances at the court of Burgundy might be inferred from the fact that Louis de Bruges commissioned only one new Arthurian text for his large library (now BN, MS fr. 358-63). See C.E. Pickford, *L'Evolution du Roman Arthurien en Prose vers la fin du Moyen Age* (Paris, 1960), p. 279. Neither Charles the Bold, nor Anthoine, *grand bâtard* of Burgundy had Arthurian romances written for them (ibid., pp. 283-4).

and humanistic works had begun under Philip the Good. The work of Jean Miélot, canon of St Pierre at Lille, from 1449 onwards had brought the letters of Cicero and Italian humanistic treatises, based on classical texts, into the libraries of the duke and his nobles.[11] In 1454 Jean Mansel presented his *Hystoires Rommaines* to Philip the Good, and by 1465 Miélot had translated Roberto della Porta's *Romuléon* into French for the ducal library.[12] The history of ancient Rome was by no means a *terra incognita* at the court of Philip the Good, and the translation of Caesar's *Commentaries* for Charles the Bold in 1472 simply continued an existing tradition.[13] This was in turn based upon earlier precedent. The translations produced for Charles V and Charles VI of France in the later fourteenth century provided both a source and an inspiration for the Burgundian translators of the next century.[14] Ghillebert de Lannoy's advice to his son rested upon a literary tradition which had begun some seventy years before at the royal court of France.

Manuscripts containing the works of all those authors cited by Lannoy are found in the libraries of Burgundian nobles in the second half of the fifteenth century. The ducal library held copies of their works, often in the form of miscellanies or anthologies. Charles the Bold put Lannoy's advice into practice on campaign in 1474 by reading (or having read to him) 'Valerius [Maximus], Titus Livy or some book about Alexander the Great, or of battles'.[15] What could he have found in them which might have influenced his conduct? The collection of extracts from Livy, Cicero, Sallust and other Roman writers gathered together under the name of Valerius Maximus had been available in the French translation by Simon de Hesdin since 1375-80.[16] Addressed to the Emperor Tiberius, its nine books dealt in turn with Roman religious rites, civil and military institutions, the exercise of virtue, the achievement of happiness, judgments and the vices. Each book was illustrated by apt episodes from Roman history: Numa enacts his laws, Augustus administers justice, Marcus Cato protests against the cruelty of Sulla, Julius Caesar, Pompey and Horatius defend the state and perform deeds of prowess in battle. Such subjects caught the imagination of those who read this somewhat indigestible compilation, and

11. See R. Bossuat, 'Jean Miélot, traducteur de Cicéron', *BEC*, xcix (1938), pp. 108-33; Willard, art. cit., pp. 37-8.

12. Lacaze, art. cit., pp. 362, 363; G. Doutrepont, *La littérature française à la cour des ducs de Bourgogne* (Paris 1909), p. 142.

13. R. Bossuat, 'Traductions françaises des "Commentaires" de César à la fin du xve siècle', *Bibliothèque d'Humanisme et Renaissance*, iii (1943), pp. 253-373.

14. See L. Delisle, *Recherches sur la librairie de Charles V*, 2 vols. (Paris 1907), passim.

15. See R. Vaughan, *Charles the Bold* (London 1973), p. 163 citing a Milanese ambassador's report; Willard, art. cit., p. 36 for translations undertaken from *c*.1450 onwards. For the contents of the ducal library at this time see G. Dogaer and M. Debae, *La Librairie de Philippe le Bon* (Brussels 1967). It has also been argued that a taste for illuminated manuscripts of a new type is found at the court of Burgundy after 1450: '... from books of hours and the rather few copies of extant texts, we pass, in the middle of the century, to a period of creative lay literature ...': L.M.J. Delaissé, *A Century of Dutch Manuscript Illumination*, (Berkeley and Los Angeles 1968), p. 74.

16. See G.F. Warner, *Valerius Maximus. Miniatures of the School of Fouquet*, (London 1907), pp. 1-4.

the illuminated manuscript which belonged to Philippe de Commynes has miniatures illustrating these themes.[17] Commynes was perhaps thinking of such volumes when he wrote, echoing Ghillebert de Lannoy, that 'one of the best ways to make a man wise is to have read ancient histories and to have learnt to conduct and protect himself ... wisely by means of the stories and examples of our predecessors'.[18] Ancient history might arouse admiration but, in Commynes' eyes, it also furnished cautionary tales of the deceitful tricks and ruses against which a ruler must be constantly on his guard.[19] In his tent outside Neuss in the winter of 1474-5 Charles the Bold could find timely warnings among the *hystoires* recounted by Valerius about the treachery of friends and allies, as well as instruction in the virtues.

It is evident from the great library of Louis de Bruges that the classical writers cited by Lannoy would not have been unfamiliar to a member of the Burgundian or Flemish nobility. Louis de Bruges, lord of La Gruthuyse (d.1492), descendant of the lineage of Bruges-d'Aa and unrelated to the ducal family, kept his books at his great town-house in Bruges, and his collection compares very favourably with that of the dukes themselves.[20] It is a manifest contradiction of the notion that there was a marked difference between the literary taste of members of the nobility, and that of the ducal lawyers and financiers at the court of Burgundy. 'The nobles perpetuated medieval traditions,' writes Professor Bartier. 'The lawyers resorted above all to classical sources both sacred and profane.'[21] Guillaume Hugonet, chancellor of Burgundy, possessed manuscripts of Caesar, Vegetius, Titus Livy, Seneca, Pliny, Valerius Maximus and Cicero.[22] Louis de Bruges had works by all of these, with the exception of Pliny. Unlike the *légiste* Hugonet, however, he

---

17. BL, MS Harl. 4374-5; Warner, op. cit., Pls. I-VIII. The *grand bâtard* and Jacques d'Armagnac, duke of Nemours, both possessed illuminated copies of the text: see A. Boinet, 'Un bibliophile du xve siècle: le grand Bâtard de Bourgogne', *BEC*, lxvii (1906), p. 258; Warner, op. cit., pp. 14-15 (BN, MS fr. 41).

18. P. de Commynes, *Mémoires*, ed. J. Calmette and G. Durville, ii (Paris 1924), pp. 128-9: 'l'ung des grandz moyens de rendre ung homme saige d'avoir leü les hystoires anciennes et apprendre à se conduire et garder et entreprendre saigement par les hystoires et exemples de noz predecesseurs.'

19. Commynes, op. cit., ii, 128. His remark stemmed from Charles the Bold's 'folly' in putting himself into Louis XI's custody at Peronne in October 1468. Despite the alleged influence of his mother, Isabella of Portugal, on the young Charles, his youthful readings at her behest had evidently (for Commynes) had little effect on his behaviour. See C.C. Willard, 'Isabel of Portugal: patroness of humanism?', *Miscellanea di studi e ricerche sul Quattrocento francese a cura di Franco Simone* (Turin 1966), pp. 540-2.

20. See J. van Praet, *Recherches sur Louis de Bruges, seigneur de la Gruthuyse* (Paris 1831), especially the inventory of his library, pp. 84-264. One manuscript (BN, MS fr. 356-7, a fourteenth-century copy of *Guyron le Courtois*) is wrongly attributed to Louis de Bruges by Van Praet (pp. 178-9). See R. Lathuillière, *Guiron le Courtois* (Geneva 1966), pp. 66-7. For an analysis of Louis' books (100 manuscripts, of which 28 are literary texts) see Pickford, op. cit., pp. 279-80.

21. J. Bartier, *Légistes et Gens de Finance au xve siècle. Les Conseillers des ducs de Bourgogne Philippe le Bon et Charles le Téméraire* (Brussels 1955), pp. 278-9.

22. Ibid., p. 278. For an inventory of Hugonet's books see P.L. Gachard, 'Les livres du chancelier Hugonet', *Bulletin de la Commission Royale d'Histoire*, Ier sér., ii (1856), pp. 120-7. These were largely in Latin.

possessed Aristotle's *Economics*, Ovid's *Metamorphoses*, Ptolemy's *Cosmographia*, Orosius' *Roman History*, Quintus Curtius' *History of Alexander the Great*, Leonardo Bruni's *History of the First Punic War* and a volume of Roman histories derived from Lucan, Suetonius and Sallust.[23] These were in French translations, some stemming from the editions produced for the French royal library in the second half of the fourteenth century, others from the work of contemporary French and Flemish translators. Louis de Bruges' library was nothing if not wide-ranging and eclectic, and clearly did not exclude texts by classical authors or contemporary works inspired by ancient history. The text of his Quintus Curtius, translated by the Portuguese Vasco de Lucena in 1468, began:

> In the history of Alexander it is evident that kingdoms increase through virtue and diligence, and decline through idle lassitude, and here it is proved by [his] conquest of all the Orient ...[24]

The exercise of virtue is once again set before the nobility. The path to honour was thought to be that followed by the ancients, and virtuous conduct was to be inculcated through education. These 'lordly amateurs of learning' found lessons for present action in the classical past – it was to Sallust or Livy that they turned in search of edifying and useful knowledge.[25] Ghillebert de Lannoy may have had the following passage from Sallust's *Catiline War* in mind when he exhorted his son to follow the deeds of the Romans. Writing of the early Roman state, Sallust observed that it

> waxed incredibly strong and great in a remarkably short time, such was the thirst for glory that had filled mens' minds. To begin with, as soon as the young men could endure the hardships of war, they were taught a soldier's duties in camp under a vigorous discipline, and they took more pleasure in handsome arms and war horses than in harlots and revelry. To such men, consequently, no labour was unfamiliar, no region too rough or too steep, no armed foeman was terrible; valour was all in all. Nay, their hardest struggle for glory was with one another; each man strove to be first to strike down the foe, to scale a wall, to be seen of all while doing such a deed. This they considered riches, this fair fame and high nobility. It was praise they coveted, but they were lavish of money; their aim was unbounded renown, but only such riches as could be gained honourably ...[26]

23. See Van Praet, op. cit., pp. 136-9, 155-6, 200-4, 220-2, 227-8, 231-3. The latter was a version of the *Faits des Romains*.

24. Ibid., pp. 220-2: 'Comment es hystoires d'Alexandre puet apparoir que les Royaumes croissant par vertu et diligence et declinent pour vicieuse laschete et illec se preuve a este conquist tout orient.' For the work of Vasco see R. Bossuat, 'Vasque de Lucène, traducteur de Quinte-Curce, 1468', *Bibliothèque d'Humanisme et Renaissance*, viii (1946), pp. 197-245; for Portuguese influence, through the duchess Isabella, on Burgundian literature C.C. Willard, 'Isabel of Portugal and the French translation of the "Triunfo de las Doñas"', *Revue Belge de Philologie et d'Histoire*, xliii, II (1965), pp. 961-9.

25. See Hexter, art. cit., pp. 61-2; Lacaze, art. cit., pp. 363-4: '... il ne s'agissait plus de récits romanesques, mais de "traités de Prince" qui envisagaient l'Antiquité sous un angle différent.' A certain 'de-mythification' of the Alexander legend was apparently under way at this time, especially in Vasco de Lucena's work: ibid., p. 359; Doutrepont, op. cit., pp. 178, 182-3.

26. Sallust, *The War with Catiline*, tr. J.C. Rolfe (London 1931), pp. 13, 15.

The emphasis on valour, competition between men for reputation, a rigorous military training, and the quest for honour above all material reward, provided themes upon which fifteenth-century nobles could profitably ponder. The lessons of Roman history were perhaps especially relevant at a time when war was conducted on a commercial basis and when the pursuit of profit and material reward could outweigh the desire for honour and renown. Some form of reaction may have been under way against the materialistic and mercenary chivalry of the age.[27]

Commynes formulated a further reason for the study of *hystoires anciennes*: a lettered and well-read noble would not be misled by the ready advice of the 'clercs et gens de robbe longue' who surrounded him as counsellors. 'They have,' he wrote, 'a law in their mouths or a story for every occasion.'[28] An educated noble would be able to distinguish good advice from bad and would not be deceived by their learned examples. Through this process of educational self-help, a noble might learn to think for himself, distrust flatterers and serve the prince in a more effective manner. There is in such comments an awareness that the political and military rôle of those who were noble by birth and descent was changing. The contemporary controversy over the nature of true nobility was perhaps the most striking symptom of that change.

In his recent study of fifteenth-century chivalry and literature Professor Benson observed that the 'knightly class' (in this context, the nobility) faced a series of threats during the later Middle Ages. 'The almost inevitable response of the nobility was an insistence on those qualities which set them apart as a class and an emphasis on the ideal of noble conduct that defined that class.'[29] They were under pressure, he argued, from demographic reverses, the social ambitions and the aspirations of those below them, and by the power of the liquid capital which they themselves experienced such great difficulty in preserving. Professor Bartier has produced a wealth of evidence for the displacement of ancient noble families in the Burgundian lands by newly ennobled families, mostly ducal officers and financiers, such as the Hugonet, Goux, Coustain, Clugny, Molain and, above all, the Rolin.[30] A *plèbe nobiliaire*, he concludes, was created, especially among the middle and lower nobility whose lands, like those of the Châteauvillain family, lay exposed to the worst ravages of warfare.[31] The spectacle of men buying their way into its ranks was not a new one for members of the French and Flemish nobility. Nevertheless, a

27. See C.A.J. Armstrong, 'Sir John Fastolf and the law of arms', *War, Literature and Politics*, p. 56.

28. Commynes, op. cit., i, pp. 129-30: 'A tous propos ont une loy au bec ou une hystoire.'

29. L.D. Benson, *Malory's Morte Darthur* (Cambridge, Mass. 1976), p. 143. Professor Benson sees the primary source of the 'ideal of noble conduct', and hence of 'virtue' in chivalric romances rather than in the more formal didactic literature of the period (ibid., p. 144).

30. Bartier, op. cit., pp. 228-42.

31. Ibid., pp. 230-5, 269-70; A. Bossuat, 'Les prisonniers de guerre au xve siècle: la rançon de Guillaume de Châteauvillain', *Annales de Bourgogne*, xxiii (1951), pp. 7-35.

redistribution of wealth after the epidemics of the fourteenth century and the comparative ease with which great fortunes could be made (especially in the Flemish towns) seems to have made the hereditary nobility particularly conscious of the ascent of *parvenu* families. These had manifestly not 'lived nobly' – they had not followed the profession of arms, but had bought patents of nobility with the profits of legal or financial office. A ducal ordinance of Philip the Good reflected the views of the hereditary nobility when, in 1438, he enacted that new nobles were to pay taxes and their children could only claim exemption if they followed a military career.[32] Noble status demanded noble conduct – the sons of *bourgeois* and civil servants were thus obliged to take up arms if they were to escape taxation and maintain their places in the ranks of the *noblesse*.

An emphasis on the qualities of 'true nobility' pervades much of the didactic literature of honour and virtue. Birth, it was argued, was no longer sufficient in itself to gain a man honour and renown. In 1449, Jean Miélot translated the *De Nobilitate* of the Italian humanist Buonaccorso da Pistoia for Philip the Good, in which the nature of true nobility was debated.[33] The Latin text had been written in 1429 and dedicated to Carlo Malatesta of Rimini, and became known as *La Controverse de Noblesse* in Miélot's translation, of which six fifteenth-century manuscripts survive.[34] The work takes the form of a debate before the Roman Senate between an idle man of noble birth, and an active Roman citizen of obscure and humble origin, for the hand of a lady. Here nobility of birth is set beside nobility of 'virtue', as defined by a civic humanist of the early Renaissance. Professor C.C. Willard has seen such ideas as unsympathetic towards the hereditary nobility of the Burgundian court and especially favourable to the rising civil servants and newly-ennobled *bourgeois*.[35] In her view treatises like the *Controverse* 'corresponded to the views of such men as Gros, Bladelin and Rolin', and commercial contacts between Florence and Bruges are adduced to explain the transmission of ideas and the similarity of the audiences which received them.[36] However, such an argument ignores the fact that both

<hr />

32. C.A.J. Armstrong, 'Had the Burgundian government a policy for the nobility?', *Britain and the Netherlands*, ed. J. Bromley, E.H. Kossmann, ii (1962), p. 18.

33. See Willard, 'The concept of true nobility', pp. 37-8. It was translated into English by John Tiptoft, earl of Worcester, in *c*.1480, and printed by Caxton in 1481 (ibid. pp. 34-5) as *The Declamacion of Noblesse*.

34. Ibid., pp. 37-8; Hans Baron, *The Crisis of the Early Italian Renaissance* (Princeton 1966), pp. 420-3.

35. Willard, 'The concept of true nobility', p. 45. Professor Willard's article provides a salutary antidote to the view that the court of Burgundy in the fifteenth century was a stronghold of 'decadent' medievalism.

36. Ibid., pp. 45-6. It is, however, noteworthy that the Senate's judgment is not recorded and the author leaves the question open to debate. Part of the *De Nobilitate* seems to argue for active participation in politics, public office and war as a qualification for nobility – a view that would correspond to the attitudes of the 'old' nobility at the court of Burgundy: see Baron, op. cit., pp. 420-1.

Latin and French versions of the treatise were dedicated to a hereditary noble, and that nobility of birth and nobility of 'virtue' were not always thought to be mutually exclusive. Similarly, there were other definitions of 'virtue' besides that which stemmed from the Aristotelian and Ciceronian concept of civic duty.

It is here that notions of the traditional rôle of the nobility – as a hereditary military class, members of an order or estate of chivalry – were bound to undergo some modifications. Nobility 'de vertu et bonnes moeurs' was emphasised, not to the exclusion of birth, but as an essential adjunct to hereditary status. In the romance *Histoire des Seigneurs de Gavres* (1456), the mother of the hero says to her son as he goes off to war: 'you are noble by lineage; you should be even more so by *vertus*, because nobility of good deeds (*bonnes meurs*) is worth so much more than nobility of birth.'[37] The argument seems to be that inherited nobility is justified, enhanced and sustained by virtuous conduct. Ghillebert de Lannoy took up the theme when he wrote in his *Enseignements Paternels*: 'Nobility proceeds first of all from the noble and worthy virtues of our ancient fathers.'[38] A stark antithesis between birth and virtue may have been acceptable to the humanistic circles of early Renaissance Italy, but it hardly corresponded to the prevailing notions of nobility at the court of Burgundy. Perhaps the idea of an inherited virtue, directing and informing the present behaviour of a noble, represented one reaction of the hereditary nobility to the many challenges to their position. They had the support of the dukes, insofar as the profits of ducal service in war, diplomacy, at court, and in offices throughout the Burgundian domains could entirely offset dwindling seigneurial revenues.[39] The Croy, Brimeu, Lannoy, Lalaing and Créqui families rode out the economic storm with notable success, largely by means of the pensions and rewards which accrued from ducal service. If 'virtue' carried any meaning for such men, it stood for an ideal of noble conduct which set them apart from the rest of their society. Civic and chivalric humanism blended to create an ideal compounded of concepts of personal honour and public service.

There was nothing intrinsically novel about such an ideal. In his *Book of the Order of Chivalry* (*c.*1310) Raimon Lull had written that the knight must lead a virtuous and exemplary life, putting his noble qualities at the service of a prince.[40] The notion that chivalry possessed a public function is well expressed

---

37. BR, MS 10,238, fo. 8r: 'Estes nobles de lignye, encores deves plus estre de vertus, car la noblesse des bonnes meurs vault trop mieulx que la noblesse des parens.' A similar notion is found in the *Livre des Faits* of Jacques de Lalaing, printed in G. Chastellain, *Oeuvres*, ed. Kervyn de Lettenhove, viii (Brussels 1866), p. 18.

38. Lannoy, op. cit., p. 460: 'Noblesse vint premierement par les nobles et dignes vertus de nos anciens pères.'

39. Bartier, op. cit., p. 269. See also Armstrong, '... policy for the nobility?', pp. 20-1 for the dependence of the nobility upon court and household service for fees and pensions. In the *comté* of Flanders this was built upon an existing tradition of public service among nobles.

40. See Raimon Lull, *The Book of the Ordre of Chyvalry* (tr. Caxton), ed. A.T.P. Byles (London, *EETS*, o.s. clxviii, 1926), pp. 29-30.

in Caxton's translation of Lull: 'To a knyght apperteyneth that he be lover of the comyn wele. For by the comynalte of the people was the chyvalrye founded and establysshed. And the comyn wele is gretter and more necessary than propre good and specyall.'[41] Lull's discourse on the origins of the order of chivalry mistakenly stressed its popular and elective basis, in which the *miles* was so called because he had been chosen from every thousand of the Roman people.[42] Better and more extensive knowledge of Roman history in the fifteenth century led to elaborations and revisions of Lull's assertions and, as I have suggested, a marked emphasis on the Roman concept of discipline and service in both peace and war. True nobility came to be seen as the exercise of 'virtue', which led inexorably to the service of the prince. The origins of 'virtue' were disputed: if it was not inherited by one born noble, it must be instilled and inculcated by education. To serve the prince, therefore, the noble must become learned, as well as skilled in arms. In the council where the business of state was done, he must beat the clerks and lawyers at their own game.[43] Chastellain was well aware of their presence and their threat to his class. Speaking of the non-noble members of the ducal council, he wrote:

> This set the author especially ... against many clerks and officers; not all of them, but certain were raised up high, who were not nobles, either by birth or by conduct (*moeurs*), who were often occupying ... the seats and dignities of true nobles in heart and in deed ...[44]

To Chastellain a 'true noble' was one born noble. Such was the nature of fifteenth-century government that, to retain his place in the ducal service, a noble needed training in the arts of persuasion. Jean de Lannoy, Ghillebert's cousin, wrote to his infant son that he regretted his lack of learning acutely, because:

> No day passes that I do not regret this deeply, and especially when I find myself, with others, in the council of the king ... or of ... the duke of Burgundy, and I know not nor dare not speak my opinion after the clerks, eloquent legists and *ystoryens* who have spoken before me. For I do not know the order or manner of

41. Ibid., p. 113.

42. Ibid., p. 15. The *Instruction d'un Jeune Prince* has a similar account of the origins of knighthood (Lannoy, op. cit., pp. 406-7), as does an anonymous treatise printed in *Parties Inédites ... de l'oeuvre de l'héraut Sicile*, ed. P. Roland (Mons, 1867), pp. 64-6. Although neither is a direct copy, these two works are closely related. For a comparison between the Roman *equites* and the medieval knight, see H. Delbrück, *History of the Art of War within the Framework of Political History*, tr. W.J. Renfroe, i (Westport/London, 1975) pp. 60, 267-8. These Roman troops fought, as knights did, on both horseback and foot.

43. Hexter, art. cit., pp. 62-5.

44. 'Cecy met l'acteur notamment et tout de gré à l'encontre de plusieurs clercs et officiers, non tous, mais aucuns hautement promus, qui non nobles, ne de sang, ne de moeurs, occupent les sièges et dignités souvent en court des vrais nobles en coeur et en fait ...' Chastellain, op. cit., vi, 402-3.

speaking and can say nothing but 'Master Jean or Master Pierre has spoken well, and I am of his opinion' ... Whence I have often felt deep shame and humiliation in my heart.[45]

In the French royal council, Jean, count of Dunois and Pierre de Brézé, *grand sénéchal* of Normandy, were noted for their fine speaking:[46] keeping up with the churchmen and civil servants was thus not peculiar to the court of Burgundy. Nobility of virtue, of good deeds and exemplary conduct, was to be cultivated by those born into the *noblesse* so that they might excell over those not so favoured by the accident of birth. It was by such means that the hereditary nobility of France and the Burgundian lands validated the image which they cherished of themselves. The concept of honour has been defined as 'the value of a person in his own eyes, but also in the eyes of his society; it is the estimate of his own worth, his claim to pride.'[47] Self-esteem and pride in antiquity of lineage was supported by the esteem and respect of others, both peers and inferiors. To be honoured a man's behaviour had to be honourable, and a hereditary nobility had to be reminded of its obligations and responsibilities.

The moralists set out an ideal of noble conduct; the more cynically-minded might argue that this could sometimes be nothing other than self-interest sheltering under the cloak of service to the 'public weal' (as some did in 1465). Nevertheless, the emergence of a literate, educated nobility, competing for a place in the prince's service with the 'eloquent legists and *ystoryens*' had given rise to a new literature. This was eclectic in its sources, drawing upon both classical and medieval writings, but finding the most relevant material in Greek and Roman history. A series of didactic treatises and exhortations, dating from *c*.1440 onwards, sought to instruct the French and Burgundian nobility in the qualities required by *noblesse de vertu et bonnes meurs*. Of these, I propose to examine four of the most important, concluding with a brief discussion of a work lying outside this Burgundian corpus – Jean de Bueil's *Le Jouvencel*.[48] The four works are the anonymous *Enseignement de Vraie Noblesse* (1440);[49] the *Instruction d'un Jeune Prince*, attributed either to Ghillebert de Lannoy or

45. 'Dont nest jour que je nen aie ung mervelleux regret; et par espetial touttes les fois que je me treve, avoec les aultrez, au conseil du Roy ... et parellement de mon ... seigneur le Duc de Bourgogne; et je ne scay, ne je n'ose dire mon oppinion, aprez les clers eloquens legistes et ystoryens, qui devant moy ont parlé. Car je nay pas la manière, ne lordre de parler, et ne scay aultre chose dire, fors que maistre Jehan ou maistre Pierre a bien dit et que je suis de son oppinion ... De quoy, mainteffois, ay eut grant honte et grant vergongne a mon ceur ...' Baudoin de Lannoy, *Jean de Lannoy le Bâtisseur, 1410-1492*, (Paris, 1937), pp. 120-1, cit. Hexter, art. cit., p. 63. The letter was written in May 1465.
46. See J. Chartier, *Chronique de Charles VII*, ed. Vallet de Viriville, ii (Paris 1858), p. 105; Chastellain, op. cit., vii, pp. 37-65, 72 and iii, 347.
47. J. Pitt-Rivers, art. cit., p. 21.
48. J. de Bueil, *Le Jouvencel*, ed. C. Favre, L. Lecestre, 2 vols. (Paris 1887-9).
49. BR, MS 11,047, fos. 1r-37r. For another copy with the title *Imaginacion de vraye noblesse* see BL, Add. MS 15,469, fos. 3r-30v.

Chastellain;[50] Ghillebert de Lannoy's *Enseignements Paternels*;[51] and the *Traité de Noblesse* by the Castilian noble Diego de Valera, translated by Hugues de Salve, *prévôt* of Furnes in Flanders.[52]

The anonymous *Enseignement de Vraie Noblesse* is fortunately datable from internal evidence. Its author speaks of a pilgrimage which he made from Lille to Notre-Dame-de-Hal in Hainault, during which he had a vision of a lady, personifying Imagination, dressed in 'all the colours that a painter, however skilled, could ever use in his paintings'.[53] This apparition supposedly took place on 5 May 1440, between Enghien and Hal, and the lady's purpose was to give a message to the 'princes and knighthood of Christendom' about the nature of true nobility.[54] Together with the origins and duties of knighthood, this was naturally the principal subject of his treatise. The affinities between his work and the *Instruction d'un Jeune Prince* are striking, especially in the fourth part of the treatise, concerning knighthood, which exactly reproduces the *Instruction*.[55] True nobility is defined similarly in both treatises: a man cannot be truly noble without 'Virtues and good conduct' (*vertus et bonnes meurs*) and four personified virtues are selected – 'prudence, justice, continence, and *force* that some call *magnanimité*'.[56] The author of the *Instruction* adds that by *force* some mean 'magnanimity, boldness of heart or force of courage'.[57] By means of these cardinal chivalrous virtues, a man may find both salvation in the next world and renown upon earth. The *Enseignement* offers perhaps the clearest statement of the primacy which nobility of virtue should assume:

> Such is the state of affairs today that many people do not look to the good conduct (*bonnes meurs*) and virtues of individuals, which is a great failing and stupidity, but only to the lineage from which they descend, saying that such-and-such is noble through his father and not through his mother, or that he lacks a half or a quarter ...[58]

50. Lannoy, op. cit., pp. 325-435.

51. Ibid., pp. 447-72.

52. BR, MS II. 7057, fos. 1r-74v. This illuminated version belonged to Anthoine, *grand bâtard* of Burgundy: it bears his arms, surrounded with the collar of the Golden Fleece (fo. 1r) and his motto, *Nule ne sy frote* (fo. 74v). The manuscript was later owned by his grandson Adolphe, whose motto, *Nul ne laproce*, is found on the same folio. For another copy of the text, see BR, MS 21,551-69.

53. BR, MS 11,047, fo. 2v: 'de toutes les couleurs que oncques paintre tant fust soubtil employast en ses paintures.'

54. Ibid., fo. 1r.

55. Cf. ibid., fos. 29r-36v and Lannoy, op. cit., pp. 403-17. This forms the eighth chapter of *L'Instruction*, headed *Cy parle de l'ordre et estat de chevalerie et comment on le doit entendre*. In the *Enseignement* it forms part IV, entitled *Quel estat est ordre de chevalerie et a quoy elle doit servir* (fo. 29r). The relationships between these texts and the work cit. supra., n. 40, have not been established, nor the chronology of their composition established.

56. BR, MS 11,047, fo. 9v.

57. Lannoy, op. cit., p. 354.

58. BR, MS 11,047, fo. 15r: 'le temps est tel au jourduy que pluseurs ne regardent pas aux bonnes meurs et vertus des personnes, qui est default et simplesse grant, mais comme folz seulement au lignaige dont ilz sont descendus en disant tel est noble de par son pere et non de par sa mere ou quil y en fault moitie ou quartier.'

This theme is developed in the *Instruction*, dated between 1439 and 1446.[59] The author stresses that he is writing not only for princes but for other *grans seigneurs*, and we know that some of them possessed copies of the treatise.[60] Of the four cardinal virtues the last is judged to be especially valuable in time of war, and provides a means whereby the rigours of a military calling may be endured. 'Magnanimity', or bravery, he writes,

> is the fourth of the virtues that one must greatly honour, for princes and knights of high repute never performed enterprises nor bold deeds of arms worthy of memory without its accompaniment, aid and comfort. This force of courage, or bravery, belongs especially to princes and knights, for by its nature they are armed for everything that can happen: encounters with lance, bombard, cannon, storm at sea, harshness of winter, or heat of the sun; neither the great host of his enemies, nor towns and castles enclosed with walls and high towers, can dismay him, hinder his enterprises, nor defend his enemy ... the shedding of his own, or others' blood cannot dismay or frighten him; death seems a small penalty to endure in order to gain honour and great renown ...[61]

Physical courage and fearlessness are thus considered a talisman against the horrors of war; allied to 'franchise' (integrity) it leads to honourable conduct in battle which is 'sans reproche'.[62] 'He who loves honour and fears shame,' comments the author, 'would rather suffer death than be reproached for committing cowardice, treason or any other evil deed ...'[63] Cowardice and *lèse-majesté* appear as the cardinal sins of a nobleman.

The author is anxious to stress that the order and estate of knighthood constitutes the hands and arms of the prince, and that a knight should be constantly ready to serve and obey that prince.[64] Self-help and feudal

---

59. For a discussion of authorship and dating see Potvin's Introduction: Lannoy, op. cit., pp. liii-lxxi.

60. Ibid., pp. 335, 350. Copies were owned by Philip the Good (BR, MS 10,976); Charles the Bold (Bibliothèque de l'Arsenal, MS 33); Louis de Bruges (BN, MS fr. 1216).

61. Ibid., pp. 356-7: 'Magnanimité est le iiiie des vertus que on doit moult honnourer, car princes ne chevaliers de haulte renommée ne firent oncques entreprise ne vaillance en armes dignes de mémoire sans sa compaignie, aide et confort. Ceste vertu, selon nostre langaige, vault autant à dire que force de courage ou hardement, qui appartient espéciallement aux princes et chevaliers, car de sa nature elle est resconfortée de tout ce qui poeut advenir: rencontrée de lance, bombarde, canon, tourment de mer, dureté d'yver, chaleur de soleil; ne le grant nombre de ses ennemis, villes ne fortz chasteaux, encloz de murs à haultes tours, ne le poevent esbahir, ne empeschier ses entreprinses, ne garantir son ennemy, puis qu'il l'a enchassé; l'effusion du sang, de lui ne d'aultres, ne le poeut esbahir ne doubter; la mort luy samble petite paine à endurer, pour acquérir honneur et bonne renommée.' For fourteenth-century notions of chivalrous prowess, including *magnanimitas*, see G. Mathew, *The Court of Richard II* (London 1968), p. 118 and 'Ideals of knighthood in late fourteenth-century England', *Studies presented to F.M. Powicke* (Oxford 1948), p. 358.

62. For 'franchyse' in fourteenth-century English literature see Mathew, *Court of Richard II*, p. 123, where it is defined as 'a form of generosity of spirit ... close linked with "fellowship"'.

63. Lannoy, op. cit., p. 358: 'Et cilz qui aime honneur et crainte honte, vouldroit autant souffrir mort que d'estre reprochié d'avoir commis lacheté de corps, traïson ne aultre vilain cas ...'.

64. Ibid., pp. 403-4, 408.

independence have been outlawed. Chivalry finds its justification through service in a just war, that is, in a war waged on the authority of a sovereign prince against Christians or infidels. Honour and renown can be attained only in such wars and the possession of those qualities has, for the author, an eminently practical purpose. Perhaps as part of a reaction against the mercenary chivalry of his day, in which ransom and booty provided a major incentive to wage war, he declares that 'if it should happen that a prince or good knight should fall into the hands of a worthy man (*preudomme*) his ransom is much less'.[65] He illustrates his point by telling a story of the crusading hero Hugues de Tabarie, who was captured and put to ransom by the Sultan, but released greatly enriched with infidel gold because he had convinced his captor that this was the manner in which a *preudomme* should behave towards his peers in the order of knighthood.[66]

Ghillebert's de Lannoy's *Enseignements Paternels* dates from between 1430 and 1440, and the work is found with the *Instruction* in some manuscript miscellanies of the period.[67] This fatherly exhortation is couched in moralistic and hortatory terms, and Ghillebert makes three main points about the means by which his son may attain 'high and perfect honour'.[68] First, a true noble must always speak cautiously and wisely; secondly, he must fear the dishonour which results from base and cowardly actions; thirdly, he must abstain from the excesses of the flesh.[69] As in the *Instruction*, a fear of reproach is paramount. The very greatest honour accrues from death in battle, and personal valour is clearly the hall-mark of the truly noble. The self-sacrifice of Louis de Robesart who, as a member of the Order of the Garter, refused to retreat and was killed near Amiens, is used as an example of this quality at its most exalted level.[70] Every noble, writes Ghillebert, should ask himself the following questions when he wished to undertake anything:

> Lord God, will I say or do anything that will bring shame to me or to the lineage from which I have come ...? Will nobility be lacking in me? Will I be such that I will not dare to be found with other good, noble and valiant men, and speak when my turn comes in all assemblies? As for myself, I wish to live and die as a noble man should. If I am in battle, I would prefer that I should be found among the slain than ... be written down among the fugitives.[71]

65. Ibid., pp. 424-45.

66. Ibid., pp. 417-25. The author's source was, he claims 'aulcunes croniques de la conqueste de la sainte terre que fist le vaillant cristien Godefroy de Buillon' (p. 417). Cf. BR, MS 11,047, fos. 36v-37r where Hugues de Tabarie is made to write a treatise on the creation of knights for Saladin.

67. For examples see BN, MS fr. 1216; Bibliothèque de l'Arsenal, MS 33; BN, MS fr. 1957; Van Praet op. cit., p. 149.

68. Lannoy, op. cit., p. 447.

69. Ibid., pp. 448-9.

70. Ibid., pp. 457-8.

71. Ibid., p. 460: 'Beau sire Dieu, diray je ou feray je chose dont il me puist venir honte, ne au lignage dont je suis partis et yssus?'

The emphasis upon the recording of those who fled a field of battle is note-worthy, and will be returned to later. Nobility of birth (for the Lannoys were nothing if not hereditary nobles) demanded more than a complacent exercise of inherited privilege. If necessary it required sacrifice of self to a just cause, in the pursuit of honour and renown, irrespective of the effects of such an event upon the transmission of a noble inheritance. Death in battle could deprive a family of a male heir, but the extraordinary degree of honour which might thereby accrue was, for Lannoy, clearly compensation enough. The Lalaing family offers an example of a noble lineage which appears to have put such notions into practice,[72] with unfortunate results for the descent of the patrimony. Yet the prevailing ethos and the prospect of financial ruin through the payment of ransom combined to render a glorious death more appealing than dishonourable security. War was the preserve of *noblesse* and, for Ghillebert, a means of preserving and increasing wealth. In war, he writes, 'one can honourably enrich oneself'.[73] An abstention from trade, money-lending and manual labour marks off the true noble from his *bourgeois* contemporaries. By 'haunting and following war' a 'wise, valiant and virtuous man can ... take a prisoner of such great power in land and lordship that he will be and remain rich all his life, and even those of his successors'.[74] With the other 'hazards and good fortunes of war, from which he can honourably enrich himself' the noble could be assured of economic security.[75] His virtuous conduct would also commend him to the service of his prince and, as we have seen, royal and ducal office offered another rich source of profit.[76] Nobility of virtue might furnish nobility of birth with a lifeline and an insurance against adverse economic circumstances. How far such advice could be converted into practice remains open to question. Nevertheless, with such admonitions and exhortations in their minds, members of the fifteenth-century nobility, like their fourteenth-century forebears, might find the pursuit of certain kinds of financial profit quite consistent with the ideals of chivalry and the achievement of honour and renown.[77]

The fourth work of didactic literature concerning the concept of true nobility

72. See *infra*, pp. 98-9.
73. Lannoy, op. cit., p. 471.
74. Ibid., p. 471: 'par hanter et porsiévir la guerre, il poeut advenir à ung saige vaillant homme et vertueux qu'il prende en quelque besongne ung prisonnier de sy grant puissance de terre et de seignourie qu'il en sera et demourra riche toute sa vie, voire et tous ses successeurs.' This sentiment seems somewhat at odds with that expressed in the *Instruction* (ibid., pp. 424-45). 'Honourable' enrichment from a ransom presumably meant that the sum demanded should not be excessive, with crippling financial consequences for the prisoner.
75. Ibid. p. 471: 'Encores y a il pluseurs aultres hasars et bonnes fortunes de guerres dont on poeut honnourablement soy enrichir ...' For discussion see Bartier, op. cit., pp. 254-6.
76. Lannoy, op. cit., p. 471: '... moyennant lesdites vertus demourées en toy, ton prince, qui en orra parler et qui les apercevra par effect, te commettra en tel office et sy hault, dont tant de biens et pourfis te porront venir que tu seras riche et puissant et sans a nulz faire tort, et feras venir tous tes amis en grant honneur et souveraine richesse.' See also Hexter, art. cit., pp. 64-6.
77. See J. Barnie, op. cit., pp. 71, 95-6.

which appeared in the middle of the fifteenth century is Diego de Valera's *Traité de Noblesse*. It is the only one of those considered here in which the author is named. Diego de Valera was born in 1412 and served the kings of Castile, writing a *Tratado de las Armas* (about the law of arms). His treatise on nobility was dedicated to Juan II of Castile,[78] and its composition must therefore date from before 1454. As a young noble, skilled in arms and the tournament, he frequented the court of Burgundy, and his treatise includes a prologue in which he refers to contemporary debates about the nature of nobility. He claims he has heard such discussions not only at the Castilian court but 'in many other households of most exalted kings, illustrious princes and ... barons'.[79] His aim, apart from the conventional avoidance of idleness, is to enable 'virtuous nobles' to attain 'sovereign honour', and to inspire commoners to the same end through the exercise of virtue.[80] Nobility is thus deemed to be open to the virtuous, and Juan II is described as one who is not only noble by birth but is a 'mirror of all the virtues'.[81] Nobility is granted only by princes and symbolised by coats of arms. The examples which Diego de Valera gives of this practice concern those who have been ennobled for good deeds in war and in the tournament. The Emperor Sigismund, he declares, granted arms (and hence nobility) to many in his own presence, including Orsalamian, whom he ennobled at a tournament, although he was a butcher's son; Filippo Maria Visconti of Milan ennobled the *condottiere* Niccolo Piccinino and received him into the ducal household as a reward for his service in war.[82] Virtue is defined as military prowess, and Diego devotes a substantial part of his treatise to a discussion of the bearing of coats of arms in battle, their granting and loss.[83] Arms, as the emblems of nobility, can be lost by a man who forfeits his nobility through crime or dishonourable behaviour. Ignoble conduct cannot be tolerated even among those of high birth, and Roman examples are adduced to illustrate the perils and penalties suffered by those who forfeited their nobility 'through crime or vile behaviour'.[84] Diego's aim is essentially twofold: first, to warn the hereditary noble that he cannot rest upon the laurels of ancient lineage, but must constantly seek to gain the honour of his contemporaries through the exercise and display of virtue, above all in war and tournament; secondly, to ensure that

78. Willard, 'The concept of true nobility', pp. 39-40.

79. BR, MS II. 7057, fo. 2r: 'en beaucop dautres maisons de tres-haulz roys et illustres princes et treshaulz barons.' Given the identity of the recipient of this presentation copy it is interesting to note that illegitimacy and its implications for both inheritance and the bearing of coats of arms are discussed: fos. 47v-48v, 68v-69r.

80. Ibid., fo. 3r.

81. Ibid., fo. 3v.

82. Ibid., fos. 63r-63v. Spanish examples of grants of arms by Juan II's father are given on fo. 63v. Piccinino bore the name of Visconti from 1439 (the year of his adoption) until 1441 or 1442. His medal by Pisanello describes him as 'capitaneus maximus et Mars alter': see G.F. Hill, G. Pollard, *Renaissance Medals from the Samuel H. Kress Collection* (London 1967), p. 8 cat. no. 4.

83. BR, MS II. 7057, fos. 61v-66v. The work of Bartolus of Sassoferato is frequently cited in this part of the text.

84. Ibid., fos. 66r, 51r: 'par delit ou vil office.'

the recruitment of non-nobles to the ranks of *noblesse* was not determined by
wealth, but by military virtue. New nobility was to be welcomed, but it was to
be on the old nobility's terms.

The ennobling qualities of war – ennobling because they test a man's worth
in conditions of extreme personal danger – find their consummate late-medieval
expression in Jean de Bueil's *Le Jouvencel*.[85] Written in about 1466, this
allegorical military romance, or *roman à clef*, sets out the attitudes of one
fifteenth-century noble and soldier towards his calling. At the end of an
evening's merry-making, the Jouvencel says:

> What a joyous thing is war, for many fine deeds are heard and seen in its course,
> and many good lessons learnt from it. When war is fought in a good cause, it is
> fought for justice and the defence of right. I believe that God favours those who
> risk their lives by their readiness to make war to bring the wicked, the oppressors,
> the conquerors, the proud and all who deny true equity, to justice. War ... is a
> proper and useful career for young men, for which they are respected by both God
> and man. You love your comrade so much in war. When you see that your quarrel
> is just and your blood is fighting well, tears rise to your eyes. A great sweet feeling
> of loyalty and pity fills your heart on seeing your friend so valiantly exposing his
> body to execute and accomplish the command of our Creator. And then you
> prepare to go and live or die with him, and for love not to abandon him. And out of
> that there arises such a delectation, that he who has not tasted it is not fit to say
> what a delight it is. Do you think that a man who does that fears death? Not at all;
> for he feels so strengthened, he is so elated, that he does not know where he is.
> Truly he is afraid of nothing.[86]

Such sentiments are common to the literature and the reality of war at many
periods. To be called a 'noble fellow' by friend or foe on the field of Waterloo
was the highest accolade.[87] For fifteenth-century soldiers and writers, nobility
stemmed from 'noble courage', demonstrated and tested in war.[88] The *Jouvencel*

85. See G.W. Coopland, 'Le Jouvencel (re-visited)', *Symposium*, v, I (1951), pp. 137-85.

86. 'C'est joyeuse chose que la guerre; on y öit, on y voit beaucoup de bonnes choses, et y
apprent moult de bien. Quant elle est en bonne querelle, c'est justice, c'est deffendre droicture. Et
croy que Dieu ayme bien ceulx qui exposent leur corps a vouloir faire la guerre et faire la raison aux
ingratz et descongneuz, aux prosternés et orgueilleux, et qui vont contre bonne equité. Ceulx qui se
peinent de les réprimer sont à louer. Et, quant la guerre prent en cest entendement, c'est ung
plaisant mestier et bon à jeunes gens. Car ilz en sont amez de Dieu et du monde. On s'entr'ayme
tant à la guerre. On pense en soy-mesmes: Laisseray-je ad ce tirant oster par sa cruauté le bien
d'autruy, où il n'a riens. Quant on voit sa querelle bonne et son sang bien combatre, la larme vient à
l'ueil. Il vient une doulceur au cueur de loyaulté et de pitié de veoir son amy, qui si vaillament
expose son corps pour faire et accomplir le commandement de nostre Createur. Et puis, on se
dispose d'aller mourir ou vivre avec luy, et pour amour ne l'abandonner point. En cela vient une
delectacion telle que, qui ne l'a essaiée, il n'est homme qui sceust dire quel bien c'est. Pensez-vous
que homme qui face cela craingne la mort? Nennil; car il est tant reconforté, il est si ravi qu'il ne
scet ou il est. Vraiment il n'a paour de rien.' *Le Jouvencel*, ii, pp. 20-2. My translation partly follows
The Waning of the Middle Ages, p. 73.

87. See Keegan, op. cit., pp. 189, 201.

88. 'Noblesse qui est vertu et bonnes meurs ... et ceste ont acquis et acquierent plusieurs par
leurs vaillances et proesses, car on dit communement que noblesse vient de noble corage ...' (*La fleur
des batailles Doolin de Maience*, 1501, cit. Willard, 'The concept of true nobility', p. 43.)

is, of course, a self-justificatory work and its eulogy of war and of what today might be called 'battle psychosis' rings hollow when the controversial question of the nature of a just cause is raised by the sceptical. Yet the elevated sentiments of loyalty, pity and self-sacrifice which Jean de Bueil found in war furnish meaning to the bland and often undefined 'virtue' admired by the authors of prescriptive literature. At one point in the book, the Jouvencel addresses his comrades upon the subject of the nobility conferred by the career of arms. Those not born noble, he claims, can become so through the 'exercise and profession of arms, which they follow, and which is in itself noble'.[89] Arms ennoble a man, whoever and whatever he is, as long as he is prepared to 'fight to the death with [his] leader in order to acquire the state of *noblesse*'.[90] A hereditary noble may receive confirmation of his true nobility by being knighted, even by a 'simple knight', for his bravery on the battlefield.[91] Not only could a man gain personal nobility in this way, but personal salvation too. The *Jouvencel* repeats the earlier *Livre de Chevalerie* of Geoffroy de Charny (*c*.1352) claiming that young men should pursue 'noble skill and exercise of arms, through which one can certainly acquire one's salvation'.[92] Jean de Bueil's stress upon the rigours of a military training, the privations of a soldierly existence and the skills demanded of the man-at-arms make him the fifteenth-century successor to Charny, whose writings he may well have read. It is instructive to note that this element in the chivalric tradition was part of that handed on to Renaissance nobles and soldiers – the *Jouvencel* went through five printed editions between 1493 and 1529.[93] This legacy of precept and example, and the contemporary emphasis upon Roman discipline and the exercise of virtue, imparted both life and meaning to the cult of chivalry at a period of radical change in the conduct and practice of war.

The value of didactic literature, however, to an activity as practical as warfare has recently been questioned. In his study of Renaissance Italy, Dr Mallett asks: 'Was example more important than experience to the Italian soldier?'[94] It is a question which is equally valid for Northern Europe. The fighting-man's experience of war, and the lessons learnt from it, demand attention. 'Knightly warfare,' it has been argued 'was probably already nearly a century out of date by the time of Agincourt' (1415).[95] Why, and how far, the practice of war had

---

89. *Le Jouvencel*, ii, p. 80: 'par exercice et mestier des armes, qu'ilz suyvent, qui est noble de soy-mesme.'

90. Ibid., p. 82: 'qui combatent jusques à la mort avec leur chief pour acquerir l'estat de noblesse.'

91. Ibid., p. 114. A man could only be knighted on the battlefield, not at an assault: for the significance of this ruling see infra., pp. 94-5, 168.

92. Ibid., i, p. 5: 'noble stille et exercice des armes, esquelles on peut bien faire et acquerir son sauvement.' See also G. de Charny, *Le Livre de Chevalerie*, in J. Froissart, *Oeuvres*, ed. Kervyn de Lettenhove (Brussels 1867-77), i, pt. II, pp. 463-533, esp. pp. 511-12.

93. Coopland, art. cit., pp. 137-8.

94. M. Mallett, op. cit., p. 176.

95. Keegan, op. cit., p. 317 and *inf.* pp. 100-1.

allegedly become an exercise in anachronism, will be discussed in a later chapter. The fifteenth and early sixteenth centuries were not lacking in theoretical literature about war. There can be little doubt that military treatises were read by those who fought – their libraries bear witness to that. Their influence has, however, been called into question because 'only a very limited instruction derived from the book was regarded as sufficient since, as the texts say, "war is to be waged by the eye".'[96] War defied every attempt to reduce it to textbook models: practical necessity, rather than awareness of classical precedent or contemporary theory, determined the structure of armies and the course of battles. Nevertheless, the impact of ideas drawn from didactic literature was clearly felt among the later medieval and early Renaissance nobility, but their force was exerted over personal attitudes and behaviour, rather than the organisation and techniques of war.

96. P. Contamine, 'The war literature of the late middle ages', *War, Literature and Politics*, p. 121: 'la guerre se fait a l'ueill.'

CHAPTER TWO

Orders of Chivalry in the Fifteenth Century

The influence of chivalry on war and politics in the later Middle Ages has been dismissed as minimal. As an exercise in lip-service to an outworn ideal, or as mere posturing, the cult of chivalry has not lacked its detractors. 'In the fourteenth and fifteenth centuries,' wrote Huizinga, 'the real importance of chivalric orders, which were founded in great numbers, was very slight, but the aspirations professed in founding them were always those of the very highest ethical and political idealism.'[1] These new secular orders, beginning with the Order of the Garter, founded by Edward III of England in 1348, have been written off as part of a bizarre social diversion, an exercise in decadent aristocratic frivolity, or as a 'primitive and sacred game'.[2] According to that view, illusion once more distorted and clouded reality to such an extent that the aspirations professed by their founders resounded with insincerity. Yet Huizinga himself was not entirely convinced by his own dismissive arguments. 'The membership of an order of chivalry constituted a sacred and exclusive tie,' he observed, and cited the strong religious overtones clearly audible in some of these associations.[3] His final view was set out in *Homo Ludens* (1938) when he concluded:

> The chivalry of Medieval Christendom as we know it expends itself in artificially keeping up or even deliberately refurbishing certain cultural elements handed down from a long-forgotten past. But the sumptuous apparatus of codes of honour, courtly demeanour, heraldry, chivalric orders, and tournaments had not lost all meaning even towards the close of the Middle Ages.[4]

Exactly what that meaning was, Huizinga does not tell us. He sees chivalric orders only in the most general terms, as part of the 'play-element of culture' where they form a residue of 'primeval initiation-rites' that have outlived their original purpose and significance. They survive as expressions of the 'primitive

1. *The Waning of the Middle Ages*, p. 83.
2. *The Waning of the Middle Ages*, p. 86; P.S. Lewis, 'Une devise de chevalerie inconnue, créée par un comte de Foix? Le Dragon', *Annales du Midi*, lxxvi (1964), p. 81.
3. *The Waning of the Middle Ages*, p. 84; also *Men and Ideas*, pp. 203-4, where the order of the Star (1351) is described as 'the culmination of chivalric romanticism' (p. 204).
4. *Homo Ludens*, p. 126.

conception of a club, of a game, of an aristocratic federation', lingering on as artificial attempts to act out an anachronistic dream of knightly conduct.[5] Apparently it did not occur to Huizinga that the order of chivalry, like other medieval institutions, might undergo changes which are not necessarily to be interpreted in terms of decay or decline.

The fact that men resigned from chivalric orders in the later Middle Ages, on the grounds that continued membership was incompatible with their political loyalties argues at least a *prima facie* case for a certain seriousness of purpose. In August 1377, Enguerrand de Coucy, earl of Bedford, surrendered his Garter insignia to Richard II on such grounds,[6] and in January 1450 François de Suriennes, called *l'Arragonais*, did likewise after the sack of Fougères in March 1449.[7] Suriennes had been very wary of taking part in that ruse, which broke the Anglo-French truce, because it might be 'a reproach upon the said order'.[8] In the event, he sent back the Garter to Henry VI, claiming that although he had served him 'as loyally as any knight of my estate could serve his natural and sovereign lord', subsequent events had forced him to withdraw from English obedience and 'hold myself only subject to the king of Aragon because he is my natural lord'.[9] To that extent his surrender of the Garter through the hands of Longueville Herald was symbolic of his change of allegiance. His example was followed by two former subjects of the English crown, both Gascon nobles, in the reign of Edward IV. In 1462 Jean de Foix, earl of Kendal, resigned from the order, and in August 1475, Gaillard de Durfort, lord of Duras, did likewise, and returned to the France of Louis XI.[10] All these men were compromised, as allies or subjects of the crown of France, by their membership of the Garter, which was 'the sovereign order of the king of England'.[11] If the wearing of the Garter had not had distinct political connotations, there would have been no need for them to surrender it. The extent to which an overt or disguised political purpose and function lay behind the foundation and perpetuation of fifteenth-century orders of chivalry needs to be considered in relation to other fraternities than the Garter.

Historians have on the whole tended to underrate the political value and significance of orders such as Philip the Good's *Toison d'Or*, founded on 10 January 1430, or René of Anjou's *Croissant*, established on 11 August 1448. 'Although the Golden Fleece helped,' writes Professor Vaughan, 'in the process

---

5. *The Waning of the Middle Ages*, p. 83; *Homo Ludens*, pp. 110-26 for his final conclusions on the 'ludic function' of war.

6. G.F. Beltz, *Memorials of the most noble Order of the Garter* (London 1841), pp. 152, cliii.

7. Ibid., p. clxi. For Suriennes' career see A. Bossuat, *Perrinet Gressart et François de Suriennes, agents d'Angleterre* (Paris 1936), pp. 324-5, 348-9. Also M.H. Keen and M.J. Daniel, 'English diplomacy and the sack of Fougères in 1449', *History*, lix (1974), pp. 375-91.

8. J. Stevenson, *Letters and papers illustrative of the Wars of the English in France*, i (Rolls Series, London 1861), p. 285 (letter of Suriennes to Henry VI, 15 March 1450).

9. Ibid., i, p. 276 (letter of Suriennes to Charles VII, January 1450): 'je ne me tien subget se nest au dit roy Darragon, pour ce quil est mon naturel seigneur.'

10. Beltz, op. cit., pp. clxiv (Foix), clxv (Durfort).

11. See Jean Chartier, *Histoire de Charles VII*, ed. D. Godefroy (Paris 1661), p. 463.

of making, or keeping, friends and allies among the aristocracy and ruling houses of Burgundy and Europe, the court ... played a far more important rôle.'[12] The latter had a far greater membership which was 'drawn from other strata of society besides the upper ranks of the aristocracy'.[13] Yet the very exclusiveness of orders such as the *Toison d'Or* provided a means whereby the real props of any fifteenth-century régime might be secured and strengthened. In politics, it was the nobility who mattered – their loyalty and their service were still crucial to the support of any dynasty. There may well have been 'other and less cumbersome ways by which a magnate could collect clients and *alliés*',[14] but the binding oath to an order of chivalry was not to be taken, nor broken, lightly. A distinction must first of all be made between two types of order: those formed of equals and those of unequals. The fraternity of knights, regarding each other as brothers-in-arms, seems to have increasingly given way during the fifteenth century to an association acting under a 'sovereign'. This posits an immediate political function for an order of chivalry. It has been suggested that the new orders reveal a 'hierarchy of political values, sustained by the sovereign for the service of the kingdom' – or by a duke, count or other great lord for the service of his dynastic and territorial ambitions.[15] Distinctions of rank between members within an order became pronounced, and were signified by differences of seating order, costume and insignia. The order of chivalry was not exempt from that process of stratification which has been observed at work elsewhere among the fifteenth-century nobility.[16]

A second area of differentiation lay between those nobles who were subjects of the founder or sovereign of an order, and those who were not. Most of the more celebrated royal and princely orders – the Garter, the *Toison d'Or* and the *Croissant* among them – had both subject and non-subject members within their ranks, but the former were in a clear and substantial majority. The aim of an order which enlisted only subjects or vassals was clear. A prior claim to the loyalties of the member might be enforced at a time when more traditional bonds were suffering a process of erosion.[17] The ties of vassalage were largely a thing of the past. Loyalty had become negotiable, and the increasingly materialistic nature of the relationship between lord and man – cemented largely by money payments in the form of pensions and annuities – may have lain behind the attempt to invoke the ties of chivalry. The cash nexus was not enough to hold a man's allegiance, nor to prevent him from slipping into a rival

12. R. Vaughan, *Philip the Good* (London 1970), p. 162.
13. Ibid., loc. cit.
14. P.S. Lewis, *Later Medieval France. The Polity* (London 1968), p. 200.
15. J. Heers, *Fêtes, Jeux et Joûtes dans les sociétés d'Occident à la fin du Moyen Age* (Montréal/Paris, 1971), p. 37.
16. See K.B. McFarlane, op. cit., pp. 122-6, 268-78; for the Low Countries, L. Génicot, 'La noblesse dans la société médiévale, à propos des dernières études relatives aux terres d'Empire', *Le Moyen Age*, lxxi (1965), pp. 115, 548.
17. For a discussion of such tendencies in fourteenth-century France, see R. Cazelles, *La Société Politique et la Crise de la Royauté sous Philippe de Valois* (Paris 1958), p. 436: 'la fidelité n'est plus une obligation naturelle, mais un simple lien contractuel qu'on brise à sa guise.'

camp. The crucial questions of loyalty and disloyalty, of fidelity and *lèse-majesté*, were as much part of the rationale and justification for orders of chivalry as they were for the treason trial and *lit-de-justice*.

For men who were neither subjects nor vassals of an order's sovereign or head, the bonds which the order created were more flexible and consequently less directly advantageous to a sovereign as a political investment. To offer the insignia of an order of chivalry was a common weapon in the diplomatic armoury of later medieval and Renaissance rulers. An alliance or a marriage might be secured in this way. Under Edward IV of England, for example, the Garter was offered to eight foreign rulers and nobles: Francesco Sforza, duke of Milan; Ferdinand I, king of Naples, and his chamberlain, Don Iñigo d'Avalos; Charles the Bold of Burgundy; Federigo da Montefeltro, duke of Urbino; Ferdinand, king of Castile and Aragon; Ercole d'Este, duke of Ferrara, and John II, king of Portugal.[18] There is little to suggest that their political behaviour was much influenced by their membership of the order. Most had little in common with Edward IV except their enemies, however proudly Federigo of Urbino might sport the Garter insignia in Joos van Ghent's portrait of him.[19] For the non-subject member of an order of chivalry, if he was the equal of its head, there was little in the bond except cordial, diplomatic friendship. Yet a lesser noble might find his position compromised if the head of an order of which he was a member and his own sovereign lord were in dispute or at war. Some orders, as we shall see, made special provision for such cases in their statutes, clearly aware that the claims exerted by such chivalrous associations might create tensions which could not but influence political behaviour.

To arrive at any conclusions as to the political value of orders of chivalry in the fifteenth century, an analysis and comparison of their statutes, composition and function is necessary. The orders of the *Toison d'Or* and the *Croissant* lend themselves to detailed examination, and comparisons can be drawn between them and the order of the Garter. Copies of their statutes, and the surviving manuscript registers of their chapters and councils, provide the major sources of evidence.[20] To contemporaries, there was evidently a hierarchy of chivalric

18. Beltz, op cit., pp. clxii-clxxvi; C. Ross, *Edward IV* (London 1974), p. 274.

19. See J. Pope-Hennessy, *The Portrait in the Renaissance* (London/New York, 1966), pp. 161-2 and figure 179. This double portrait of Federigo and his son Guidobaldo dates from 1476. Raphael's St George in his painting of *St George and the Dragon* (Washington, National Gallery of Art), also wears the Garter: see B. Berenson, *Italian Painters of the Renaissance. 2. Florentine and Central Italian Schools* (London, 1968), pl. VIII and figure 216. This was presumably intended as a compliment to the ducal house of Urbino.

20. See Baron de Reiffenberg, *Histoire de l'Ordre de la Toison d'Or* (Brussels 1830), passim. The manuscript evidence relating to the order which I have drawn upon is largely to be found in B.R., MS II. 6288, 'Ordonnances de l'Ordre de la thoyson d'Or' (statutes); MS 11205 (poem on the order); and Registers 1 and 2 of the Archiv des Ordens vom Goldenen Vliesse, Vienna. I am indebted to Mr C.A.J. Armstrong for kindly allowing me to use his microfilm of these registers. Much manuscript material relating to the *Croissant* is to be found in BN, MS fr. 25204 (statutes and armorial of the order), MS Clairambault 1241, pp. 905-20 (seventeenth-century miscellany of documents and drawings concerning the order). See plate 4.

laisser et laisseront tout autre ordre ex
ceptez empereurs roys et ducs qui auec ce
present ordre pourront porter lordre dont ilz
seront chief par ainsi que ce soit du gre et con
sentement de nous ou de nos successeurs
souuerains et des freres de lordre prise en
leur chapitre et non autrement Et pareil
lement nous et nz successeurs souuerains
de ce present ordre en cas semblable. pour
rons sil nous plaist porter lordre des dessuz
diz Empereurs roys et ducs auec le nre en
demoustrance de vraye et fraternelle amour
lung enuers lautre. et pour le bien qui en
pourra venir.

iij

Item pour auoir cognoissance dudit
ordre et des cheualiers qui en seront
Nous pour vne fois donnerons a chascun
des cheualiers dicellui ordre vng colier or
fait a nre deuise Cest assauoir par pieces
afacon de fusilz touchans a pierres dont
pertent est incelles ardans et au bout di
cellui colier pendant semblance dune thoi

associations, as there was a hierarchy of angels and a hierarchy of battles. The aged Olivier de la Marche, that ardent exponent of the *Toison d'Or*'s superiority, wrote in his *Epistre pour tenir et celebrer la noble feste du Thoison d'Or* (1500), that a distinction was always to be made between a true *ordre* and a mere *devise*.[21] When a prince gave a certain *devise* (that is, a livery collar or other emblem) to an unlimited number of nobles without issuing written statutes or prescribing 'feasts and solemnities', he did not create an order of chivalry. La Marche cited the example of the kings of England, who had a proper order in the Garter, but also a *devise*, which was given to many nobles and ladies.[22] He was referring to the livery collars distributed by the Lancastrians, Yorkists and Tudors in the form of *SS* insignia; the chain of suns and roses, with the lion of March as a pendant; and the collar of red and white roses.[23] These were in no sense orders because they lacked a fixed membership, written statutes, and regular meetings or chapters. Nor, he continued, were the *Croissant, Camail, Porc-Epic, Hermine*, nor the *devises* created by the kings of Aragon or Cyprus, true orders.[24] As for the *Fer de prisonnier*, the *Ecu vert à la dame Blanche*, or the *Dragon*, such ephemeral fraternities did not even qualify for mention by La Marche.[25] His sole concern was with an exclusive *ordre de prince*, which the Archduke Philip the Fair had inherited from his Burgundian predecessors, and which should never be allowed to lapse.

That order was founded as an 'order and fraternity of chivalry or amiable company of a certain number of knights' and it was as a 'noble company and fraternal union' that La Marche successfully urged its continued existence upon the Habsburgs.[26] A member of the order spoke in May 1468 of its institution as one means of gaining, and keeping, the 'good will and love' (*bonne grace et amour*) of the sovereign,[27] and La Marche endorsed its usefulness by telling Philip the Fair that, as a result, he and his predecessors had had 'great and noble fraternal alliances' with emperors, kings, dukes, counts, barons and knights of great renown.[28] Yet the order was not founded upon fraternal equality. Like the religious military orders of the Temple and the Hospital of St John, with their Grand Masters, the *Toison d'Or* possessed its unique sovereign

21. O. de La Marche, *Mémoires*, ed. H. Beaune, J. d'Arbaumont (*SHF*, Paris, 1883-88), iv, p. 161.
22. Ibid., iv, pp. 161-2.
23. See e.g. A. Hartshorne, 'Notes on collars of SS', *Archaeological Journal*, xxxix (1882), pp. 376ff.
24. La Marche, *Mémoires*, iv, p. 162.
25. See *Choix de pièces inédites relatives au règne de Charles VI*, ed. L. Douët-d'Arcq, i (*SHF*, Paris, 1863), pp. 370-4; *La Chronique du bon duc Loys de Bourbon*, ed. A.N. Chazaud (*SHF*, Paris, 1876), pp. 8-15; Lewis, art. cit., pp. 77-84 for the *Dragon* and a bibliographical survey of the statutes of chivalric orders in late medieval France; P. Contamine, 'L'Histoire militaire et l'histoire de la guerre dans la France médiévale depuis trente ans', *Actes du 100e Congrès National des Sociétés Savantes*, i (Paris, 1977), pp. 71-93 for a recent bibliography.
26. La Marche, *Mémoires*, iv, p. 163; BR, MS II. 6288, fo. 7r.
27. AOGV Reg. 2, fo. 4r. The words were those of Jean, count of Nevers.
28. La Marche, *Mémoires*, iv, p. 159.

in the person of the duke of Burgundy.[29] In 1424, Philip the Good had refused to accept the Garter, not wishing to pledge himself further than was expedient to the cause of Henry VI of England, and Chastellain thought that he had founded the *Toison d'Or* to escape another offer of the Garter from John, duke of Bedford.[30] There may well have been a covert political purpose of this kind behind the institution of the order, and it certainly imitated the English order in many respects, with its statutes, chapters and officers, including a king-of-arms and a pursuivant. There were to be 24 members apart from the sovereign (later increased to 31); they were to be noble in both name and arms, and without reproach.[31] The *Toison d'Or* was indeed the Burgundian Garter.

Why Philip the Good chose the Golden Fleece as the emblem for his new order remains obscure. There can be no doubt that the legend of Jason's seizure of the Fleece on the island of Colchis, aided by the charms of Medea, lay at the root of his choice. The story, with its dubious pagan and necromantic associations, as well as Jason's deception and desertion of Medea, hardly provided an edifying moral foundation for the new order.[32] By November 1431, Jean Germain, bishop of Châlon and first chancellor of the order, had proposed a worthier patron, the biblical Gideon, for, as Jean du Clercq noted, Jason had broken a promise.[33] Whatever the precise significance of Philip the Good's choice, the Fleece itself was held to embody the virtues ostensibly cultivated by the order. Guillaume Fillastre, bishop of Toul and its second chancellor, spoke of the Fleece as an incarnation of magnanimity, and the notion of knightly quest was to be associated with it.[34] Just as the Grail, or the ring of the Nibelungs, had been the objects of a quest, so Jason and the Argonauts were seen as models of knight-errantry in search of a rich and precious prize. Whether or not there were crusading intentions behind the order, the idea of chivalrous adventure was not lacking. None of this was, perhaps surprisingly, couched in an Arthurian mould, nor, as we shall see, did the order of the *Croissant* make any allusion to the knights of the Round Table.[35] To establish an order under the ambiguous patronage of Jason and Gideon was perhaps symbolic of that uneasy

29. B.R., MS II. 6288, fo. 9r (art. 4). For the Grand Master of the Temple see *La Règle du Temple*, ed. H. de Curzon (*SHF*, Paris, 1866), pp. xvi-xx.

30. Chastellain, op. cit., vii, p. 216: 'Pour evader les Anglois et de leur ordre, mist sus le sien propre, la Toison d'Or.'

31. BR, MS II. 6288, fos. 7r-7v; cf. Beltz, op. cit, p. clviii and H.S. London, *The Life of William Bruges, first Garter King of Arms* (Harleian Society, London, 1970), pp. 43-4 for contacts between Bruges and Jean Lefèvre, lord of St-Rémy, before 1431. Lefèvre was appointed *Toison d'Or* king of arms in November 1431.

32. See G. Doutrepont, 'Jason et Gedéon, patrons de la Toison d'Or', *Mélanges Godefroid Kurth* (Liège/Paris, 1908), ii, pp. 191-208; Le vicomte Terlinden, 'Les origines religieuses et politiques de la Toison d'Or', *PCEEBM*, v (1963), pp. 35-46.

33. Doutrepont art. cit., p. 196.

34. Ibid., p. 207.

35. See *infra*, p. 52; for the possible decline of interest in Arthurian literature at the courts of Burgundy and Anjou, Pickford, op. cit., p. 279 and *supra*, p. 16, n. 10.

juxtaposition of Christian and pagan mysteries that was so characteristic of Renaissance culture.[36] By 1448 Philip the Good had commissioned tapestries from the Tournai workshops depicting the 'history of Gideon or of the Golden Fleece', and in 1456 Raoul Lefèvre's *Livre du preux Jason et de la belle Medée* sought to justify Jason's treatment of Medea and to christianise the story.[37] One might conclude that Philip's choice of the Fleece may have stemmed from some topical and quite ephemeral episode, possibly deriving from an entertainment or *entremet* devised for the marriage celebrations of the duke and Isabella of Portugal in January 1430.

A certain Burgundian traditionalism, however, permeated the original statutes of the order. The dedicatee was to be St Andrew, patron saint of Burgundy, and the order's insignia was exceptional in that it incorporated the sovereign's personal livery collar into the new device of the *Toison d'Or*. Since the capture of John of Nevers (later John the Fearless) by the Turks in 1396, the flint and fire-steel, striking sparks, had been one emblem of the ducal house.[38] This was apparently adopted as part of a vow made to avenge John's capture and to recover the Holy Places from the infidel. Philip the Good had revived the badge as his own personal emblem by 1421, and the foundation statutes insisted that the collar of gold flints and steels, as well as the pendant fleece, were to be worn daily.[39] The duke's sovereignty over his order was thus made plain. Unlike the Garter, the *Toison d'Or* was not independent of the sovereign's own *devise*, but inextricably bound up with it, for members of the order were to be fined for wearing the pendant alone. The duke was not merely one brother in a fraternal alliance, but the 'head, chief and sovereign' of a body which was designed to strengthen existing bonds between a great magnate and those who wore his livery. If you appeared in public wearing the collar of the *Toison d'Or*, you were the duke of Burgundy's man.

The foundation statutes of the order are uncompromisingly exclusive in their emphasis upon personal loyalty to the duke alone. Its members were to abandon membership of all other chivalric associations, pledging themselves on oath to the *Toison d'Or* and its sovereign alone.[40] Difficulties in the enlistment of other great princes had led by November 1440, however, to the addition of an exception in favour of 'emperors, kings and dukes', who were permitted to bear 'the order of which they are head' as well as the *Toison d'Or*.[41] The exception

36. V. Tourneur, 'Les origines de l'Ordre de la Toison d'Or et la symbolique des insignes de celui-ci', *Bulletin de l'Académie Royale de Belgique. Lettres*, 5e série, xlii (1956), pp. 300-23.

37. Doutrepont, art. cit., pp. 200, 202.

38. E.E. Rosenthal, 'The invention of the columnar device of the Emperor Charles V at the court of Burgundy in Flanders in 1516', *JWCI*, xxxvi (1973), p. 204.

39. F. Deuchler, 'Zur Burgundischen Heraldik und Emblematik', *Die Burgunderbeute und Werke Burgundischer Hofkunst* (Bernischer Historisches Museum, Bern, 1969), p. 36; BR, MS II. 6288, fos. 8r-8v. See plate 13.

40. Ibid., fo. 8r (art. 2). See plate 4.

41. Ibid., fo. 8r; AOGV Reg. I, fo. 27v (30 November 1440).

appears to have been made first for Charles, duke of Orléans, elected in 1440, so that he might bear his own *devise* of the *Camail* without infringing the statutes of the *Toison d'Or*. Philip the Good was in turn permitted to bear the order of any other such prince as a 'token of true and fraternal love one towards the other'.[42] He accordingly received the order of the *Camail*. Charles of Orléans was too valuable an ally to lose in 1440, when Philip the Good was plotting against an embattled Charles VII.[43] The exclusive adherence of great lords of high status was clearly impossible, and obviously detrimental to the conclusion of diplomatic alliances. An inflexible rule of abdication from any other order, as had been required from the Knights Templar by their statutes,[44] was inappropriate, and could not further the cause of the house of Burgundy with its peers. To its subjects and vassals, on the other hand, this rule was inflexibly applied. There could be no deviation in the loyalty of those bound by this 'corporate retainder' to the service of the Burgundian dynasty.[45] A Burgundian noble, from whatever area of the ducal lands he came, could not serve two masters.

His service was essentially personal in nature.' The statutes of the order stipulated service in war for 'reasonable wages' if the duke's lands or subjects were attacked, or if he should undertake a crusade.[46] All members were to be forewarned of a ducal intention to wage war, except in 'secret and hasty enterprises'.[47] No member who was a subject or vassal of the duke was to indulge in warfare, nor make long journeys abroad, without informing him, and the duke was to prevent internal conflict within the order. This precept was obeyed, for example, in May 1468 when Jean I, duke of Cleves, was accused in the chapter of commencing

> war against my lord Adolf, young duke of Guelders, his nephew, brother of the order, which is against the fourth chapter of the ordinances of the said order, by which the brother-knights ... are held, and promise at their initiation, to show good and true love to the sovereign and to each other, and to ... advance the honour and profit and prevent the harm and dishonour of those of the said order ...[48]

Jean of Cleves had also raided the lands in Brabant of his younger brother Adolf, lord of Ravenstein and fellow-knight of the order 'without defiance or

---

42. Ibid., fo. 27v.
43. M.G.A. Vale, *Charles VII* (London 1974), p. 85.
44. *Règle du Temple*, no. 670.
45. C.A.J. Armstrong, '... policy for the nobility?', p. 25.
46. BR, MS II. 6288, fos. 9v–10r (art. 5).
47. Ibid., fo. 10r.
48. AOGV, Reg. 2, fo. 46r; BR, MS II. 6288, fo. 10v: 'la guerre contre monseigneur Adolph, jeune duc de Ghelres, son nepveu, confrere de lordre, qui est contre le ive chapittre des ordonnances dudit ordre, par lequel les chevaliers confreres sont tenus, et promettent a leur entree, davoir bonne et vraye amour au souverain et lung a lautre, et vouloir pourchasser et avancer a leur povoir lonneur et prouffit, et eschiever la dommaige et deshonneur de ceulx dudit ordre ...'.

reasonable cause'.[49] The chapter invoked the eighth article of the statutes and decided to enforce submission of these disputes to the sovereign. If both Cleves and Guelders refused to come to heel, Fusil, the order's herald, was to bear a summons to them to present themselves at the next chapter to answer charges against them.[50] Civil war within the Burgundian domains could not be tolerated, and the *Toison d'Or* was one means whereby an aggressive and competitive nobility might not only be united, but disciplined. Such measures were of course inapplicable to members who were not subjects, vassals or clients of the duke. The statutes recognised that if he made war against the lords of non-subject members, the latter were to 'preserve their honour and defend their natural lord and his lands …'[51] There was a prior claim upon the allegiance of men such as Friedrich, count of Mörs, subject of the German emperor, and founder member of the order, which could override his obligations to the *Toison d'Or*.[52] As in the contemporary *alliances* contracted between the counts of Foix and men 'who were not [their] subjects', limitations had to be imposed upon the terms of their service.[53] That no exception was made in favour of the crown of France for Burgundian subjects and vassals was, conversely, a clear and unequivocal expression of the duke's desire to be truly sovereign, not merely over the *Toison d'Or*, but over his scattered and heterogeneous lordships. Though technically subjects of the Lancastrian, and then the Valois, monarchy, Burgundian nobles were effectively prevented, through the 'corporate retainer' imposed by the order, from serving the king against the duke.

Should they do so, an infringement of the statutes to which they had sworn a solemn oath would be committed. A man could be expelled from membership of the order on three grounds: heretical religious beliefs; the crime of treason or *lèse-majesté*; and flight from a battle or encounter in which banners had been unfurled.[54] The last clause echoed the statutes of John the Good's order of the Star (1351) and was clearly designed to prevent desertion of a cause on the field of battle, which was censured by Ghillebert de Lannoy in his *Enseignements Paternels*.[55] The writers of treatises for the edification of the nobility and those who framed the statutes of the *Toison d'Or* were at one in their condemnation of

49. AOGV, Reg. 2, fo. 46r.

50. Ibid., fo. 46v.

51. BR, MS II.6288, fo. 12r (art. 11): 'garder leur honneur et deffendre leur naturel seigneur et ses pays.'

52. Armstrong, '… policy for the nobility?', p. 27; Vaughan, *Philip the Good*, p. 161.

53. P. Raymond, 'Rôles de l'Armée rassemblée … par Gaston Phoebus, comte de Foix en 1376', *Archives Historiques du Département de la Gironde*, xii (1870), p. 141; P.S. Lewis, 'Decayed and non-feudalism in later medieval France', *BIHR*, xxxvii (1964), pp. 161-74; M.G.A. Vale, *English Gascony, 1399-1453* (Oxford, 1970), pp. 167-70, 173-4.

54. BR, MS II. 6288, fos. 12r-12v (arts. 14, 15, 16).

55. C.A.J. Armstrong, 'La Toison d'Or et la loi des armes', *PCEEBM*, v (1963), pp. 71-7. For the effects of this obligation on the behaviour of members of the order of the Star at the battle of Mauron, August 1352, see *Chronicon Galfridi le Baker de Swynebroke*, ed. E.M. Thompson (Oxford 1889), i, p. 120 and ii, p. 287. Cf. Lannoy, op. cit., p. 460.

heresy, treason and dishonourable conduct in battle.[56] One might reasonably suspect a certain identity of assumption, intention and interest among them. If the elevated notions of honour and virtue expressed in the treatises had any impact whatsoever upon the actual behaviour of nobles, an order of chivalry could provide a means whereby those ideals might be translated into practice. Members were expelled from the *Toison d'Or* in 1431 and 1473 for cowardice in battle, and in 1468 on (exceedingly dubious) grounds of sorcery and abuse of the sacraments.[57] Just as Sir John Fastolf was deprived of the order of the Garter for his allegedly craven conduct at Patay in June 1429,[58] so Louis de Châlon, prince of Orange, Jean de Montagu-Neufchâtel and Louis de Châteauguyon lost their insignia of the *Toison d'Or* as a result of their flight from the fields of Anthon and Bussy.[58a] In England, Henry VIII's revised Garter statutes of 1522 defined the grounds for 'reproach' and consequent dismissal in exactly the same terms as the *Toison d'Or*.[59] Personal valour and loyalty to the sovereign had merged to produce orders of chivalry which were peculiarly appropriate to the political climate of their time. The secular orders made no less rigorous demands than the order of the Temple, whose rule asserted that 'if a brother leaves his *gonfanon* [banner] and flees for fear of the Saracens, he is expelled from the house'.[60] Contemporaries referred to the 'religion' of the *Toison d'Or*, and its records suggest that they were right to do so.[61]

The knights of the *Toison d'Or* were a select and exclusive body. Limited in number, they constituted a kind of peerage among the nobility of the Burgundian lands. La Marche supported the limitation of membership to 31 nobles because, he wrote, 'if there should be more knights, more contentious matters could arise between those knights that do not make for their unity nor for the furtherance of the intentions of the [order's] head.'[62] Internal dissensions might disrupt a larger body, and, given the lack in the Burgundian lands of a central representative institution on the English pattern, with its house of peers, entry into the ranks of this exclusive élite had to be severely restricted. Membership, like that of the Garter, was by election through secret ballot of the knights meeting together in chapter. The names of candidates were recorded by the *greffier*, and their 'estate and merits' were discussed by the assembled

56. *Supra*, pp. 15, 26-7.

57. Armstrong, '... loi des armes', pp. 73-6; AOGV Reg. 2, fo. 21r; *infra*, pp. 50-1.

58. Monstrelet, *Chronicles*, ed. T. Johnes (London 1840), p. 555; *Chronique*, ed. Douët-d'Arcq, iv, 331-2.

58a. Armstrong, '... la loi des armes', pp. 73-6.

59. Beltz, op. cit., p. lxxxiv.

60. *Règle du Temple*, nos 574, 164: 'se frere laisse son confanon et fuit par paor des Sarrazins, il pert la maison.'

61. *The Waning of the Middle Ages*, p. 84.

62. La Marche, *Mémoires*, iv, pp. 167-8: 'plus de chevalliers y auroit et plus d'estranges choses pourroient advenir entre iceulx chevalliers qu'ilz ne seroient pas tous correspondans à l'union d'iceulx et au proffit de l'intencion du chief.'

order.[63] In May 1473, the election of five new knights took five or six days, according to one account, and the process of selection seems to have borne a close resemblance to that of the Garter.[64] In April 1429, for instance, Sir John Radcliffe was elected to the Garter after his sponsors had submitted a written account of his merits. This declared that 'he hathe brought by hys labour in knyghthood to hys soveraign lords obeysance, within the duchie of Guyen, many dyverse cytes, townes and fortresses'.[65] The materials for a roll of honour, or a chronicle, recording the 'vertus et bonnes meurs' of their members, were evidently not lacking either for the Garter or for the *Toison d'Or*.

Yet a sense of unity was lacking among the nobility of the disparate provinces of the Burgundian lands. Perhaps the most striking difference between the Flemish nobility and that of ducal Burgundy was that the former tended to live by preference in the towns, the latter on their rural estates.[66] Politically, the privileges, customs and liberties of the various provinces defied attempts at centralisation, and the Second Estate of the county of Holland or the duchy of Guelders had little in common with that of the duchy of Brabant, the Franche-Comté, or the counties of Rethel and Nevers. To create a common focus of allegiance, dependence upon the person of the duke was essential, and it was through the court and the *Toison d'Or* that such dependence was achieved.[67] The founder members of the order were drawn from a very wide geographical range, representing most territories in ducal hands in 1430. The stalls erected for the second chapter of the order, in the collegiate church of St Donatian at Bruges (30 November 1432) bore, like those in St George's, Windsor, plates displaying the arms of the members, beginning with those of the duke, 'first creator and founder of the noble order of Gideon's *Toison d'Or*', and including the heraldic achievements of the families of Lannoy, Croy, Luxembourg, Vergy, La Trémoïlle, Créqui, Brimeu, Lalaing and Charny.[68] Both senior and cadet branches were represented by three members of the house of Lannoy, two of Croy and three of Brimeu, seated, like members of the English Upper House, in one assembly.[69] If there was a movement towards the creation of a caste among the Burgundian nobility in the fifteenth century, an analysis of the composition of the chapters of the *Toison d'Or* might accurately reflect it.

If the Burgundian nobility were divided by geography, law and custom, they

63. AOGV, Reg. 1, fo. 5v.

64. Valenciennes, Bibliothèque Municipale, MS 776, fo. 71v for an account by Charolais Herald, *maréchal d'armes* of Brabant, of the chapter and festivities of 1473.

65. Oxford, Bodleian Library, Ashmole MS 1132, fo. 149a; E. Ashmole, *The Institution, Laws and Ceremonies of the Order of the Garter* (London 1672), pp. 270ff.

66. Armstrong, '... policy for the nobility?', p. 9; D.M. Nicholas, *Town and Countryside: Social, Economic and Political Tensions in Fourteenth-Century Flanders* (Bruges 1971), pp. 251-2, 350-1.

67. Armstrong, '... policy for the nobility?', pp. 21, 25-7.

68. J. Gailliard, *Inscriptions Funéraires et Monumentales de la Flandre Occidentale*, i, part 1 (Bruges 1861), pp. 23-34; W.H. St John Hope, *The Stall-Plates of the Knights of the Order of the Garter, 1348-1485* (London 1901), passim.

69. Cf. McFarlane, op. cit., pp. 274-8.

were also divided by language. The great majority of members of the order of the *Toison d'Or* were primarily French-speaking, for the administrative and courtly language of much of the Burgundian Netherlands was French, but attention has been drawn to an early copy of the order's statutes, written in Netherlandish at some date before November 1440.[70] The use of Netherlandish was certainly accepted by the order. Reinoude van Brederode, a Dutch member, thus demanded a copy of the statutes in Netherlandish and conducted his defence before the chapter of May 1456 in his native tongue. This, it has been shown, 'was intended to emphasise that a feudal family of Holland was challenging the Burgundian dynastic interest' on the issue of a disputed election to the bishopric of Utrecht.[71] It can have done little to commend the use of Netherlandish at meetings of the order to Philip the Good or Charles the Bold. French was the language of Burgundian literature and the order was created in the context of a French-speaking court. It was the *Toison d'Or*, not the *Guldenen Vlies*, to which literate contemporaries referred. An effectively united nobility was at least to a certain extent dependent upon linguistic unity and the *lingua franca* of chivalry was French. To use any other tongue at the solemn meetings of the order had become a gesture of defiance.

A further means of promoting a sense of corporate action towards a common end was the institution of religious ceremonies for the order. A brotherhood of collective devotion was thereby created. Two services were laid down for the order – vespers, followed on the morrow by a solemn requiem mass for the souls of deceased members. The elaborate liturgical observances described by La Marche, confirmed by the registers of the order, remind one of the ecclesiastical counterparts of knightly fraternities.[72] The knights of the order sat in their stalls as canons might sit in the prebendal stalls of a cathedral chapter, often taking over the choir during these ceremonies. In the course of the requiem the *greffier* was to pronounce the names of all the deceased members 'briefly touching upon their noble deeds and *gestes*', and La Marche noted that before the offertory a 'notable frere prescheur' should preach a sermon recalling the reasons for the order's foundation and exhorting its members to perpetuate this 'noble confrairie et amiable fraternité'.[73] Duly apparelled in the vestments of the order – crimson cloaks – the knights of the *Toison d'Or* were observing a secular liturgy of chivalry for which space had been appropriated within the established Church. Yet the overtones of politics intruded even into this aspect of the order's activities. An account of these religious ceremonies, composed after the Burgundian *débacle* of 1477 when the nobility divided themselves between France and the German Empire, referred to the

70. C.A.J. Armstrong, 'The language question in the Low Countries', *Europe in the Late Middle Ages*, ed. J.R. Hale, J.R.L. Highfield and B. Smalley (London 1965), p. 403.
71. Ibid., pp. 403-4.
72. La Marche, *Mémoires*, iv, pp. 166-7, 168ff.; *The Waning of the Middle Ages*, p. 84; AOGV Reg. 3, fos. 15r-16v.
73. Ibid., fo. 16r; La Marche, *Mémoires*, iv, p. 179.

arms of the five knights being in France, on the opposing side, which knights have not been summoned to the offertory ... but when their turn came to be called, the king-of-arms [Toison d'Or] ... went up to the place where the plate of their arms was, making a little bow, and thus passed on without saying a word ...[74]

The *Toison d'Or* could not be anything other than a political institution.

To its political rôle were added judicial, almost inquisitorial functions. The chapters appear to have become something resembling tribunals, in which the political and moral behaviour of the Burgundian nobility was examined and praised, or criticised and censured. At the 1468 chapter, for example, an inquisition was held into the 'virtues and good conduct' of the members, to ascertain if any had committed anything 'against the honour, fame, estate and statutes of the said order'.[75] The dukes of Cleves and Guelders were then arraigned on 'certain points touching their honour'. As most of these 'points' concerned such matters as the waging of illicit feuds, acts of *lèse-majesté*, or dishonourable conduct in war, the chapter combined some of the features of the French *parlement* and the English Court of Chivalry.[76] From its foundation, the order had indulged in 'examinations and corrections' of its members, although under Philip the Good their moral probity was not generally assessed. The duke himself, that 'homme lubrique', was hardly in a strong position to condemn his nobles for their sexual laxity, unlike his chaste and puritannical son.[77] In the chapter of November 1432, the register recorded that

today we proceeded to examine the life and government of the knights present, and of the sovereign, as in the preceding year, but there was found in none of the said brothers and companions ... nor in the sovereign, any wrong or vice to be corrected, according to the statutes and ordinances of the order.[78]

Charles the Bold's reign proved much more fruitful in moral peccadilloes and unworthy lapses. In 1468, Adolf, lord of Ravenstein, was reproved for his *lubricité*, and Anthoine, *grand bâtard* of Burgundy, for his adulterous conduct, excessive liberality and unfulfilled promises. Jean II, duke of Alençon, was warned about the possible consequences of his blasphemy and *sortilèges*; Reinoude van Brederode was implicated in two murders, but cleared himself;

74. AOGV Reg. 3, fos. 15v-16r: 'les escucons des armes des cinq chevaliers estans en France ou parti contraire, lesquelz chevaliers nont point este appellez pour aler a loffrande ... mais quant leur tour estoit pour les appeler le Roy darmes ... ala devant le lieu du tableau de leurs armes faisant petite inclinacion, et ainsi passa oultre sans mot dire ...'

75. Ibid., Reg. 2, fo 47r.

76. Ibid., fo. 46v; G.D. Squibb, *The High Court of Chivalry* (London 1959), pp. 1-9; C.A.J. Armstrong, 'Sir John Fastolf and the law of arms', *War, Literature and Politics*, pp. 55-6.

77. Vaughan, *Philip the Good*, pp. 132-3; *Charles the Bold*, pp. 158-9.

78. AOGV Reg.1, fo. 6r: 'ce jour fut procede a lexamen de la vie et gouvernement des chevaliers presens et du souverain, comme lannee precedente, mais il ne fut trouve sur aucuns desdits freres et compaignons presens ne sur le souverain quelque blasme ou vice a corriger selon les statuz et ordonnances de lordre ...'.

Pierre de Bauffremont, lord of Charny, was acused of swearing false oaths on the name of the order and on his own honour, but successfully answered the charges; and Louis de Bruges, lord of La Gruthuyse, was alerted to the danger of *corruptions* in his native land.[79] Others, such as Philippe Pot, were unstintingly praised for their 'vertus, meurs et bonne vie', and were exhorted to continue in their careers of unblemished virtue.[80] In some cases the order, probably at the duke's instigation, took action to arbitrate in family quarrels. On 12 May 1468, Jean de Neuchâtel, lord of Montagu, was required to answer accusations of rancour towards his elder brother, the marshal of Burgundy, whose offices he had, it was alleged, sought to obtain. He had 'spoken rudely in chapter about my said lord the marshal ... saying that he did not recognise him at all as the head of his house nor lord of his [heraldic] arms'.[81] He further claimed that, had it not been for the terms of his father's will, he should bear the 'full arms' of his house and enjoy one half of the lordship of Neuchâtel. He based this claim upon the regional customs of 'the place where it [Neuchâtel] is situated in Germany (*es Allemaignes*)'.[82] His fellow-knights delayed judgment, pending his reply to further points made by his brother.

A similar case of fraternal conflict was raised when Pierre de Bauffremont, lord of Charny, withdrew from the chapter, while his peers examined his conduct.[83] He had left his brother as a hostage and pledge for the payment of a ransom and the chapter considered his behaviour dilatory. His reply was that he had gone to great pains to have his brother released from prison: he had offered to sell his lands to raise the money, but had found no purchaser; he had already disbursed 16,000 *écus*, and would pay the residue as quickly as he could. The chapter demanded to see his sealed bond concerning payment, and he was required to give a precise date by which his brother would be released and his ransom fully paid.[84] Such affairs were clearly thought to be matters of honour, falling within the purview of the order. Interestingly, the rules of the twelfth-century military orders had stipulated regular disciplinary assemblies in which accusations were made by the brothers and confessions were received.[85] The brother concerned was, like a *Toison d'Or* member, to leave the chapter while his fate was decided. Once again, a degree of conscious imitation, in which the religious order furnished the secular fraternities with a model, might be

79. Ibid., Reg.2, fos. 45r, 45v, 47v, 48v, 51v, 44r.
80. Ibid., fos. 44r, 44v.
81. Ibid., fo. 47v: 'Quil a parle rudement en chapitre envers monditseigneur le mareschal ... disant quil ne le recognoissoit point pour son chief et seigneur de ses armes.'
82. Ibid., fo. 48v: 'au regard de la maison de Neufchastel selon les coustumes du lieu ou elle este situee es Alemaingnes, se ne feust par le testament et partaige fait par feu leur pere, il deust porter les plaines armes et avoir la moitie de la maison et seigneurie de Neufchastel, pareillement comme monseigneur le mareschal ...'.
83. Ibid., fo. 51r-51v.
84. Ibid., fo. 51v. For a more celebrated ransom case among the Burgundian nobility, see Bossuat, 'Les Prisonniers de guerre', pp. 7-35.
85. See *Règle du Temple*, pp. xxviii-xxix.

detected here. The order of chivalry supplied a ruler as high-minded as Charles the Bold with a partial means of control over the more wayward of his subjects.

Yet attempts could also be made by the nobles to use the order against the duke himself. As a brother-knight he was not exempt from criticism, and less than one year after his accession Charles the Bold was already answering complaints and charges at the chapter of May 1468.[86] Although this gave him an opportunity to indulge in rhetorical speeches and harangues, which he clearly enjoyed, this early exposure to criticism would hardly have endeared the order to him. No further chapter-general was held until 1473 when, to the duke's evident distaste, the same criticisms and remonstrances were not merely resubmitted, but considerably expanded.[87] All was not well in the order, and Charles was firmly requested to 'have benign regard for the statutes and ordinances ... and set his mind to them, considering that all my lords of the order are obliged to keep, observe and maintain them in their turn ...'[88] The members asked him for peace. He showed no sign of giving them anything but war. There was little hope that their remonstrances might be accepted, even less that they would be acted upon. The evidence suggests that the order became an instrument for the disciplining of subject nobles, never for effective criticism of the sovereign. As a forum for discussion, regulation and adjudication of cases concerning the allegiance and loyalty of the nobility, the order now served an overtly judicial purpose.

The political behaviour of the dukes themselves could not fail to influence that of their nobles. Philip the Good's defection from allegiance to the Lancastrian dual monarchy of England and France, for example, in September 1435 caused some members of the *Toison d'Or* considerable disquiet. On 8 December, the order was presented with a request for advice from Jean de Villiers, lord of L'Isle-Adam, in which he set out the history of his service to the house of Burgundy and the English régime since 1416.[89] He had been dispossessed from the office of marshal of France by John, duke of Exeter, imprisoned in the Bastille, released through Philip the Good's influence, and retained as his chamberlain. Although the *parlement* of Paris had vindicated him and John, duke of Bedford, had again offered him the office of marshal, thereby restoring his honour, he was still doubtful about the implications of his past behaviour. He had accepted the marshal's bâton from Bedford and sworn the customary oath, but since that date the *volte-face* at Arras had taken place. L'Isle-Adam thus addressed his petition to the duke and his fellow-knights of the order, requesting that

---

86. AOGV, Reg.2, fos. 52v-53v; Vaughan, *Charles the Bold*, p. 172.
87. AOGV, Reg.3, fos. 27r-29v; trans. in Vaughan, *Charles the Bold*, pp. 172-8.
88. Vaughan, *Charles the Bold*, p. 173.
89. AOGV, Reg.1, fos. 19r-19v. He wrote a treatise on the judicial combat for Philip the Good which was included in Olivier de la Marche's *Livre de l'advis de gaige de bataille*, dedicated to Philip the Fair: see *Traités du duel judiciaire: relations de Pas d'Armes et Tournois*, ed. B. Prost (Paris 1872), pp. 28-41. L'Isle-Adam was killed during a rising at Bruges in 1437.

considering the treaty which it has recently pleased you to make in your town of
Arras, it may please you to give me advice as to what I should do concerning the
said office, oath and my honour. Also may it please you to have pity on, and
regard for, my poor condition and estate ... seeing the danger which threatens the
country in which my lands lie, and that it is daily near to destruction.[90]

L'Isle-Adam was reassured by the duke and the order, but his predicament was
not unique. Jean de Luxembourg, lord of Hautbordin, bastard of St Pol, was
also a victim of the Burgundian change of allegiance. He similarly petitioned
the order for advice, because he had been given the lordship of Montmorency by
Bedford after the siege of Orléans in 1429.[91] The grant had been confirmed by
Henry VI, as king of France, and he had performed homage and fealty for the
seigneurie. Yet by December 1435 he told his peers that 'affairs stand otherwise
at present and are very much changed'.[92] The duke, as sovereign of the order,
was responsible for the consequences of his political actions – the compromised
honour of certain of its most distinguished members had to be satisfied and
some form of compensation for their material losses offered. It is striking that
they should have chosen the chapters of the order as a forum for discussion of
their cases. Lacking a fully sovereign court of appeal, Philip the Good may well
have encouraged his nobles to submit such cases to the order so that these were
not taken to the Paris *parlement*, where they would escape his jurisdiction.

The equivocal, if not hostile, relationship between the last two Valois dukes of
Burgundy and the crown of France constantly infiltrated the chapters of the
order after 1435. In the chapter-general of 1468, two members whose stance
towards the monarchy was thought unacceptable were arraigned. Henrik van
Borselen, lord of Veere, the Dutch captain of the Burgundian fleet, was accused
of having 'taken a pension and office from the king [Louis XI], that is to say, as
lieutenant of the late admiral on this side of the sea, although he resides outside
the kingdom and is in no way the king's subject'.[93] His son, the lord of
Boucham, had also accepted an annual pension of 1,000 francs from the king,
although he claimed to have received nothing of it for three years. Nevertheless,
the matter was interpreted as a case of unwarranted interference in Burgundian
affairs. Although van Borselen's plea that he had accepted the office under

90. AOGV Reg.1, fo. 20r: 'que veu le traictie que derrenierement vous a pleu faire en vostre ville
Darras il vous plaise moy donner conseil de ce que jay a faire touchant ladite office, serment et mon
honneur. Et aussi vous plaise ... avoir pitie et regard de mon povre fait et estat, veu le dangier qui est
ou pays ou mes terres sont assise et que chascun jour est en voie de destruction.' For the problems
posed to both French and Burgundian partisans by the treaty of 1435, see A. Bossuat, 'Le
rétablissement de la paix sociale sous le règne de Charles VII', *Le Moyen Age*, lx (1954), pp. 137-62;
'Le Parlement de Paris pendant l'occupation anglaise', *Revue Historique*, ccxxix (1963), pp. 19-40 for
grants by the Lancastrian régime to Burgundian supporters and allies.
91. AOGV, Reg.1, fo. 18v.
92. Ibid., fo. 18v.
93. Ibid., Reg.2, fo. 49v, 50r (discussion of the case by the chapter): 'quil a prins pension et office
du Roy, assavoir de lieutenant du feu admiral par mer pardeca, veu quil demeure hors du royaume
et nest de riens subgiet au Roy.'

Philip the Good with the duke's consent was upheld, the chapter forbade him
from exercising it in future. A change of ducal policy – from Philip the Good's
uneasy accommodation with Charles VII to Charles the Bold's open defiance of
Louis XI – was again at the heart of the problem. A Dutch nobleman, like his
Flemish and Burgundian peers, was not allowed to serve two masters. Ducal
sovereignty over the nobility of all the Burgundian lands was expressed at its
most forceful, however, by the resolutions of the 1468 chapter condemning the
behaviour of the duke's kinsman, Jean de Bourgogne, count of Nevers.[94] His
loyal service to the ducal house under Philip the Good had turned to rancour
under Philip's son. The chapter-general of 1468 was thus witness to a family
quarrel within the upper ranks of the house. Jean de Nevers had refused to
answer a summons to the chapter, and had sent back his collar of the *Toison
d'Or* in the hands of a pursuivant, together with two letters explaining his
resignation. One letter was addressed to the duke, the other to his brother-
knights. The second is more revealing than the first. Both were written at Tours
on 15 April 1468, and were read aloud to the order. Nevers told Charles the
Bold that from him he could expect neither justice nor goodwill and, according
to the statutes of the order, was justified in withdrawing from it. Most of the
possessions of the house of Nevers were, he claimed, unjustly held by Charles,
and he had decided to return the collar. With his brother-knights, however, he
was more forthcoming. A clash of loyalties had caused him to refuse the
summons. He was, he wrote, at Tours 'with my lord the king, my natural and
sovereign lord', who had ordered him to stay there.[95] This was an explicit
rejection of ducal sovereignty. Many people, he claimed, were astonished at the
summons

> especially because the said order is a fraternity of chivalry or amiable company,
> and by the fourth chapter of its statutes, the knights of the same promise to show
> good and true love to their head, and one towards the other, and the head towards
> the knights, and because I ... cannot obtain from my said lord and cousin any
> request which I have made ... to him.[96]

He could no longer keep his oath to the sovereign of the order, because this was
incompatible with his obedience to his sovereign lord. The statutes were
unobservable and untenable, for 'according to reason, in every oath it is
understood that the sovereign's authority should be excepted'.[97] He had no

94. Ibid., fos. 3v-5v, 20v-21r. For Nevers' 'antics' in 1467 during Charles the Bold's negotiations
with Liège, see Vaughan, *Charles the Bold*, p. 14.
95. AOGV, Reg.2, fo. 4v.
96. Ibid., fo. 5r: 'mesmement que ledit ordre est une fraternite de chevalerie, ou amiable
compaingnie, et que par le ive chapittre ... les chevaliers dicellui promectent avoir bonne et vraye
amour a leur chef, et lung envers lautre, et ledit chief envers lesdis chevaliers, et que ... ne puis
obtenir envers monditseigneur et cousin quelque devoir que jaye fait ... envers lui'.
97. Ibid., fo. 5r: 'car selon raison en tout serment ou jurement est entendu lauctorite du
souverain exceptee.'

alternative but to resign from an association which required him to disobey his 'natural and sovereign lord'. Charles the Bold's maladroit mishandling of such men made mockery of the unifying purpose of his father's order. Nevers was degraded and disgraced, his arms were taken down from their place above his stall in the church of Notre-Dame at Bruges and replaced with the following inscription, painted on a black ground, and clearly visible from below:

> The sentence delivered by the chapter of the order against the count of Nevers: The count of Nevers, summoned by letters patent of our lord the duke, sealed with the seal of his order of the *Toison d'Or*, to appear in person at the present chapter, to answer on his honour concerning a case of sorcery (*sortilège*) in abusing the Holy Sacraments of the Church, has not presented himself nor appeared. Thus he has defaulted, and in order to avoid trial, and deprivation of the order ... he has sent back the collar, and for this reason has been ... declared expelled from the said order and not called to the offertory.[98]

It was easy to disguise the true reasons for his resignation under trumped-up religious charges, and the credibility of the *Toison d'Or* as a body dedicated to the mutual welfare of its members scarcely gained from the episode. The cracks in the Burgundian edifice were already clearly visible. The register of the 1468 chapter suggests that the order was being employed not merely as an instrument of control, but of prosecution. As such, it reflects the pattern of authoritarian disregard for privileges which seems characteristic of Charles the Bold's reign.[99] It was not surprising that, in 1473, the chapter of the order requested him to 'maintain my lords [of the order] in their prerogatives', and to 'observe the things agreed to by my late lord his father'.[100] The *Toison d'Or* perhaps needed an Olivier de la Marche to argue for its continuance, not only to the duke, but to the nobility.

Unlike the Burgundian order, the second great princely order of chivalry founded in the mid-fifteenth century was relatively short-lived. René of Anjou's order of the *Croissant* died with him in 1480.[101] Its status as a true order of chivalry, however, has been disputed since La Marche's *Epistre* of 1500. He argued that the *Croissant*, unlike the *Toison d'Or*, failed to meet his criteria for a properly constituted order.[102] It had neither a fixed quota of members nor

---

98. 'La sentence baillee par chappitre de lordre contre ... le conte de Nevers: Le conte de Nevers, adjourne par lettres patentes de nostreseigneur le duc seellees du seel de son ordre de la Thoison Dor a comparoir en personne ou present chapittre pour y respondre de son honneur, touchant cas de sortilege en abusant des Sains Sacremens de leglise, ne sest presente ne comparu. Aincois a fait deffault et pour eschiver la proces et la privacion de lordre ... a renvoye le colier et pour ce a este et est declaire hors dudit ordre et non appelle a loffrande ...'. Ibid., fo. 21r; also ADN, B. 2068, fo. 107r for payments to the painters of the inscription.
99. See Vaughan, *Charles the Bold*, pp. 399-400.
100. Ibid., p. 173.
101. A. Leçoy de la Marche, *Le Roi René* (Paris 1875), i, p. 536.
102. La Marche, *Mémoires*, iv, p. 162: '... il n'avoit ne nombre ne chapitres, et n'en fut jamais la feste tenue ne celebrée; pourquoy je dis et concluz en ceste partie que ce en fust point ordre, mais la nommerons confrairie ou devise, qui certes fut belle et de grand monstre.'

regular chapters. Nevertheless, its statutes contradict La Marche, describing it as 'an order [which is] to last, God pleasing, perpetually and for ever', to consist of 'knights and esquires who shall ... be up to the number of fifty'.[103] Extracts from a register of the order, moreover, survive to demonstrate that during the years 1450-2, regular annual chapters were convened on 22 September and 'councils' on the first day of every month.[104] Although the association was founded on 11 August 1448, its statutes do not appear to have been finalised until September 1451.[105] There can, however, be no doubt that the *Croissant* was a true order, not merely a *devise* or *emprise*. Each member received a copy of the statutes, just as did the knights of the *Toison d'Or*. The reasons for René's choice of the Turkish crescent as the emblem for his order are obscure. We know that his predilection for *turquoiserie* was expressed in the pageants of his tournaments and feasts,[106] and in 1453 he assumed the device of a Turkish bow with a broken string on the death of his first wife Isabella.[107] There are perhaps two possible conjectures which can be made. First, the seventeenth-century historian of the order, Ménard, claimed that René modelled his order on that of the *Navire*, founded by St Louis and his brother, Charles of Anjou.[108] Its emblem was a chain of interlinked shells and crescents, the symbols of crusade and pilgrimage. A second possible explanation may be that the emblem was simply the visual expression of a verbal conceit. The order's motto was to be 'Los en Croissant' and was to be borne on a crescent-shaped enamelled plate worn beneath the right arm of each member.[109] The words could mean 'Honour in the Crescent' that is, in the waxing moon, or simply 'Increasing Praise'. A passage in the statutes stipulates that the 'good deeds and prowess' of the knights should be recorded so that 'their praise and renown may always be increasing (*croissant*)

103. BN, MS fr. 25205, fo. 2v. The statutes of the order are set out on fos. 2v-7r, 'ceremonies' on fos. 29r-34v, and the oaths taken by members on fos. 35r-37r. See fo. 40r for a verse rendering of these obligations:

'La messe ouir ou pour Dieu tant donner
Dire de Nostre Dame ou menger droit ce jour
Que pour le soverain ou maistre ne sarmer
Amer les freres et garder leur honneur
Feste et dymenche doit le croissant porter
Obeir sans contredit tous jours au senateur.'

104. BN, MS Clairambault 1241, pp. 905-20, a copy of 'actes, arrests et conclusions faits es conseils de l'Ordre du Croissant' extracted from the register of Jean de Charnières, first *greffier* of the order, on 17 April 1658 (p. 920). See plate 5.

105. See ibid., p. 914; B. de Montfaucon, *Monumens de la Monarchie françoise* (Paris 1731), ii, p. 258.

106. See M. Vulson de la Columbière, *Le Vray Théâtre d'Honneur et de Chevalerie*, i (Paris 1648), pp. 83-4 for men dressed as Turks at the *pas d'armes* of the *Gueule du Dragon* held by René near Saumur in 1446.

107. BN, MS Clairambault 1309, p. 139. Henri II of France adopted this emblem, as well as the crescent, at his entry into Lyon in 1548. See F. Bardon, *Diane de Poitiers* (Paris 1963), p. 42. I owe this reference to Dr T.C. Cave.

108. Leçoy de la Marche, op. cit. i, p. 531.

109. Vulson, op. cit., i, p. 107. See plate 6.

from good to better'.[110] As an apt device for the promotion and increase of honour and virtue, the Crescent was an appropriate conceit.

It was fitting that the Angevin order should be dedicated to the patron-saint of the cathedral church at Angers and of the *comté* of Anjou. The brothers were to meet on the eve of the feast of the Roman soldier-saint Maurice (22 September) and were to attend vespers.[111] An offertory of candles and monetary gifts was to be made, and an elaborate heraldic ritual was devised in which the heralds of the order wore the fictitious coat of arms invented for the saint, while the brothers gathered in chapter before his statue in Angers cathedral. On 1 October 1450, a statue was commissioned, to be 'the finest and most magnificent that can be made', flanked by the arms and crests of the brothers.[112] In January 1452, the painting of this image was discussed in chapter and 'two or three painters' were to be consulted.[113] An element of religious and quasi-religious ceremonial was very marked in the proceedings of the *Croissant*. A drawing made in 1695 shows the statue of St Maurice at Angers in which the saint, dressed in neo-Roman armour, holds a lance, with the motto 'Los en Croissant' beneath a shield bearing the *carboncle* of his arms.[114] There are close affinities between this representation and a full-length figure of the saint in a very fine Italian illuminated manuscript *Life of St Maurice*, attributed to Andrea Mantegna, presented to the order by Jacopo Antonio Marcello of Venice in June 1453.[115] This outstandingly beautiful volume also contains a miniature showing a chapter of the order of the *Croissant*, probably that of September 1452, where precisely the same statue presides over the assembly, bearing shield, lance and martyr's palm.[116] In the text of the manuscript the saint is described as 'protector and patron of *our* order', an exemplar of Christian chivalry especially appropriate for a knightly fraternity because he

---

110. Ibid., p. 111; F. Godefroy, *Lexique de l'ancien français* (repr. Paris, 1971) s.v. *croissant, croistre*. Henri II's assumption of the crescent was said to indicate that he had not yet attained his full inheritance (Bardon op. cit., pp. 43-44). A similar interpretation might be suggested for René's choice, given his plans to recover his Italian inheritance.

111. Vulson, op. cit., i, p. 111, 118-20.

112. BN, MS Clairambault 1241, p. 912. For heraldic rituals see ibid. p. 909.

113. Ibid., p. 918.

114. BN, MS Clairambault 1309, pp. 115-16. An inscription around the shield reads: 'Omnipotens sempiterne Deus qui per eam gloriosi bellam certaminis ad immortales triumphos martires tuos Mauricium sociosque eius extulisti de cordibus nostris dignam pro eorum ...' (p. 115).

115. Bibl. Arsenal, MS 940, fo. 34v. For recent and full discussion of the attribution of the miniatures to Mantegna, noting their similarity to some early works of Giovanni Bellini, see G. Robertson, *Giovanni Bellini* (Oxford 1968), pp. 18-20, 28 and pls. IIb, III, IVa. See plate 1.

116. Bibl. Arsenal, MS 940, fo. Cv; Robertson, op. cit., pl. IIb. Another representation of St Maurice, presenting René of Anjou as donor, is on a shutter of Nicolas Froment's triptych of the Burning Bush, commissioned in 1476 (Aix-en-Provence, cathedral of St-Sauveur). The saint wears a Gothicised Roman armour and carries a banner of his arms. See G. Ring, *A century of French painting, 1400-1500* (London 1949), pl. 129, p. 226; for the iconography of St Maurice, infra, p. 54. See also plate 5.

was martyred at Agaunum in the fourth century with a company of comrades (*commilitones*) drawn from the Theban legion.[117] The humanistic Latin *incipit* of the text speaks of the 'Passion of Maurice and his companions in the times of Diocletian', just as the inscription around the shield on his statue at Angers similarly thanked God for 'the immortal and triumphant martyrs Maurice and his comrades'.[118] The collective self-sacrifice of these Roman soldiers, under their commanding officer, was a particularly well-chosen ideal for a brotherhood of knights.

The dedication of the order to this military saint pervaded its ceremonies, rituals, and even the instruments through which its affairs were conducted. A seal was made for the *Croissant*, as it was for the *Toison d'Or*, which the chancellor was to apply to 'virgin white wax', signifying the saint's purity, attached to crimson silk laces, in honour of his martyrdom for the faith.[119] A surviving impression of the seal, appended to a letter of 23 September 1462 shows a half-length frontal figure of St Maurice, bearing shield and lance, which describes him as 'divus adjuctor'.[120] The saint was, like the Garter's St George, an ideal type of Christian knighthood, and the brothers of the order were exhorted to follow his example. Their own deeds were also to be enshrined in a written record. The statutes spoke of a 'book of the chronicles of the order' in which the 'good deeds and prowess' of its members, achieved by bravery in battle, should be registered.[121] The king-of-arms of the order was to ascertain those deeds so that they could be inscribed in the 'chronicles', and on 29 September 1450 René proposed that canons or chaplains of Angers cathedral be appointed to 'write the chronicles and register, the *faictes et gestes*, of those of the said order'.[122] It was, however, agreed by the chapter that the king-of-arms should 'set them down in writing very faithfully and truly, just as he has begun to do'.[123] This literary adjunct to the order's activities has, regrettably, not survived, but it was not entirely without good precedent. In 1351, the statutes of the order of the Star had required two or three clerks to record the adventures and deeds of arms of its members so that they were not forgotten, and so that 'three princes, three bannerets and three bachelors who shall have done most in the arms of war' might be elected every year.[124] The choice of the *Croissant*'s

117. Bibl. Arsenal, MS 940, fo. 2v. An edition of this short text would be most valuable.

118. Ibid., fo. 9r: 'Incipit Passio Mauritii et sociorum eius temporibus Diocletiani'. Cf. BN, MS Clairambault 1241, p. 910.

119. Vulson, op. cit., i, p. 115.

120. J. Roman, 'Le grand sceau de l'Ordre du Croissant', *Bulletin de la Société Nationale des Antiquaires de France*, lix (1897), pp. 183-6, (engraving of the impression p. 184). See BN, *pièces originales*, t. 1478, no. 20, for the letter, nominating André de Haraucourt a member of the order.

121. Vulson, op. cit., i, p. 111.

122. Ibid., p. 117; BN, MS Clairambault 1241, p. 910.

123. Ibid., p. 910. At René's *pas d'armes* in 1446, two kings-of-arms rode in the procession to the lists 'tenans leurs livres ou cartulaires d'honneur et de noblesse en leurs mains, pour y descrire et exalter les nobles faits d'armes et les valeureux combats qui se feroient au lieu ou les lices estoient dressees.' Vulson, op. cit., i, p. 83.

124. See L. Pannier, *La noble maison de St-Ouen ... et l'Ordre de L'Etoile d'après les documents originaux* (Paris 1872), p. 93, nn. 1, 2.

Plate 5. A meeting of a chapter of the Order of the *Croissant* (1452). Paris, Bibliothèque de l'Arsenal, MS 940, fo. Cv.

herald as its historian is consonant with what is known of the literary work of Jean Lefèvre, lord of St-Rémy, herald of the *Toison d'Or*.[125] Historical writing of a chivalric kind thus received a considerable impetus from the newly-founded orders of chivalry.

The *Croissant* shared the social exclusiveness of the *Toison d'Or*. It was composed of princes, marquises, counts, *vicomtes*, and those descended from 'ancient knighthood', all of them bearing the four quarters of nobility.[126] It was perhaps a little more broadly-based than the *Toison d'Or*, because esquires were thought worthy of admission. The *Croissant* displays many of the qualities of a multiple brotherhood-in-arms, in which social distinctions between nobles were largely eliminated. Members were to contribute to the payment of each other's ransoms and to support the widows and orphans of their comrades.[127] Unlike the practice of the *Toison d'Or*, however, mutual criticisms and accusations were not to be publicly made. One of the regulations of the *Croissant* declared that the brothers should suppress matters of shame and dishonour, unless these contravened the statutes, but should rebuke their fellow-knights privately and as soon as possible after the event.[128] There were to be no scenes of mutual accusation and recrimination in the chapters of the *Croissant*. Nor was there a 'sovereign' set over the order. Its head was dignified with the title of Senator, elected annually to preside over meetings of the order.[129] This might suggest that the *Croissant* was not primarily designed to bolster and enhance the political ambitions and prestige of René of Anjou. Every known Senator was, nevertheless, a loyal servant of the Angevin dynasty. The first was Guy de Laval, lord of Loué, who was followed in 1449 by René himself; in 1450 by the Italian Giovanni Cossa, count of Troya and lord of Grimaldi; in 1451 by Louis de Beauvau, seneschal of Anjou; in 1452 by Bertrand de Beauvau, lord of Précigny; in 1453 by René's son Jean, duke of Calabria, and in 1454 by Ferry de Grancy, count of Vaudemont, in Lorraine.[130] These men represented the governing class of the Angevin domains, and were drawn from the *comtés* of Anjou and Provence, the duchy of Lorraine and the kingdom of Naples and Sicily. The officers of the order were, similarly, recruited from amongst the dynasty's servants – the treasurer, Etienne Bernard, was also treasurer of Anjou; the *greffier* was René's secretary Jean de Charnières; and Jean Breslay,

125. See J. Lefèvre de St-Remy, *Chronique*, ed. F. Morand (*SHF*, Paris, 1876-81), *passim*.

126. Vulson, op. cit., i, p. 107; cf. BR, MS II. 6288, fo. 7v for the *Toison d'Or*.

127. Vulson, op. cit., i, p. 112. Cf. these clauses with the stated aims of an association of Gascon lords created on 4 February 1360: see H. Morel, 'Une association de seigneurs gascons au quatorzième siècle', *Mélanges ... a Louis Halphen*, ed. F. Lot *et al.* (Paris, 1951), pp. 523-6; M.G.A. Vale, 'A fourteenth-century order of chivalry: the *Tiercelet*', *EHR*, lxxxii (1967), pp. 332-41, esp. 337-8.

128. Vulson, op. cit., i, p. 108.

129. Ibid., i, pp. 109, 113-14.

130. For a list of members, with names and arms of the senators for 1448-53, see BN, MS fr. 25204, fos. 41r-56v. See also Leçoy de la Marche, op. cit., i, p. 533. Cf. plate 6.

Plate 6. Arms and crest of Raymond, lord of Sault, from a book of the Statutes and Armorial of the *Croissant* (1448-53). Paris, Bibliothèque Nationale, MS fr. 25204, fo. 41.

juge ordinaire of Anjou, was appointed chancellor.[131] It was unlikely that any of them would prove unreasonably obstructive to Angevin ambitions in France or Italy.

The *Croissant* was unusual among secular orders of chivalry for its stress upon the religious bonds and duties of its members. Penalties were imposed for neglecting the canonical hours, and for not hearing a daily mass.[132] By September 1455, René had founded a daily mass for the order at a newly-constructed altar of St Maurice in Angers cathedral, where a special chapel was set aside and furnished with stalls, stall-plates and embroidered armorial cushions for the brothers.[133] Their scarlet robes were kept by the cathedral chapter, who then received them for conversion into vestments after their deaths.[134] As a religious fraternity, closely bound to a cathedral chapter, the order resembled the guilds and corporations of the age. With a fixed place of meeting for its conclaves and chapters, elaborate religious ceremonies, and a convivial purpose, the *Croissant* was the aristocratic equivalent of the bourgeois *confrérie*.

Unlike the bourgeois assocations, however, an order as socially exclusive as the *Croissant* could not fail to be exploited for political ends. The statutes were framed with the prior claims of a sovereign to a member's loyalty firmly in mind. Jean de Nevers would have been better served by the *Croissant* than by the *Toison d'Or*, because its regulations explicitly forbade a brother to bear arms for anyone but his sovereign lord.[135] René of Anjou did not conceive the order of the *Croissant* as a means of detaching himself from the crown of France. He was, unlike the duke of Burgundy, a titular king in his own right (of Naples and Sicily) and sovereign over the *comté* of Provence. The *Croissant* was devised at a time when the thoughts of the houses of Anjou and Orléans were increasingly turning towards Italy. The Aragonese conquest of Naples in 1442 and the vacancy in the duchy of Milan in 1447 meant that the political ambitions of two of the greatest magnates in France were closely bound up with events in the Italian peninsula.[136] Despite such differences of purpose, the *Croissant* was not

131. Ibid., i, pp. 534-5. For a dispute within the chapter over the appointment of Etienne Bernard as treasurer (because he had not yet settled his accounts as treasurer of Anjou), see BN, MS Clairambault 1241, pp. 910-11 (29 September 1450).

132. Vulson, op. cit., i, pp. 107-8; BN, MS fr. 25204, fos. 41r-56v.

133. BN, MS Clairambault 1309, p. 79 (24 September 1455) extracted from a register of St Maurice at Angers (1454-81). René's desire to establish a religious foundation for the order (as Edward III had endowed the college of canons at Windsor) is first recorded in September 1450 (BN, MS Clairambault 1241, p. 909). For lists and drawings of the stall-plates and armorial cushions (*quarreaux*), see MS Clairambault 1309, pp. 109-11, 113, 117-41, 147-245. Each cushion displayed the embroidered arms and devices of each member. That of Jacopo Antonio Marcello had *banderoles* with the motto *Alta vita* surrounded by intertwined vines (p. 179).

134. Ibid., pp. 80, 87, 93. In February 1477 one chasuble, three stoles and two maniples were made for the chapter from the robes of the lords of Bournon and Du Plessis-Clairambault (ibid., p. 99).

135. Vulson, op. cit., i, p. 109.

136. See Vale, *Charles VII*, pp. 104-6, 112.

dissimilar, in other respects, to the *Toison d'Or*. The grounds on which a member might be expelled from the order bear close affinities to the 'causes for reproach' listed in the Burgundian order's statutes. There were five reasons for expulsion, three of them identical to those proposed for the *Toison d'Or*: conviction of heresy; treason; flight from a battle in which banners had been unfurled; defeat in a judicial combat fought over a matter of honour; and the bearing of arms singly, or in the company of confederates, against a sovereign lord.[137] Moreover, the sovereign's banner had to be unfurled and the sovereign present in person on the battle-field, for dishonour to be incurred.[138] As René was himself most likely to be the sovereign in question, given the nature and composition of the order, such rulings were perhaps less likely to pose problems of conflicting allegiance than did the statutes of the *Toison d'Or*.

Of the thirty-two knights of the *Croissant* listed in a manuscript armorial of the order composed soon after 1453, only three were neither subjects nor vassals of René.[139] These were Francesco Sforza, duke of Milan; Jacopo Antonio Marcello of Venice and Johan, count of Nassau and Saarbrücken. The first and last of these were princes in their own right, whose aid might be valuable to Angevin interests in Italy and on the western frontier of the German empire.[140] Marcello was a useful agent of René's schemes in the peninsula. The other Italian members of the order – Giovanni and Gaspar Cossa – were barons of the kingdom of Naples, exiled after the Aragonese victory of 1442.[141] Giovanni became seneschal of Provence, 'drawn', according to the inscription upon his Italianate tomb at Tarascon, 'by the effulgence of king René'.[142] These men certainly attended meetings of the *Croissant* and, although a crude numerical count tells us little, the fact that both chapters and councils took place regularly is of some significance. The chapters were attended by twelve members in September 1450, by seventeen members in September 1451, and by sixteen members in September 1452.[143] The meetings of the council were more spasmodic and less well attended – twelve members on 29 September 1450, six on 22 December 1450, nine on 24 March 1451 and nine on 16 January 1452.[144] Much of the business transacted on these occasions was of a procedural and ceremonial

137. Vulson, op. cit., i, p. 110; BN, MS fr. 25024, fo. 5v; cf. Beltz, op. cit., p. lxxxiv.

138. BN, MS fr. 25024, fo. 5v.

139. Ibid., fos. 41r-56v. A list of additional members, elected since 1453, can be compiled from other sources, including MS Clairambault 1309, pp. 94-7, 169, 243. Four names can be added from this source.

140. P.M. Perret, *Histoire des relations de la France avec Venise*, i (Paris 1896), pp. 243-76; Vaughan, *Philip the Good*, pp. 293-4.

141. See A.J. Ryder, 'The evolution of imperial government in Naples under Alphonso V', *Europe in the Late Middle Ages*, pp. 332-57.

142. His tomb is in the crypt of the church of St-Marthe, Tarascon, and records his death at the age of 76 in October 1476. On 11 September he was still reputed alive, but his armorial cushion had already been taken into safe-keeping by the chapter of St Maurice at Angers (see MS Clairambault 1309, p. 97).

143. See BN, MS Clairambault 1241, pp. 905, 916, 919.

144. Ibid., p. 907, 913, 915, 918.

kind, although a resolution taken at the council of 16 January 1452 may have had wider implications.[145] Each member of the order was to be informed of the content of its statutes and the obligations which he had assumed. It was ordered that the *greffier*'s clerk should produce 'ten or twelve little parchment books of the oaths contained in the statutes ... and ... the pursuivant should carry them to the brothers ... who should be told by the Senator that every knight and esquire should take the trouble to know the contents of the said little books.'[146] Just as the statutes of the *Toison d'Or* and the Garter were sent to each newly-elected member, so were those of the *Croissant*, perhaps with a view to disallowing claims of ignorance of the order's regulations in cases of proposed expulsion.

There are no known cases of expulsion from the *Croissant*, but there is one well-documented instance in which political events impaled one member on the horns of a dilemma. Professor Millard Meiss has argued that the gift of the Latin *Life of St Maurice* to the order by Jacopo Antonio Marcello in June 1453 was 'designed to effect an immediate political or military purpose', namely to 'help forestall a military campaign that its employer feared he might lose.'[147] Marcello described himself in the manuscript as 'provisor exercitus' and addressed his accompanying letter to the order 'from the most happy camps of the most illustrious Doge of the Venetians' on 1 June 1453.[148] He was writing from the army drawn up by Venice, in alliance with the Aragonese régime in Naples, to oppose a combined attack by Milan, Florence and René of Anjou.[149] Marcello's loyalty to his *patria* – Venice – was pitted against his obligation to the order of the *Croissant*. His position was further complicated by his having held the office of *praefectura maritima* at Naples under Angevin rule.[150] He had been elected to the *Croissant* on 26 August 1449, with Francesco Sforza, on the latter's recommendation.[151] Marcello was then said by Sforza to be a fervent advocate of the Angevin claim to Naples. By February 1452, however, Italian politics had

145. Ibid., p. 918.

146. Ibid., p. 918: 'x ou xij petits livrets en parchemin contenus au chapitre de lordre ... et que le poursuivant les porter aux seigneurs freres ... et par le Senateur leur sera faict dire que chacun chevalier et escuyer mette peyne de scavoir le contenu desdits livrets.' These books of oaths may have resembled BN, MS fr. 25204, fos. 35r-40r. See plate 6.

147. M. Meiss, *Andrea Mantegna as Illuminator: an episode in Renaissance art, humanism and diplomacy* (New York/Hamburg 1957), pp. 1, 2. See also 'A lost portrait of Jean de Berry by the Limburgs', *Burlington Magazine*, cv (1963), pp. 51-3. See plates 1, 5.

148. Bibl. Arsenal MS 940, fo. 5r. Marcello was the leading Venetian military *provveditore* from 1438 to 1454, responsible for the payment and discipline of the army, and commanded it briefly in 1450 in the absence of the captain-general, Sigismondo Malatesta. His appointment as *provveditore* was confirmed by the Senate on 3 April 1453. He was a prominent candidate for the dogeship in 1457 and served once more as *provveditore* in 1463 at the siege of Trieste. Later he became captain-general of the fleet and died at Gallipoli in 1484. I owe this information to the kindness of Dr M.E. Mallett.

149. Meiss, *Mantegna*, pp. 4-5. For an account of the 1453-4 campaign, see Leçoy de la Marche, op. cit., i, pp. 274-87. An exchange of letters between René and the *provveditori* of Venice is printed ibid., ii, pp. 275-7.

150. Meiss, *Mantegna*, p. 2.

151. Ibid., p. 3; BN, MS fr. 25204, fo. 43r.

undergone such transformations that he found himself in the untenable position of serving Venice against both René and Sforza. A strict interpretation of the statutes of the *Croissant* entitled him to do this, for loyalty to a sovereign lord or master took precedence over all other bonds.[152] Yet Marcello was clearly much troubled in his conscience. It was his great good fortune that the course of subsequent events did not compel him to serve against René in person. The alliance between Milan, Florence and the Angevins fell apart, and hostilities had ceased by January 1454.[153] It is impossible to assess the effect of this diplomatic gift on the behaviour of René and Giovanni Cossa, his lieutenant. Cossa was addressed directly on one illuminated page of the manuscript, in the words which Marcello placed beneath his own profile portrait:

> If my hopes do not deceive me
> You, Cossa, will not make my country ungrateful.[154]

Did this mean that Marcello intended to withdraw at a critical moment, leaving the Venetian army leaderless, or that the Angevin invasion would lead to accusations against him by the Republic? Whatever its precise significance, the timing of the gift – at the very moment when René and Cossa were preparing to leave Aix-en-Provence for Italy – suggests that it was intended to influence their behaviour, and that of the senator and other members of the order. It was not the first, nor the last time that a precious manuscript was used for a political purpose.[155] Perhaps as a result of his gratitude for his release in 1454, Marcello sent René a *mappamondo* in 1457, with a manuscript of Ptolemy's *Cosmographia* and, in 1459, Guarino da Verona's translation of Strabo's *Geography*.[156] This manuscript contains two dedication miniatures, one showing Guarino presenting the book to Marcello, and the other depicting Marcello offering it to René.[157] However, such gifts were not Marcello's monopoly: a French

152. Vulson, op. cit., i, p. 109; BN, MS fr. 25204, fo. 36v where a member is enjoined 'promectez et jurez de ne porter armes pour nulles quelconques querelles de homme qui vive excepté seulement pour vostre souverain seigneur, et aussi pour vostre maistre que vous avez de present et pourriez avoir pour l'avenir, se vous ne cuidez en vostre conscience que la partie pour la quelle vous vous armerez ait meilleur droit et querelle que son adversaire.' A certain freedom of conscience seems to have been admitted by the latter part of this oath.

153. Meiss, *Mantegna*, p. 16; Perret, op. cit., i, pp. 157-64.

154. Bibl. Arsenal, MS 940, fo. 38v. This is a cryptogram of doubtful meaning and obscure interpretation: see Robertson, op. cit., p. 20 n. 2. The portrait faces an allegorical representation of Marcello as the saviour of Venice (fo. 39r): ibid., pls. IIIb, IVa.

155. See e.g. M. Meiss, *French Painting at the Time of John, duke of Berry: The Boucicaut Master* (London, 1968), pp. 42-3, 116.

156. Meiss, *Mantegna*, pp. 30-3. The latter is now at Albi, Bibliothèque Rochegude, MS 4: see Leçoy de la Marche, op. cit., ii, pp. 181-2.

157. See Robertson, op. cit., p. xxvi and p. 50. The miniatures are generally attributed to Lauro Padovano; Mantegna and Marco Zoppo have also been proposed: see Meiss, *Mantegna*, pp. 30-51; G. Fiocco's review in *Paragone (Arte)*, xcix (1958), pp. 55-8. Marcello was a close friend of many humanists of the period, receiving dedications from George of Trebizond, Gian Maria Filelfo and Baptiste Guerino, as well as Guarino da Verona. A portrait of him by Giovanni Bellini was in the collection of Gieronimo Marcello in the 1520s (ex inf. Dr Mallett.)

translation of the *De Temporibus* by the Florentine humanist Matteo Palmieri, originally dedicated to Piero di Cosimo de Medici, was sent to René's second wife Jeanne de Laval by Giovanni Cossa.[158] The literate and cultured chivalric fraternity of the *Croissant* thus achieved the unexpected distinction of patronising and disseminating the humanistic literature of the Renaissance.

There are two other known instances in which political pressures made themselves felt upon the order. The proposed election of the lord of Montjean was discussed in the chapter of September 1450.[159] It had been discovered that he had sided with the Dauphin Louis against Charles VII, and had accompanied the rebellious Jean II, duke of Alençon, to seek out Louis in Poitou.[160] His election to the order was deferred while Guy de Laval, lord of Loué, was sent to Charles VII, to discover whether it was 'cas de reproches', and hence a contravention of the statutes, for a noble to be in the Dauphin's party against the king. It was. To serve against one's sovereign lord in this way was evidently thought to disqualify a man from election to the order, and Montjean's name is never recorded among its members. Secondly, the attempted suppression of the *Croissant* by Pope Pius II in 1460, on the grounds that Jean, duke of Calabria, was using it to recruit Neapolitan nobles into his service, endorses the fact that the *Croissant*, no less than the *Toison d'Or*, could be an instrument of politics.[161] Pius II's suspicion was justified. A record of the names of twenty-one barons of the kingdom of Naples who were enlisted as members of the *Croissant* by Jean of Calabria in 1459, to serve against Ferrante of Aragon, bears out the fears of the Aragonese and their allies.[162] Behind the solemn rituals and lavish display lay an identifiable political purpose. There is no reason to suppose that that purpose was invented in 1459 by Jean of Calabria. René of Anjou was no less aware of the potential usefulness of a chivalric order than were his son and his Burgundian contemporaries. It was, perhaps, the only formal means whereby chivalric values might be enlisted and harnessed to the service of a sovereign. The *Toison d'Or*, the *Croissant* and the Garter were each tuned to the respective political needs of the dukes of Burgundy, the king of Naples and Sicily, and the kings of England. An order of chivalry could act as a means whereby chivalrous ideas were transposed into political reality.

158. See BN, MS Clairambault 1309, p. 127 bis; P. Durrieu, 'Les MSS à peinture de la bibliothèque de ... Cheltenham', *BEC*, 1 (1889), p. 401.

159. BN, MS Clairambault 1241, p. 907.

160. Ibid., p. 907. For Louis' opposition towards his father in 1450, see Bibl. Arsenal, MS 2695, fo. 6v, showing a confrontation between the dauphin and the constable Richemont in the frontispiece of Richemont's copy of Honoré Bovet's *Arbre des Batailles*. The MS was begun at the end of the siege of Cherbourg, August 1450 (fo. 136v). See plate 2.

161. Leçoy de la Marche, op. cit., i, p. 535.

162. BN, MS Clairambault 1241, p. 948.

CHAPTER THREE

Chivalric Display

i. The tournament and its function

It was argued in the previous chapter that secular orders of chivalry offered a means of transposing chivalric ideas into the world of political reality. The most fantastic, extravagant and impractical expressions of those ideas, however, have been sought by historians in the world of the tournament. As we shall see, much has been made of the artificiality and unreality of the display which accompanied the later medieval tournament.[1] Unlike their modern successors, fifteenth-century writers were not so convinced of the military uselessness of such chivalric diversions. In 1497, a tournament at Sheen palace offered Henry VII of England's courtiers the opportunity to 'learn the exercise of the deeds of arms' and the king had already proclaimed a tournament there in 1492 to test their military skills before his French campaign of that year.[2] He was acting upon sound fifteenth-century precedents. Christine de Pisan had also addressed herself to the question of training a nobility for war in her *Livre de la Paix*, begun in September 1412.[3] A peace treaty between the warring factions of Armagnacs and Burgundians, made at Auxerre one month earlier, had aroused the optimistic hope that the French nobility would now present a united front against the English.[4] Military preparation was essential, and Christine proposed means of ensuring that the nobles would 'always be practised in arms'. Apart from annual musters and reviews, she suggested that *tournois et joûtes* should be proclaimed in every diocese of the kingdom of France. These were to take place once, twice, or three times a year and their cost was to be met by a levy on royal revenues in the *bonnes villes*. They were, furthermore, to be an indispensable attribute of living nobly, because, she wrote, 'no one should be reputed noble who does not attend this exercise'.[5] Age and corpulence were to be the sole grounds for exemption. To make her point more forcefully, she cited the example of Bernabo and Giangaleazzo Visconti of Milan, who had used

---

1. For some examples of this tendency, see *infra*, nn. 8, 9, 10, 11.
2. G. Kipling, *The Triumph of Honour: Burgundian Origins of the Elizabethan Renaissance* (Leiden 1977), p. 118.
3. Christine de Pisan, *The 'Livre de la Paix'*, ed. C.C. Willard, (The Hague 1958), pp. 134-5.
4. See R. Vaughan, *John the Fearless* (London 1966), pp. 97-8.
5. Christine de Pisan, op. cit., p. 134.

such methods in Lombardy to good effect, and she quoted Seneca on the value of military preparedness.[6]

There was nothing strikingly original about her proposals. The tournament had long been acknowledged as a school of prowess in arms, and the French crown was no stranger to its sponsorship. In May and June 1411, for example, Charles VI had spent the large sum of 2,400 francs equipping members of his household for jousts at the royal *hôtel* of St Pol during the feast of Pentecost.[7] To formalise such practices throughout the kingdom, however, was a new departure, and if, as historians generally allege, the tournament had 'lost all contact with the realities of warfare',[8] it is curious that Christine should advocate this form of combat.

Huizinga's conclusion that the tournament's character as 'a contest of force and courage had been almost obliterated by its romantic purport'[9] in the later Middle Ages, has been generally accepted. In its later medieval form, we are told, the tournament had become a 'hollow pastime', part of a code of chivalry which was 'a ridiculous anachronism, a piece of factitious making-up'.[10] This contrasted sharply with the serious business of war, which demanded skills and techniques that bore no relation to the playful, even frivolous activity of the lists. In this way an antithesis has been created between the early and later medieval tournament, in which the latter is seen as a decadent survival, symptomatic of a more general malaise.[11] In later medieval society – so the argument runs – war had parted company with the circumscribed and meticulously regulated conventions observed in the tournament. Towards the end of his life, Huizinga still argued for a distinction between the earliest tournaments – 'held in deadly earnest and fought out to the death' – and their fourteenth- and fifteenth-century equivalents.[12] Yet he was less certain about the evidence for polarised attitudes towards warfare and the tournament in the later Middle Ages. In *Homo Ludens* he wrote that 'fighting, as a cultural function, always presupposes limiting rules, and it requires, to a certain extent anyway, the recognition of its

6. Ibid., p. 135: 'Et ses manieres belles et bonnes estoient tenus en Lombardie ou temps de messieur Bernabo et de Galiache son frere, qui puissent obtindrent leur seigneurie; Seneca: "Longue appareil de guerre fait avoir briefve victoire".'

7. BN, MS fr. 21,809, nos. 8, 21-53. These are warrants and quittances relating to the Pentecost jousts of 1411. The manuscript also contains financial documents relating to jousting expenses in 1349, 1389, 1390 and 1391, including the Marshal Boucicaut's jousts at St-Inglevert in 1389. For similar expenses at the court of Burgundy see ADN, B.4089 (1416), fos. 109r, 111v; 1933 (1425-6), fos. 166r-68r.

8. Ferguson, op. cit., p. 15.

9. *The Waning of the Middle Ages*, p. 77.

10. Ibid., p. 125. See also N. Denholm-Young, 'The tournament in the thirteenth century', *Studies in Medieval History presented to Sir Maurice Powicke*, ed. R.W. Hunt, W.A. Pantin, R.W. Southern (Oxford 1948), pp. 240-1.

11. For a representative expression of this view, see Kilgour, op. cit., p. 257; for criticism Keen, 'Huizinga, Kilgour and the decline of chivalry', pp. 4-6, 8-10.

12. *Homo Ludens*, pp. 110, 123-4, 125-6.

play-quality'.[13] His work on what he called 'the play-element of culture' had led him to reconsider the role and nature of noble 'games'. Recognising the limitations imposed by the law of arms and the dictates of honour, he suggested war was waged between antagonists who regarded each other as equals, entitled to certain privileges (such as the right to be ransomed) and bound by certain obligations (for instance, humane conduct towards prisoners of similar social rank). Later medieval warfare, fought according to such rules, looked very like the 'agonistic warfare' which he found in primitive societies.[14] He saw the tournament bound even more strictly by limiting rules: it was an exercise in seeking and applying limits upon the violent instincts of a class whose very *raison d'être* was to fight.

To Huizinga, there was a 'close connexion between warfare and the tournament, and hence play' and he illustrated it by referring to the external apparatus of fifteenth-century warfare.[15] The 'sumptuously built and gorgeously decorated camp of Charles the Bold at the Siege of Neuss in 1475' with its tents and pavillions, as described by the Burgundian chronicler Jean Molinet, reminded Huizinga of the panoply of contemporary tournaments.[16] He took the analogy no further, merely concluding that 'the sumptuous apparatus of codes of honour, courtly demeanour, heraldry, chivalric orders, and tournaments had not lost all meaning even towards the close of the Middle Ages'.[17] The connexion between warfare and the tournament was clearly acknowledged by contemporary writers, among them such practising soldiers as Geoffroi de Charny (d.1356) who put his thoughts into verse,[18] and gave the following advice to young nobles following the profession of arms:

> Tous faiz d'armes sont bons et biaux;
> Pren le premier que trouveras.
> Et bien me semble,
> Jouster te faut en ta jouvence
> Et tournoier pour cognoissance,
> Et pour la guerre.
> Illec maintieng souvent ton erre
> La vont li bon prouesce querre.[19]

All deeds of arms are fine and good; take the first that you come across. It seems to me that you should joust in your youth and tourney for recognition and for [training in] war. Let your path often lead there; there is fair prowess to be found.

13. Ibid., p. 110.
14. Ibid., p. 11.
15. Ibid., p. 119.
16. Ibid., p. 119. See Plate 27.
17. Ibid., p. 126.
18. See Charny, op. cit., pp. 463-6 and BN, MS fr. 4736, fos. 1-8r for his questions on jousts and *tournois* addressed to the knights of the order of the Star.
19. A. Piaget, 'Le Livre Messire Geoffroi de Charny', *Romania*, xxvi (1897), pp. 394-411, ll. 731-8.

Clearly Charny saw the tournament as a means of preparation for war, that was especially valuable in the training of young squires.

For those who exhorted the French and Burgundian nobility to exercise their proper calling in the fifteenth century, the tournament also remained the 'school of prowess'. Olivier de la Marche echoed Christine de Pisan's words when he wrote: 'arms of *plaisance* are performed in order to practice the use of weapons and to perpetuate the profession of arms, to train the body, and to learn how to assert oneself for the defence of the public weal.'[20] Despite their laments about the decay of chivalry, his contemporaries and successors were well aware of the purpose of the tournament. In *Les anciens tournois et faictz d'armes* of 1459, Anthoine de la Salle criticised the prevailing softness among the nobility and their taste for tapestries representing 'hunting and hawking ... shepherds and sheep, or amourous games' rather than 'fine histories ... famous battles and conquests of the brave.'[21] He was in no doubt, however, as to the value of what he called the 'courtoise bataille' fought out in the lists. Besides his nostalgia for the ancient days of chivalry, an objective practicality is to be found.[22] Royal and ducal patronage of the tournament seemed to him one means of reviving a dying chivalry. In 1484 William Caxton translated Lull's *Order of Chivalry* into English. In his preface Caxton advocated public 'jousts of peace', fought with rebated or blunted lances, to be held two or three times a year by royal command, so that 'every knight should have horse and harness, and also the use and craft of a knight ... to tourney one against one, or two against two' for prizes.[23] This was a more or less exact repetition of Christine de Pisan's advice, but Caxton still believed that it would improve the discipline of the nobility and promote military efficiency. The writing and copying of beautifully illuminated treatises on the tournament could also have similarly practical – as well as aesthetic – ends. In 1489, Louis de Bruges presented an illuminated manuscript of René of Anjou's *Traité de la Forme et Devis d'un Tournoi* to Charles VIII of France.[24] Beneath the first miniature, a verse reads:

Pour exemple aulx nobles et gens d'armes
Qui appettent les faitz d'armes hanter
Le sire de Gruuthuuse duyt es armes
Volut au roy ce livre presenter.[25]

20. 'Les armes de plaisance se font pour exercer les armes et pour continuer le mestier, pour habiliter les corps et apprendre a valoir pour la defense du bien publique.' O. de la Marche, *Le Livre de l'Advis de gaige de bataille* printed in Prost, op. cit., pp. 23-4.
21. Ibid., p. 197: 'chasses et voilleries ... pastoureaulx et brebis, ou d'amoureux deduitz' rather than 'belles ystoires ... illustres batailles et conquestes des vaillans.'
22. Nostalgia for an imaginary chivalric world is especially marked in the work of Sir Thomas Malory, but it has been argued that his 'conception of the role and purpose of chivalry is practical rather than idealistic'. See E. Vinaver, *The Rise of Romance* (Oxford 1971), p. 123.
23. See *Selections from William Caxton*, ed. N.F. Blake (Oxford 1973), p. 112.
24. Van Praet, op. cit., pp. 265-72. The manuscript is now BN, MS fr. 2692-3.
25. Ibid., pp. 269-70; BN, MS fr. 2692, fo. 1r. See plate 7.

As an example to nobles and men-at-arms who desire to frequent deeds of arms, the lord of Gruthuyse, skilled at arms, wishes to present this book to the king.

This work, too, was offered with a didactic purpose which saw no essential dichotomy between 'deeds of arms' performed in warfare and at the tournament.

In fourteenth-century Flanders, moreover, the significance of the tournament as an intrinsic part of the code of chivalry had been expressed by the formal contracts which bound knights to the service of the counts. A series of agreements between Louis de Nevers and some of his life-retainers, made between 1338 and 1349, gave them *fief-rentes* in return for certain services.[26] A contract with Jean de Noyelle, a household knight, laid down that

> ... he should serve us well and loyally as long as we live, in war, *tournoi* and jousts and in all other things belonging to a knight ... which we shall require of him, and after our death he must serve our son Louis in the same manner. And he should be mounted for war and tournament in such a way that for the *restaur* [compensation] of his tournament horse we shall pay him that same sum of money as our other knights. And for his warhorse, if he shall lose it, we shall pay him our marshal's price. And when we shall summon him for the tournament we are obliged to give him for his expenses twelve *gros tournois* per day ...[27]

Another household knight, Jean de St-Quentin, was retained during his life-time for war and tournament on 2 September 1338.[28] On 20 November 1349, the count confirmed a grant of a *fief-rente* worth 1,000 *livres tournois* for life to Louis de Namur, knight, who had served valiantly at Crécy and been created a banneret. Henceforth he was to serve 'before all and against all, in all conditions of war, joust and *tournoi*'.[29]

By the fifteenth century, the tournament had assumed a complex form, in which three distinct kinds of combat were practised: the joust, the *mêlée* and the hand-to-hand fight on foot.[30] The *mêlée* took place at the stage of a tournament specifically known as the *tournoi*. Jousts and foot combats might follow or precede the *tournoi*, and all three types of encounter could be undertaken at a *pas d'armes*.[31] This combined combat with theatrical display, where the participants

26. ADN B.4065; 1327-49, *pièces comptables*, Flanders and Artois. For a similar English contract of 1318, see Denholm-Young, 'The tournament in the thirteenth century', p. 240, n. 2.

27. ADN B.4065, no. 7249 (25 April 1338), endorsed 'Par monseigneur le conte present le seneschal de Flandre et le seigneur de Hussalis'.

28. Ibid., no. 7275, with a *reconnaisance* by Jean de St-Quentin to observe the agreement 'en bonne foy', dated 4 September 1338.

29. Ibid., no. 7634. These contracts are a practical manifestation of the views of Geoffroi de Charny on the mutual interaction of war, joust and *tournoi* in a chivalric vocation. See *supra*, pp. 65-6, *infra*, pp. 91-2.

30. For one of the best recent accounts of the development of the tournament, see R. Harvey, *Moriz von Craûn and the Chivalric World* (Oxford 1961), pp. 113-216.

31. See F.H. Cripps-Day, *A History of the Tournament in England and France* (London 1918), pp. 82-90; Viscount Dillon, 'Barriers and foot combats', *Archaeological Journal*, lxi (1904), pp. 276-308; S. Anglo, *The Great Tournament Roll of Westminster* (Oxford 1968), pp. 19-40, esp. pp. 29-34.

acted out the fiction of defending a passage, bridge, or cross-roads against all challengers. The *pas d'armes* was a later medieval *Gesamtkunstwerk* binding together the arts of war and peace, and employing allegory, poetry, ceremonial and music to achieve its dramatic effects.[32] The kind of exercise recommended by Christine de Pisan as a means of military training, however, comprised only the joust and the *tournoi*. Both were fought on horseback, but authorities such as René of Anjou considered the *tournoi*, fought with the sword – the knightly weapon *par excellence* – superior to the joust, fought with the lance.[33] Contestants taking part in a *tournoi* for the first time were to pay a separate fee to the heralds, although they had previously jousted, 'because the lance cannot set free the sword.'[34] On the other hand, a noble who had already taken part in a *tournoi* but not a joust, was exempt from payment. In René's book, the jousts are cried only after the *tournoi* has ended.[35] The joust demanded prowess in individual combat; the *tournoi* required participants to fight as members of a group. Both stemmed from the mounted warfare of the twelfth century: the joust imitated the encounters in which knights exercised their skill with the lance against each other before battle, while the *tournoi* sought to simulate fierce hand-to-hand fighting between two groups, or *conrois*, ranged in close order under one banner.[36]

The early medieval tournament had an important military function. It trained knights in the handling of sword and lance, provided opportunities for the display of martial prowess during periods of peace or truce and accustomed men to fighting in groups. It could even influence tactics, and could sometimes act as a substitute for private war, as did a tournament held on the frontier of the *comtés* of Burgundy and Nevers in 1172.[37] It was a sham fight, a mock battle, but one which closely resembled 'real' warfare. Men and horses suffered death and mutilation, as they did in war. The blood-letting of a heroic age may make some appeal to the imagination, but the wanton squandering of lives in the twelfth-century *tournoi* hardly seems one of the more admirable features of the civilisation that Huizinga saw as the supreme medieval achievement. Repeated prohibitions by both popes and kings reveal the popularity of tournaments among the feudal baronage and knightly classes, as well as the sovereign's

32. A. Planche, 'Du tournoi au théâtre en Bourgogne. La pas de la Fontaine des Pleurs à Châlon-sur-Saône, 1449-50', *Le Moyen Age*, lxxxi (1975), pp. 97-128.

33. See the *Traictie de la forme et devis dung tournoy par le Roi René*, printed in Cripps-Day, op. cit., pp. lxxxvii-lxxxviii. The text is also printed, with reproductions of the illuminations in BN, MSS fr. 2692-3, 2695 in E. Pognon, *Livre des Tournois – Traité de la forme et Devis d'un Tournoi* (Paris 1946).

34. Cripps-Day, op. cit., p. lxxxviii.

35. Ibid., pp. lxxxvi-lxxxvii.

36. See J.F. Verbruggen, 'La tactique militaire des armées de chevaliers', *Revue du Nord*, xxix (1946), pp. 164-8; *The Art of Warfare in Western Europe during the Middle Ages* trans. S. Willard, S.C. Southern (Amsterdam 1977), pp. 32-9.

37. Verbruggen, 'L'art militaire en Europe occidentale du ixe au xive siècle', *Revue Internationale d'Histoire Militaire*, iv (1955), pp. 488-9; J-F. Lemarignier, *Recherches sur l'hommage en marche et les frontières féodales* (Lille 1945), pp. 160-2.

Plate 7. René of Anjou's *Livre des Tournois*. This manuscript was written and illuminated for Louis de Bruges, lord of la Gruthuyse, and presented to Charles VIII of France by him in 1489. The illumination shows Louis de Bruges offering the book to Charles, surrounded by the court of France. Paris, Bibliothèque Nationale, MS fr. 2692, fo. 1r.

inability to prevent them.[38] The destruction of men and horses in what were often no more than formalised private feuds and vendettas could not be tolerated by monarchies newly aware of their sovereignty and concerned for the manpower (and horsepower) of their forces. With the rise of so-called Arthurian 'Round Tables' in the second quarter of the thirteenth century, however, some of the dangers of the tournament were mitigated.[39] Blunted weapons were introduced and the encounters between knights strictly bound by rules. If attempts to lessen the dangers of mortality in the tournament are symptomatic of 'decadence' in the cult of chivalry, the process had already begun by about 1230. Moreover, contemporaries already bemoaned the extent to which chivalry had fallen short of its ideals. In the 1290s, Henri de Laon, in his *Dit des Hyraus*, lamented the fact that knights and squires sought only to win horses from their opponents at tournaments, not to put their endurance to the test.[40] Greed and pride ruled the contest, he alleged, and it was no longer a proof of military capacity. Huizinga might therefore have profitably looked to a period much earlier than the fifteenth century to find evidence for 'decadence' in the code of chivalry.

If it were to be an effective training-ground for war, the kind of combat found in the tournament had to resemble that of the battlefield. It is argued that, by the fifteenth century, individual combat at the joust no longer put to the test the qualities desired in a man-at-arms. However, some contemporary evidence undermines this view. In Jean Bouchet's *Panegyric du Chevallier sans Reproche* (1527) the aspiring warrior is advised by the goddess Minerva to learn to endure hardship and 'to exercise himself in handling the lance',[41] if he would win 'honour without reproach'. The Italian wars of 1494-1559 were still fought by heavy cavalry for whom training in handling the lance was of paramount importance. As a result of improved techniques, which will be discussed below,[42] the danger of death in a joust was greater than it had been previously. The formal distinction between 'jousts of war' (*à outrance*) and 'jousts of peace' (*à plaisance*), that had been made from the mid-fourteenth century, became all the more telling because of this new increased risk.[43] The former were fought with pointed lances, to disable an opponent; the latter with rebated lances fitted with coronals, to splinter the lances or unhorse the adversary. In Germany, the

38. See Cripps-Day, op. cit., pp. 39-41; N. Denholm-Young, *The Country Gentry in the Fourteenth Century* (Oxford 1969), pp. 135-44.

39. R. Cline, 'The influence of romances on the tournaments of the Middle Ages', *Speculum*, xx (1945), pp. 205-6; N. Denholm-Young, 'The tournament in the thirteenth century', pp. 253-4, 264-5.

40. A.R. Wagner, *Heralds and Heraldry in the Middle Ages* (2nd ed., Oxford 1964), p. 30.

41. J. Bouchet, *La Panegyric du Chevallier sans Reproche* (Paris, P. le Noir, 1527), pp. 48-9.

42. See *infra*, pp. 115-19.

43. See Cripps-Day, op. cit., pp. 46-7; Denholm-Young, 'The tournament in the thirteenth century', p. 261. For John Tiptoft, earl of Worcester's ordinances of 29 May 1467 'to be observed in all manner of justes of peace royall in England' see Cripps-Day, op. cit., pp. xxvii-xxx.

former type came to be known as the *Rennen* or *Scharfrennen*, the latter as *Gestech* or *Stechzeug*.[44] War armour was distinct from tournament armour, as René of Anjou observed, although he recommended war saddles for the joust if they were high at the back.[45] Mobility was less important than safety in the joust, and the massive weight of surviving jousting helms and reinforced tournament suits (most of them of German origin) suggests that the joust was simply too dangerous a game to play in lighter, more mobile war armour.[46] In war, men needed to be able to move more freely. In the 'joust of peace' they were virtually imprisoned in their saddles and, by the early sixteenth century, did not even need to lower their lances into the lance-rest because of the introduction of the *queue*, which held the rear end of the weapon completely rigid.[47] The addition of a further safety measure – the tilt, or barrier erected down the length of the lists to prevent collisions between opponents – in about 1420, provided the model for the Renaissance version of the 'joust of peace'.[48] The object of the exercise was to splinter as many lances as possible, and points were scored for good strokes, and lost for bad or foul ones. All this survived well into the seventeenth century, although the death of Henry II of France at a joust in 1559 also killed the tournament as a military exercise for princes.[49] It was probably no coincidence that the introduction of elaborate safety devices into the joust had followed closely upon the appearance of the lance-rest.[50] Improvements in the techniques of mounted warfare between 1390 and 1420 had given rise to changes in the character of the games played by the nobility.

Despite these innovations men still died or were injured in the fifteenth-century tournament. In 1445, Pierre de Bueil was killed in a joust at the court of Charles VII at Nancy, and Philippe de Poitiers, lord of La Ferté, was wounded and disarmed by Louis, lord of Contay, during the Anglo-Burgundian marriage celebrations at Bruges in 1468.[51] Olivier de la Marche's account suggests that this was an unusual occurrence at a 'joust of peace' and that no one knew what procedure to follow. Philippe de Poitiers was defending the *Pas de l'Arbre d'Or* against all-comers, and a substitute had to be found if the joust was to continue. The judges appointed the next challenger, Francesco d'Este, to act in Poitier's

44. See C. Blair, *European Armour* (London 1958), pp. 160-1; also *Wallace Collection Catalogues. European Arms and Armour*, ed. J.G. Mann, (London 1962), i, p. 17. See plates 8, 9, 21.

45. Cripps-Day, op. cit., p. lxxiv.

46. See *infra*, pp. 119, 185 and plates 14, 15, 19, 20.

47. For an early sixteenth-century example, see *Wallace Collection Catalogues*, i, plates 6, 7 and p. 18.

48. Blair, op. cit., pp. 158-9. For an illustration of the tilt at Henry VIII's Westminster jousts of 1511, see Anglo, op. cit., pl. XVI.

49. Kilgour, op. cit., p. 39.

50. See *infra*, pp. 117-18.

51. See La Marche, *Mémoires*, iii, p. 182. Gaston, prince of Viane, son of Gaston IV, count of Foix, was killed at a joust at Libourne in October 1470: see Guillaume Leseur, *Histoire de Gaston IV, comte de Foix*, ed. H. Courteault, 2 vols (*SHF*, Paris 1893) ii, pp. 254-5.

Plate 8. Joust 'of peace' (*Gestech*) from the *Mittelalterliches Hausbuch* (*c.* 1480), fos 20v-21r. Photo: Bodleian Library.

Plate 9. Joust 'of war' (*Rennen*) from the *Mittelalterliches Hausbuch* (*c.* 1480), fos 21v-22r.
Photo: Bodleian Library.

place, but the course was abandoned when his horse refused.[52]

In war, however, the desire for a minimal degree of comfort and greater mobility resulted in risks which would never have been taken in the tournament. The aged John Talbot, earl of Shrewsbury, was cut down at Castillon in July 1453 armed only in a brigandine; Charles the Bold's wound at Montlhéry was due to the absence of an essential piece of armour.[53] According to Commynes and Jean de Haynin, the count was wounded by a sword-thrust in the throat, because his beaver, or chin-piece, had fallen off and he had evidently not paused to replace it.[54] The scar remained with him until the end of his life. But even a prince as rash as Charles did not expose himself to the dangers of the tournament without a full complement of jousting armour. In his marriage jousts of 1468 he appeared in the lists 'fully armed, his helm on his head, his shield at his neck.'[55] The display of individual prowess was not to be at the expense of personal safety.

The popularity of the joust in the fourteenth and fifteenth centuries may partly result from the fact that it offered greater opportunities for performing notable feats in public than did the collective *tournoi*. In the opportunity for individual display in combat, the joust resembled the judicial duel, and it is interesting that the writers of treatises and compilers of tournament miscellanies often included texts relating to the judicial duel, such as Philip the Fair's *ordonnance* of 1306.[56] The terminology of the joust is also linked to that of the judicial duel or *gaige de bataille* and similar cries, for example, were made at a trial by battle as at a tournament, and a suspicion sometimes emerges from the accounts of celebrated combats of the period that the protagonists were motivated by more than the competitive instinct. The 'feats of arms' between Anthony Woodville, lord Scales, and Anthoine, *grand bâtard* of Burgundy, staged at Smithfield in June 1467, were the product of a challenge originally issued in April 1465.[57] The Bastard was engaged in Franco-Burgundian wars until the spring of 1467, and his appearance was all the more eagerly awaited. In the event, suggestions of foul play were made – especially concerning Scales's behaviour during the *tournoi* – and the officers of the field had great difficulty in stopping the foot combat between the two nobles, even though Edward IV had

52. La Marche, *Mémoires*, iii, p. 182; for the portrait of Francesco by Rogier van der Weyden where he holds a hammer and a ring that probably allude to a tournament in which he had participated, see E. Kantorowicz, 'The Este portrait by Roger', *Selected Studies* (New York 1965), pp. 366-80. See plate 10.
53. See Mathieu d'Escouchy, *Chronique*, ed. G. Du Fresne de Beaucourt (*SHF*, Paris 1863), ii, p. 41.
54. Commynes, op. cit., p. 30.
55. La Marche, *Mémoires*, iii, p. 189.
56. For examples see Viscount Dillon, 'On a MS Collection of ordinances of chivalry of the fifteenth century, belonging to Lord Hastings', *Archaeologia*, lvii (1901), pp. 29-70; BL, Lansdowne MS 285; BN, MSS fr. 5867, 387, 1280.
57. See S. Anglo, 'Anglo-Burgundian feats of arms; Smithfield, June 1467', *Guildhall Miscellany*, ii (1965), pp. 271-3.

Plate 10*a*. Rogier van der Weyden: Portrait of Francesco d'Este of Ferrara (*c.* 1450). New York, Metropolitan Museum of Art.

Plate 10*b*. Rogier van der Weyden: Portrait of Francesco d'Este of Ferrara. Reverse of the panel, showing the crest and arms of Francesco d'Este. New York, Metropolitan Museum of Art.

ordered it to end.[58] Anglo-Burgundian relations were not notably eased by these events, which accompanied diplomatic negotiations. Similarly, fifteenth-century rulers still considered putting their quarrels to the trial of battle. Olivier de la Marche, in his *Livre de l'Advis de gaige de Bataille*, tells us that Philip the Good twice wished to engage in judicial duels: once, in 1425, against Humphrey, duke of Gloucester, and again in 1443, against Frederick II, elector of Saxony.[59] Neither combat took place and La Marche was at pains to dissuade nobles from putting their lives at risk in this way. In 1398 sixty-year-old Sir Otho de Grandson had been killed in a judicial duel with Gerard d'Estavayer, although his age would have exempted him from answering his opponent's challenge.[60] His death, like Charles the Bold's wound at Montlhéry, resulted from part of his armour being left off. La Marche was in no doubt that 'armes chevallerreuses et de plaisance' were admirable, for they put the fighting qualities, horsemanship and honour of the nobility to the test.[61] He saw the *gage de bataille*, however, as nothing but the pursuit of private feuds outside the normal processes of a prince's justice.

The desire of the nobility to display their powers and skill in joust, tilt or even *tournoi*, might appear to have no relevance to the practice of warfare, but contemporary evidence seriously undermines this conventional view. The stress laid upon one-to-one combat in the lists is matched by the emphasis on personal fame achieved by highly individualistic war-time behaviour. The practice of fighting in groups at the *tournoi*, moreover, suggests certain analogies with the conduct and organisation of war during the fifteenth and early sixteenth centuries. A certain parallelism had always existed between the tournament and warfare, perhaps most convincingly expressed by Geoffroi de Charny in his *Livre*, where the joust, *tournoi* and battlefield were all seen as integral parts of a chivalric existence.[62] In his eyes there was no qualitative difference between them, for they were all *faits d'armes*, distinguished only by degree. To be truly noble, a man must indulge in all three forms of combat.

The Renaissance cult of fame merely took over such notions, classicised them a little, and handed them on to a new generation of soldiers and courtiers. In his manual of noble behaviour, *The Courtier*, Castiglione eulogised Guidobaldo, duke of Urbino (1472-1508) whom he saw as the ideal ruler, despite his physical infirmity. Of Guidobaldo he wrote:

> ... the greatnesse of his courage so quickened him, that where hee was not in case with his person to practise the feates of Chivalrie, as he had done long before, yet did he take verie great delight to behold them in other men ... And upon this at

58. Ibid., p. 280.
59. Prost, op. cit., pp. 21-2.
60. Ibid., pp. 6-7; *Histoire générale de la royale maison de Savoye*, ed. S. Guichenon (Lyon 1660), ii, pp. 243-9.
61. Prost, op. cit., pp. 2-5, 23-4.
62. BN, MS fr. 4736, fos. 1r-8r; Contamine, *Guerre, Etat et Société*, pp. 184-5.

Tilt, at Tourney, in playing at all sorts of weapon, also in inventing devices, in pastimes, in Musicke, finally in all exercises meete for noble Gentlemen, every man strived to shew himselfe such a one, as might deserve to bee judged worthie of so noble assembly.[63]

Participation in tilt and tourney was evidently one of the courtier's essential attributes, but the emphasis upon public display of prowess was not confined to the lists. To be 'well seene in armes' meant that a man should display similar qualities in war. In Book II, Castiglione wrote:

... where the Courtier is at skirmish, or assault, or battaile upon the lande, or in such other places of enterprise, he ought to worke the matter wisely in *separating himselfe from the multitude*, and undertake notable and bolde feates which hee hath to doe, with as little company as he can, and in the sight of noble men that be of most estimation in the campe, and especially in the presence and (if it were possible) before the very eyes of his king or great personage he is in service withall ...[64]

The value placed on individual prowess and achievement in warfare represents one legacy of medieval chivalry to Renaissance thought. The challenges 'to break a lance' with their opponents, given by the *chevalier* Bayart during the Italian campaigns of 1494-1559 and English noblemen during the Spanish wars, demonstrate the peculiar longevity of chivalrous ideas.[65] In 1492 the young Bayart took part in a *pas d'armes* at Aire in Picardy, together with 46 other nobles, all serving in Charles VIII's standing army.[66] The spirit of the Elizabethan Accession Day Tilts, stage-managed by Sir Henry Lee, is redolent of that of the Burgundian court of the previous century.[67] The need to be 'well seene in armes' led to an increase in the extravagance of costume at the tournament, taking its cue from the Burgundian jousts of the 1460s. The exponent of 'feates of Chivalrie,' wrote Castiglione, should have 'proper devises, apt posies, and wittie inventions that may draw unto him the eyes of the lookers on as the Adamant stone doth yron.'[68] Despite the rival claims of administration, government and letters, it was still the duty of a true nobleman to follow the profession of arms. War, tilt and tourney continued to be seen as three facets of a style of life and code of behaviour which, as Castiglione remarked, was thought to 'depende uppon Armes'.[69]

63. B. Castiglione, *The Book of the Courtier*, trans. Sir Thomas Hoby (repr. with an introduction by J.A. Whitehead, London 1974), p. 19.
64. Ibid., pp. 95-6 (my italics).
65. *L'histoire du Gentil Seigneur de Bayart*, ed. M.J. Roman (*SHF*, Paris 1878), passim.
66. Contamine, *Guerre, Etat et Société*, p. 498.
67. F.A. Yates, 'Elizabethan chivalry: the accession day tilts', *JWCI*, xx (1957), pp. 4-25. For continuity between the Burgundian *pas d'armes* and Tudor tournaments, see S. Anglo, *Spectacle, Pageantry and Early Tudor Politics* (Oxford 1969), esp. ch. 3; J.G. Russell, *The Field of the Cloth of Gold* (London 1969), pp. 104-41; (most recently) Kipling, op. cit., pp. 116-36.
68. Castiglione, op. cit., p. 96.
69. Ibid., p. 97. This contradicts the assertions of Ferguson, op. cit., pp. 222-6.

Further analogies between tournament practice and the reality of war can be drawn. Combat between two or more groups of knights in the *tournoi* brought the participants even closer to the battlefield than the joust did. Geoffroi de Charny, for example, spoke of the danger of death in the *tournoi*, which he thought was greater than in the joust. Sicily Herald believed that in 'ancient' times, men tourneyed against each other in *batailles* or field units, using all the weapons of war.[70] Ransoms were taken at the *tournoi* in the form of captured horses, and men such as William Marshal could make fortunes from their winnings. By the late fourteenth and fifteenth centuries the *tournoi* was a less life-like imitation of war, and its material rewards took the form of jewels given as prizes to the best contenders on each side.[71] It was fought with blunted swords and maces, although on some occasions, such as the Bruges tournament of 1468, a course with lances was run. There, the fifty contestants were drawn up 'en bataille' in two groups of twenty-five and, according to La Marche 'at this encounter there was many a lance-stroke (*attainte*) given and many [lances] broken, and many horses brought to the ground'.[72] This is reminiscent of scenes of warfare, such as that depicted in Uccello's *Rout of San Romano*, or in the engravings of the pitched battles of the Italian wars. In this way, the *mêlée* could be re-enacted at the tournament. René of Anjou's treatise describes the confused free-for-all which could break out. Servants on foot and on horse stood ready to lead their masters out of the combat (which could last from two to four hours) to refresh themselves.[73] If their master was unhorsed, or his horse fell, it was their task to re-mount him. Should they be unable to do so, given the weight of his tournament armour, they were to guard and protect him as he lay on the ground. The *tournoi* was a supreme test of physical stamina and endurance – qualities which were also at a premium in war. Despite the accompanying ritual, there was nothing effete about these contests, fought in heavier armour than was the rule on the battlefield.

In the *tournoi*, the group could be as important as the individual. Alliances and relationships contracted in war might be carried over into the tournament. At Bruges in 1468 and at Valenciennes in 1473, Jacques de Luxembourg, lord of Fiennes, appeared in the lists accompanied by a retinue in his livery and bearing his device.[74] These were members of his family, with the exception of Francesco d'Este, 'brother-in-arms and companion' of Jean of Luxembourg,

70. See *Parties inédites ... de l'oeuvre de Sicille, héraut d'Alphonse V, roi d'Aragon*, ed. P. Roland (Mons 1867), pp. 184-5.
71. For the distribution of prizes by Charles VI of France to those who jousted best in tournaments held in 1390 and 1391, see BN, MS fr. 21, 809, nos. 17, 19, 54, 55. These took the form of rings, clasps and jewels presented to the knights and esquires who were declared winners on both sides of the contest *de dehors* and *de dedans*.
72. La Marche, *Mémoires*, iii, p. 192.
73. Cripps-Day, op. cit., pp. lxxxiv-lxxxv.
74. La Marche, *Mémoires*, iii, p. 177; Valenciennes, Bibliothèque Municipale MS 776, fos. 70r,v.

Plate 11. Tournament scene from the Book of Hours of Yolande de Lalaing (*c.* 1440). Bodleian Library, MS Douce 93, fo. 80v.

Plate 12. Crucifixion, with a tournament scene and archery contest, from the Book of Hours of Yolande de Lalaing (*c.* 1440). Bodleian Library, MS Douce 93, fos 100v-101r.

lord of Sottenghien.[75] The retinue, or team, followed their master at each of his appearances. Relationships formed in war were even more directly reflected by the behaviour of two knights from Hainault – Jean de Ligne, lord of Rély and Jacques, lord of Harchies – who appeared together in the lists, wearing the same livery and device. This was because 'in war or in peace, they had always been companions'.[76] They wore doublets of violet velvet trimmed with black, and their horse-coverings were of the same colours, charged with silver bells and with gilded letters. Brotherhood-in-arms was thus not confined to the field of battle. Nor was combat in small groups, bearing the livery of the lord under whom they were serving. An anonymous treatise on the tournament laid down that five men should fight under a lord's banner, four under a pennon.[77] On the eve of the tournament all were to process under each banner, wearing the same livery. Sicily Herald thought that each banner or pennon should have three or four contestants serving under it and wearing the same livery.[78] Above all others should be the two 'sovereign banners', that is, those of the two lords – appellant and defendant – who had proclaimed the contest. This form of organisation is set out in the record of a tournament held in the market-square at Bruges on 11 March 1393, in which the lords of La Gruthuyse and of Ghistelles were appellant and defendant.[79] Each lord had a company of about 50 Flemish nobles, divided into five *lignes*, or groups. Each *ligne* was under the banner of a knight banneret and fought together as a band in the *mêlée*. The two teams consisted of the relatives, allies and companions in war of the two lords.[80] The tournament again perpetuated the fraternity of the camp and castle. Mutual bonds were cemented by the *tournoi* – as they were by orders of chivalry – and a record was set down for posterity in the manuscript commissioned by Louis de Bruges in 1489. The rolls of arms compiled at, and after, earlier tournaments were paralleled at the end of the Middle Ages by such splendidly illuminated volumes.[81]

The function of the banner and pennon in the *tournoi* was similar to its role in war. A king, duke, count or baron bore both banner and pennon; bannerets bore a banner alone; nobles who were not barons or bannerets bore only a

75. Jean de Haynin, *Mémoires, 1465-77*, ed. D.D. Brouwers (Liege 1905-6), ii, p. 217. See also Kantorowicz, art. cit., p. 374.

76. La Marche, *Mémoires*, iii, pp. 177-8.

77. BN, MS fr. 1280, fo. 127r.

78. *Parties inédites*, p. 194.

79. Van Praet, op. cit., p. 265.

80. Ibid., pp. 266-84. The Gruthuyse team included the following bannerets in each *ligne*: Robert van Liverghem; Henry van Berghen; Jan van den Gruthuse; Jean de Ghistelles, lord of Dudzeele (killed fighting the Liègois in 1430) and Jacob Breidel. The Ghistelles team included William van Hallewin, uncle of Jean IV de Gruthuyse, *bailli* of Alost; Gilles Braderic, Jacob van Melant, Franse Slinger and Roeland van Levenghem. There were four bastard sons serving in the Gruthuyse team. For another account of a tournament at Bruges which lists the members of each side, see BL, MS Lansdowne 285, fos. 44r-66r.

81. See N. Denholm-Young, *History and Heraldry, 1254-1310* (Oxford 1965), pp. 1-16.

pennon. This was a usage of war as well as of the lists.[82] The banner or pennon could serve as a rallying point in both forms of combat; as a means of identifying the lodgings of a contestant in a tournament and the billet of a captain in war; and as a device to begin and end a combat. Those fighting at a *tournoi* under the same banner gave mutual aid to each other when hard pressed. One of the functions of the cries given during combat was to summon aid, as during a battle. These were given by the contestants themselves, or by the heralds of their march of arms. Some *tournois* were evidently organised on a geographical pattern, with the participants grouped together into *lignes, bannières* or other bodies according to the heraldic marches to which they belonged.[83] This was how the arms of the French nobility were recorded by Gilles le Bouvier, Herald of Berry, in his *Armorial* of *c*.1450.[84] Names, crests and cries were set out in this *Registre de Noblesse* as if for a tournament. The shouts of 'Passavant!', 'Au feu! Au feu!', or 'Foix et Béarn!' might have been heard as much in the *mêlée* as on the field of battle.[85]

One of the most serious problems faced by the organisers of a sham fight in the fifteenth century was the difficulty of bringing it to an end. Contemporary writers were unanimous on this question. To keep order in the lists was no easy matter, and the observance of the strictest and most precise rules was urged upon contestants. The authority of the king-of-arms and heralds was here supreme, and steps were even taken to limit the number of blows struck with sword and mace during a *tournoi*.[86] At the *pas d'armes* of the *Perron Fée* at Bruges in April 1463, the lists were kept by the household archers of Philip the Good, and those who entered them without permission of the judges of the contest did so at their peril.[87] There were a number of means of bringing the free-for-all of a *tournoi* to an end. An arrow might be thrown into the lists by the lord under whose authority the combat was taking place. Philip the Good did this in 1435 crying 'Hola! Hola!' to indicate the end of a foot combat.[88] The appearance of an arrow in one of Roger van der Weyden's most celebrated portraits might identify its subject and explain the picture. The knight of the Golden Fleece who is shown holding what may be part of the apparatus of tournament has been variously identified as Anthoine, *grand bâtard* of Burgundy (d.1504), Jacques de Lalaing (d.1453), and the Portuguese Jean de Coïmbra (d.1458).[89] All these Burgundian courtiers had participated in tournaments under Philip

82. BN, MS fr. 1280, fos. 126v-127v, 129r. See *infra*, p. 97.

83. *Parties inédites*, p. 193.

84. Gilles le Bouvier, *Armorial de France* ed. Vallet de Viriville (Paris 1866), pp. 41-4.

85. Ibid., pp. 44-8.

86. See BL, MS Lansdowne 285, fo. 63r.

87. F. Brassart, *Le Pas du Perron Fée, tenu à Bruges en 1463* (Douai 1874), p. 51.

88. See Dillon, 'Barriers and foot combats', pp. 282-3; Lefèvre de St-Rémy, ii, pp. 318-19.

89. See Brussels, *Musée Royale des Beaux-Arts*, cat. no. 190, inv. 1449; M. Davies, *Roger van der Weyden* (London 1972), p. 205; G. van Camp, 'Portraits de chevaliers de la Toison d'Or', *Bulletin des Musées royaux des Beaux-Arts de Belgique*, II (1953), pp. 87-9. See plate 13.

Plate 13. Rogier van der Weyden: Portrait of Anthoine, *grand bâtard* of Burgundy (before 1464). Brussels, Musées Royaux des Beaux-Arts de Belgique.

the Good before the death of van der Weyden in 1464. Two other contemporary portraits show the sitter holding an arrow: it has been argued that these are representations of the assessors, or *juges du camp*, who are mentioned in René of Anjou's *Livre des tournois* and in the narratives of Chastellain, Lefèvre de St-Rémy, La Salle and La Marche.[90] It was their office to separate and disarm the combatants in a *tournoi* or judicial duel, throwing an arrow into the lists as a signal for quarter to be given immediately. Sometimes a white staff was used, as at the *pas d'armes* of the *Arbre de Charlemagne* in July 1443, when Philip the Good 'held a little white *bâton* in his hand, to throw at the champions and force them apart'.[91] More violent measures were sometimes necessary to prevent the more aggressive and bellicose from belabouring their opponents beyond the bounds of tolerance. At Bruges in 1468, La Marche reported:

> ... after the course run with lances ... they laid hands on their swords, and the *tournoy* began on one side and the other; which was ... fought for so long and with such *vertu* and vigour that one could not separate them; and it happened that my said lord of Burgundy ... took his helm from his head, so as to be recognised; and he went with sword in hand to divide the *mêlée* which recommenced first on one

90. F. Buttin, 'La Flèche des Juges de Camp', *Armes Anciennes*, iii (1954), pp. 57-64.
91. La Marche, *Mémoires*, i, p. 297.

side and then on the other; and, in separating them, he spared neither relative, nor Englishmen, nor Burgundian (all of) whom he divided by force. The said *tournoy* being ended, both sides ranged themselves in battle order, and by request fought ... one to one, two to two and three to three. But my said lord always separated them.[92]

Force majeure was sometimes the only means of restraining the excessive zeal of participants in a *tournoi*, although René of Anjou wrote that they could leave the lists still fighting and continue the rout as far as their lodgings.[93] Sicily Herald thought that the combat should end when the heralds declared who had gained most ground, but some combatants still fought on. Sometimes, he wrote, 'one then sees the best feats of arms, for the best men, who still have strength and wind, remain there, but they gain nothing as far as the winning of prizes is concerned'.[94] The signal for the ultimate end of the combat was the sounding of trumpets and the furling of banners. Anthoine de la Salle was censorious about those 'young and disorderly nobles' who ignored the withdrawal of the banners.[95] They gained nothing – not even honour – by remaining in the lists. He was adamant that what he called the *behourt d'épées* should not be fought from personal hatred or ill-will, but only to 'increase the honour of all those who wish to come, advancing the very noble profession of arms, and giving pleasure to all noble ladies and men of honour'.[96] The forcefulness of his strictures suggests that the *tournoi* was not all it should have been and that the lists could still offer opportunities for feuding and the paying off of old scores. The sovereignty of kings and princes had not yet entirely eliminated feudal independence or private feud among the fifteenth-century nobility. Without the tournament the inclination towards violence found in every medieval nobility might have erupted more often into open defiance and civil war.

92. Ibid, iii, pp. 194-5: 'Après la course des lances passée, ilz mirent la main aux espées, et commença le tournoy d'une part et d'aultre; lequel tournoy fut feru et bastu si longuement et par telle vertu et rigueur, qu'on ne les pouvoit deppartir; et convint que mondit seigneur de Bourgoingne, qui icelluy jour avoit tournoyé et jousté, et qui, à la verité, s'estoit grandement porté à toutes les deux fois, se desarmast de la teste, pour estre congneu; et vint l'espée au poing pour deppartir la meslée qui recommonçoit puis de l'ung des bouts, puis de l'aultre; et à les deppartir n'espargna ne cousin, ne Angloix, ne Bourguignon, qu'il ne les fist par maistrise deppartir. Et, ledit tournoy rompu, se mirent en bataille les ungs devant les aultres, et par requeste combatirent par plusieurs fois ung à ung, deux à deux et trois à trois. Mais toutesfois mondit seigneur tousjours les deppartoit.'

93. Cripps-Day, op. cit., p. lxxxv.

94. *Parties inédites*, p. 197: 'et aulcunes fois on y voit les plus beaux fais darmes, car les meilleurs et qui plus ont force et alaine y demeurent, pour eulx mieulx monstrer; mais ce ne leur vault riens quant a pris gaignier'.

95. B.N., MS fr. 5867, fo. 19v.

96. Ibid., fo. 21v: 'pour acroistre honneur a tous ceulx qui y vouldront venir, en recordant le tres noble mestier des armes, et donnant plaisir a toutes nobles dames, damoiselles et gens donneur'.

ii. Heraldic display: the tournament and the funeral ceremony

Compared with the bold and simple coats-of-arms that had characterised the tournament and battlefield since the mid-twelfth century, later medieval heraldry appears strikingly more complex and elaborate. This strong contrast has prompted the assumption that heraldry no longer enjoyed an important practical rôle, but was becoming increasingly decorative and less functional, merely 'the artistic expression of chivalry'.[1] The change resulted largely from the increasing tendency for the laws of inheritance to work in favour of male heirs: the coat-of-arms on shield and surcoat was no longer purely an aid to recognition, but also a show-case of descent where hereditary devices might be displayed. The distinction between 'jousts of war' and 'of peace' came to be reflected in the armorial devices considered appropriate for battle and tournament.[2] By the mid-fourteenth century 'arms of peace' and 'arms of war' were clearly established and the two types are first reflected in nobles' wills and testaments and in the accounts of their funeral ceremonies.

A testator would often give his executors precise instructions about the arrangement of his funeral ceremony, and the occasion always offered opportunity for impressing peers, neighbours and inferiors with the wealth and status of a nobleman and his house. The lavishness of some of these displays was frowned upon by some puritannical nobles, as well as by the more impecunious. In his will of 15 March 1361, Henry of Grosmont, first duke of Lancaster, told his executors that he desired 'nothing vain nor extravagant, such as armed men, covered horses, nor other vain things' at his burial, and Richard Fitzalan, fourth earl of Arundel, repeated the injunction in his will of 4 March 1392.[3] The Church, however, supported and indeed encouraged the practice of making gifts in money, weapons, heraldic achievements and military equipment to a burial-place.[4] Some of these items could be sold back to the deceased's kin, but the donation of the best horse as a mortuary gift or 'corse-present' had a symbolic as well as material value, and the offering of arms and accoutrements at the altar was a token that the Church recognised that a noble-man's duty was to fight.[5] The counts of Flanders and Guînes, in their wills of

---

1. E.F. Jacob, *Essays in later medieval History* (Manchester 1968), p. 153.
2. See *supra*, pp. 70-1 and plates 8, 9.
3. J. Nichols, *A Collection of all the Wills ... of the Kings and Queens of England* (London 1780), pp. 84, 121. For other instances see N.H. Nicolas, *Testamenta Vetusta*, i (London 1836), pp. 62, 75, 94, 109, 118.
4. See F.H. Cripps-Day, 'On armour preserved in churches', *A Record of European Arms and Armour*, ed. G. Laking, v (London 1922), pp. 151-273; *Fragmentaria Armamentaria*, iv *Church Armour* (*Addenda*) (Frome 1939), pp. i-v, by the same author. For a dispute over the giving of such mortuary gifts between the prior and convent of Malton, Yorks., and the widow of a burgess of the town, see Borthwick Institute, York, Cause Papers G.290, dated 1528, but citing evidence from as early as the 1470s.
5. See C. Gaier, *L'Industrie et le Commerce des Armes dans les anciennes principautés belges du xiiie siècle à la fin du xve siècle* (Paris 1973), pp. 72-5.

1244 and 1249, thus bequeathed armour and weapons to their burial-churches, and the custom continued into the next century.[6] In England, William de Beauchamp willed in January 1269 that a 'barded horse ... with warlike equipment' should be led before his body in his funeral *cortège*, and in his will of September 1296 his son gave 'two great horses, viz. those which shall carry my armour at my funeral' to the Franciscans.[7] Such gifts occur frequently during the following two centuries. An element of formal chivalric display which was to outlive the Middle Ages and the Reformation entered the ceremony of the Requiem.[8] It was expressed through elaborate heraldic ceremonies in which the introduction of armorial bearings, weapons, warhorses and fully-armed men was not thought to be incongruous nor incompatible with reverence for the peace and sanctity of God's house. It was yet another embodiment of the religious aura which still surrounded the cult of chivalry.[9]

The wills of English peers and knights, and the funerary helms and hatchments preserved in many parish and cathedral churches, amply testify to the practice.[10] On 6 November 1347, for example, Thomas Chaworth, a Nottinghamshire knight, bequeathed his 'most venerable palfrey', armed with his arms, to go before his body when he was buried.[11] He was so much in debt that he was uncertain of his ability to meet his funeral expenses, but he desired his hapless executors to ensure that he was buried in a manner befitting one of his status. A few months earlier, in June 1347, the exalted and affluent John de Warenne, earl of Surrey, made his will at Conisborough castle, and desired burial in his ancestral church of St Pancras at Lewes.[12] His interesting and lengthy will contains this injunction:

> I require four of my great horses to be armed with my arms, two for war, and two for peace, [to go] before my body on the day of my burial; those of war should be barded, and ... should remain in, and be given to, the aforesaid church of St Pancras with my [heraldic] arms in which those who shall ride them shall be clad ...[13]

The procession of chargers ridden by men dressed in the arms of the dead man

6. Ibid., p. 73.

7. M.H. Bloxam, *Fragmentaria Sepulchralia* (Oxford 1840-50), p. 132; Nicolas, op. cit., pp. 51, 52.

8. See A.R. Wagner, *Heralds of England* (London 1967), pp. 106-9. Although a statute of 21 Henry VIII commuted mortuary gifts into money payments, the practice of bearing arms and armour in funeral processions continued throughout the sixteenth century.

9. See *supra*, pp. 31, 43, 45, 58.

10. Bloxam, op. cit., pp. 134-5; Cripps-Day, 'On armour preserved in churches', pp. 151-273; J.G. Mann, *The Tomb and Funeral Achievements of Edward the Black Prince* (Canterbury 1972), pp. 15-20; Gaier, op. cit., pp. 72-3.

11. Borthwick Institute, Abp. Reg. 10, fo. 324v (probate April 1348).

12. Borthwick Institute, Abp. Reg. 10, fos. 316r-v (probate 26 July 1347).

13. Ibid., fo. 316r: 'Et jeo devys quatre de mes grauntz chivaux destre armetz de mes armes, les deux pour guerre, et les autres deus pour pees devant mon corps le jour de mon enterrement, dount ceux de guerre soient covertz de fer et que ... demoergent et soient donez a leglise de Saint Pancratz avantnommee ove mes armes dount ceux que les chivaucherount seront armetz.'

became a striking part of the funeral ceremony in the second half of the fourteenth century. In May 1394, Sir Brian Stapleton, knight of the Garter and a veteran soldier, willed that at his funeral in the priory of Healaugh Park there should be

> a man armed with my arms, with my helm on his head, and that he be well mounted and a man of good looks of whatever condition he is ...[14]

The sentiment behind such instructions was not only prompted by the desire for display. An armed effigy on a tomb might express the survival of the dignity and office of nobility or knighthood: for the same reasons, heraldic emblems recalling his ancestry, connections and alliances were conspicuously displayed during the funeral ceremony, and carved and painted on his tomb-chest.[15] The most celebrated instance in a fourteenth-century will of the bearing of arms for war and tournament is found in the testament of Edward, the Black Prince, drawn up on 7 June 1376. The prince referred to his arms 'for war, of our complete quartered coat' and his arms 'for peace, of our badges of ostrich feathers'.[16] Clearly, a noble's hereditary coat of arms – in the case of the Black Prince, the arms of England and France quartered, with a label – was to be borne in war. In peace – that is, at the tournament – his badge or *devise* of ostrich feathers was to be worn.[17] This distinction runs through the accounts of the funeral ceremonies of the English, French and Flemish nobility at this time.

So, for example, the anonymous author of a chivalric miscellany written for Louis de Bruges in 1481 set out what he knew of past procedure at noblemen's funerals. Candles, he wrote, were to be placed at the four corners of the bier or iron hearse containing the body, representing the four quarters of his inherited nobility.[18] His shield was to be carried in the *cortège* by his eldest surviving son; his crested helm by two of the greatest lords present, and his sword by worthy knights. Two horses were ridden in procession – one caparisoned with the hereditary coat of arms, the other with the man's livery and *devise*. The first was to be ridden by a noble, carrying a banner if the deceased were a baron or banneret, a pennon if he were a bachelor. Two of the 'most renowned captains

14. 'Jeo devise que jay un homme arme en mes armes et ma hewme ene sa teste et que y soit bien monte et un homme de bon entaile de quil condicion que y soit.' Borthwick Institute, Prob. Reg. I, fo. 69v (probate 26 June 1394). The parallels with the Black Prince's funeral are striking: see M.G.A. Vale, *Piety, Charity and Literacy among the Yorkshire Gentry, 1370-1480* (York 1976), p. 12.

15. Wagner, *Heralds of England*, p. 106; E. Kantorowicz, *The King's Two Bodies* (Princeton 1957), pp. 419-36. For the value of tombs as genealogical evidence of descent, see J. Weever, *Ancient Funeral Monuments* (London 1631), p. 18.

16. See Nichols, op. cit., p. 68 (transcript of the will); Cripps-Day, *History of the Tournament*, p. 63.

17. The tomb-chest at Canterbury bears alternating shields of war and peace with the Prince's two mottoes, *Houmout* and *Ich Dien*: see Mann, op. cit., pp. 7, 10 and plate 2.

18. BN, MS fr. 1280, fo. 131v. Each candle was to bear a shield of arms displaying each of the four quarters of the man's nobility. A surviving example of an iron hearse, that has preserved its mountings for candles is found over the alabaster effigies of Sir John Marmion (d. 1388) and his wife at West Tanfield, Yorks.

and governors of men-at-arms' were to lead the first horse. The second was to be ridden by another noble, accompanied on foot by two 'gracious ladies or *damoiselles sans reproche*'.[19] The connexion between *Frauendienst* and the winning of honour at the tournament was perhaps symbolised by the presence of women. The cult of chivalry did not lend itself to division into 'secular' and 'clerical' aspects or ideals – from its inception chivalry, however imperfectly practised, combined both religious and secular preoccupations in such a way that they could not be forced apart.[20] The funeral ceremony was perhaps the quintessential later medieval expression of the fundamental and complementary relationship between sacred and profane. An image of a mounted man in full armour clattering down the nave of a church to deposit the funeral achievements at the choir screen might shock those for whom pacificism is an integral part of Christian belief. Yet the men of war could appeal to the same God – the God of battles – for their justification.

The inter-relationship between the three forms of chivalric encounter – battle, joust and *tournoi* – was reflected in the lavish funeral ceremonies of Louis de Mâle, count of Flanders, in 1384.[21] Four knights armed in the count's arms of war accompanied the body; before them rode four other knights bearing his tournament *devise*, and banners of war and tournament were also displayed. At the church of St Pierre in Lille, shields, horses, axes, helms and banners for both war and tournament were offered the following day by the nobility of Flanders and their new Burgundian count.[22] The higher nobility led the way in this practice: the lesser nobility followed. An account of the funeral of a minor Flemish noble in 1391 distantly echoes these ceremonies for the very great.[23] Gerard de Mortagne, lord of Espières and Caurines, was an ancestor by marriage of Louis de Bruges, who had the account inserted in his chivalric miscellany ninety years later.[24] Two mounted esquires in black carried a pennon of war and one of the tournament to the door of the abbey; they were followed by two more esquires on warhorses, wearing the arms of peace and of war. A long list of the nobles who then offered and donated shields, helms, horses and pennons, on behalf of Gerard de Mortagne and his family, follows.[25]

19. Ibid., fos. 132r-133r.
20. See *supra*, pp. 45, 58. The church still played an important part in the organisation of tournaments in the fifteenth century. The cloister of a monastic house could be used to display banners and helms on the eve of a *tournoi*, and gifts of banners, pennons, helms and crests could be made to the church after the contest. See René d'Anjou's observations on the subject in Cripps-Day, *History of the Tournament*, p. lxxxviii. According to Sicily Herald nobles might buy back their banners and pennons from the heralds to present them to the church (*Parties inédites*, p. 195).
21. See the account of his obsequies printed from a copy of the *Chroniques de Flandres* in Louis de Bruges' collection by Van Praet, op. cit., pp. 257-9.
22. Ibid., pp. 258-9. Philip the Bold, as Louis' heir to the *comté* of Flanders, was the first to offer.
23. BN, MS fr. 1280, fos. 122r-124r.
24. The manuscript was written at the command of Gilles, king-of-arms of Flanders, in 1481 (fo. 139r). The account of Gerard de Mortagne's funeral is printed in Van Praet, op. cit., pp. 194-7.
25. Ibid., pp. 194-5.

The obsequies were attended by seventeen knights and twenty-four squires, all dressed in mourning, and were clearly thought to be among the most elaborate of their day for a man of knightly status. Thus after 1384 their Flemish inheritance did not merely give the dukes of Burgundy great wealth, but a tradition of chivalric ceremony and display which they might use for their own ends. Burgundian chivalric culture was built upon well-established foundations in the *comtés* of Flanders and Artois.

Rituals of such great pomp were of course not confined to the nobility of Flanders and England. The memorial requiem held in the abbey church of St Denis on 7 May 1389 for Bertrand du Guesclin, some years after his death, reflects French observance of these armorial customs.[26] The service was preceded by the ceremonial knighting of Louis and Charles of Anjou, with accompanying jousts. Many aspects of chivalric ritual merged in this celebration of the deeds of the Constable of France. His fellow-Breton, Guillaume de la Penne, in a poem composed about the ceremony in 1390, wrote:

> Quatre destriers, qui en l'eglise
> Furent a l'offrande menez,
> Deus en y ot de telle guise
> Comme pour un tournay armez,
> Et les aultres deus en la guise
> De guerre furent ordenez ...[27]

Four warhorses, which were brought to the offertory in the church; two were armed as if for a tournament; the other two drawn up as if for war ...

There were in fact no fewer than eight warhorses in the church, all bearing Du Guesclin's arms and emblems, of which four were offered to the abbey. Four shields, four banners, four swords and four helms of war and peace were carried by nobles, knights and esquires to the altar. The swords were reversed and handed to the clergy.[28] The written records of such ceremonies, which were soon to be kept exclusively by the heralds, evidently gave subsequent generations models to emulate.

During the fifteenth century, responsibility for ordering and executing funeral ceremonies for the nobility gradually became a prerogative of the heralds. It was part of their encroachment upon the rituals of chivalry which

---

26. See M. Barroux, *Les Fêtes Royales de St-Denis en Mai 1389* (Paris 1936), pp. 22-6, 46-9; L. Mirot, 'La Messe de "Requiem" de Du Guesclin (1389)', *Revue des Questions Historiques*, xxvi (1903), pp. 228-33. The conventual mass at which offerings were made was an innovation in the practice of the abbey.
27. Mirot, art. cit., p. 231, ll.25-30
28. Barroux, op. cit., pp. 46-8.

mirrored the decline of their functions upon the battlefield and at the siege.[29] Their genealogical and armorial expertise made the kings-of-arms, heralds and pursuivants natural stage-managers of such ceremonies. Heralds were record-keepers and custodians of precedent, and it is hardly surprising that they should have written much of the descriptive and prescriptive literature of chivalry in the fifteenth and sixteenth centuries. A description of the burial of Richard Neville, earl of Salisbury, and his son Thomas, on 15 February 1463, reveals the heralds already performing a major and important part in chivalric ceremony of this kind.[30] The earl's funeral *cortège* was met by Garter and Clarenceux kings-of-arms, and Windsor and Chester heralds, about a mile outside the town of Breshall, where they were to be buried. The heralds grouped themselves around the hearse, wearing Neville's coat of arms. The next day they played an important part in the presentation of the earl's funeral achievements, which was clearly thought to be their right,[31] and the account furnished a precedent for the burials of Sir John Lovell in 1524 and Sir Philip Sidney in 1586.[32] The engraved roll of Sidney's funeral (1587) shows five heralds wearing mourning hoods 'carrying the hatchments and dignity of his knighthood', comprising funerary helm, spurs, gauntlets, tabard, sword and shield.[33] At the 1463 Neville funeral the significance of the heralds was expressed symbolically when the earl's coat of arms, shield, sword, helm and crest were returned by the officiating priest to the son and heir, who in turn handed them to Garter king-of-arms.[34] In his will, signed in his own hand and dated 10 May 1459, Salisbury had laid down that his burial church should receive two horses, a complete suit of his armour, his coat of arms, banner, standard and other equipment 'as is the custom'.[35] His executors duly discharged his wishes, although the heralds had made their rights plain. It was they who went to the west door of the church to admit 'a man armed on horseback trapped, with an axe in his right hand, the pointe

---

29. Wagner, *Heralds of England*, pp. 34-6. R. Dennis, *The Heraldic Imagination* (London 1975), pp. 34-6; P. Adam-Even, 'Les fonctions militaires des hérauts d'armes', *Archives Héraldiques Suisses*, lxxi (1957), pp. 2-33; J.B. de Vaivre, L. Jequier, 'Eléments d'héraldique médiévale: orientations pour l'étude et l'utilisation des armoriaux du Moyen Age', *Cahiers d'héraldique*, i (Paris 1975), p. xiv: '... it was when a more rational organisation of armies ended by putting the very existence of heralds in danger that the latter drew up their treatises on *blason*.' For late examples of heralds exercising military duties by summoning towns to surrender, see C.G. Cruickshank, *Army Royal. Henry VIII's Invasion of France, 1513* (Oxford 1969), pp. 82-3, 143.

30. See *A Collection of Ordinances and Regulations for the Government of the Royal Household* (London 1790), pp. 131-3; Wagner, *Heralds of England*, pp. 106-7.

31. *Collection of Ordinances*, p. 132.

32. For the conduct of funerals, see BL, MS Stowe 152, fo. 135 ('The Manner of bureinge Great Persons in ancient tymes'); Cripps-Day, *Fragmentaria Armamentaria*, iv, p. 153, n. 1. For Sidney, see *The Heralds' Exhibition Catalogue, 1934* (London 1970), pp. 31-2.

33. Ibid., plate XV, pp. 31-2. None of these could have been worn in battle and were purely symbolic of Sidney's knighthood.

34. *Collection of Ordinances*, pp. 132-3.

35. Borthwick Institute, Abp. Reg. 20, fo. 280r (probate 23 June 1461).

downewarde' who rode to the door of the choir to offer his mount and its
trappings.[36] As exponents and guardians of the science of armory, the heralds
were extending their jurisdiction to embrace every aspect of the bearing of arms
by the nobility: ceremonies such as the Neville funeral set precedents for the
future. A description of 'the ordering of a funeral for a noble person in Henry
VII's time' is noteworthy because it explicitly distinguishes the banner and
pennon, which bore the lord's arms, from his standard 'with his beste [beast]
therein' and his guidon 'of his devise with his worde [motto]'.[37] The fourteenth-
century distinction between arms of war and peace had been fossilised in
funeral ceremonies which owed much to the tournament and its insignia.

In some regions, however, heraldic rituals had allegedly been allowed to lapse
by the late fifteenth century. In 1481, the author of Louis de Bruges' miscellany
observed that there were very few at that time who 'direct their nobility
according to the content of the rules noted here' and expressed the hope that
things would soon change for the better.[38] He hoped that someone would
appear, God willing, who might 'raise *noblesse* out of the mire' into which it had
fallen. There was no lack of candidates for such a task. Anthoine de la Salle,
Olivier de la Marche, and Louis de Bruges himself, were concerned to revive
and re-invigorate the practice of chivalry. One means of doing so, they argued,
was by restoring (or merely continuing) such customs as wearing the arms of
peace and war, and presenting them at funeral ceremonies. Anthoine de la Salle
explained the significance of arms worn during war in terms of loyalty,
obedience and honour. He wrote:

> ... when his coat of arms is on the armed knight or esquire, drawn up in *bataille*,
> upon so very noble and perilous a day, let it be known that he cannot honourably
> be disarmed without great reproach to his honour except for one of these three
> reasons: victory ... capture ... or death. And he who does otherwise puts his life in
> the prince's mercy.[39]

36. *Collection of Ordinances*, p. 132.
37. See *Queene Elizabethes Acadamy. A Boke of Precedence ...*, ed. F.J. Furnivall (EETS, London
1869), p. 29. Banners of the Trinity, of St George, of the Virgin Mary and of 'the Seynt that was his
advoure', i.e. patron, were also to be borne in the deceased's *cortège*.
38. Van Praet, op. cit., pp. 196-7.
39. '... puis que la cote d'armes est sur le chevallier, ou escuier, armée, et en bataille assemblée,
ad ce sy tres-noble et perilleux jour, sachent que sans l'une de ces troiz choses ne peult estre
honnourablement et sans grant reprouche de son honneur desarmée, c'est assavoir, par la victoire,
... la prison ... ou la mort. Et qui aultrement le fait, à la mercy du prince mect sa vie ...' Prost,
op. cit., p. 202 and BN, MS fr. 5867, fos. 9r, 6r where La Salle speaks of past usages of arms by
nobles who knew 'non seullement leurs armes, celles de leurs voisins ne celles de leurs marches,
mais se delictoient a savoir celles de leurs annemis. Car quant ilz venoient aux battailles en
fierement combattant ilz se arestoient sur lez grans seigneurs aux cotes darmes que ilz cognoissoient
ou secouroient leurs plus amis. Laquelle coutume soit par les francoiz ou par les angloiz au temps
des fortes et derraines guerres, ou parquoy que soit est aujourduy, presque toute delaissee. Et seroit
luy honte, fust en bataille ou en assault, qui sa cote darmes porteroit.' Every man used to carry his
coat-of-arms ready to don in battle or assault. La Salle's views are consistent with those of
Ghillebert de Lannoy: see *supra*, p. 15; La Marche, *Mémoires*, iv, p. 60 for similar rulings on the
display of banners.

This was an extension of the argument found in the statutes of chivalric orders, that it was *lèse-majesté* to flee from a battle in which banners had been unfurled.[40] To wear one's coat of arms was, he thought, a pledge of allegiance and a sign that one would fight to the end, whether that meant death or capture. A Roman precedent, culled from Vegetius, was cited to reinforce the argument.[41] The arms of war – a hereditary coat – obliged a man to put both personal and family interest behind his lord's interests. The honour of his house, as well as his personal pride, was at stake when he bore those arms in war.[42] This, La Salle lamented, had largely declined in his time, and should be resurrected.

Before such a revival could take place, the nobility – or at least their heralds – had to know the arms which they were entitled to bear, both in war and tournament. In the preamble to his *Armorial*, Gilles le Bouvier spoke of the effects of 'wars and divisions' within France on the knowledge of heraldry possessed by the nobility.[43] Civil war and the war with the English had driven some nobles away from their households, especially young noblemen, and 'the houses and churches where their arms were painted ... are all broken down and desolated'.[44] The books in which the kings-of-arms had recorded their coats and crests were also lacking as a result of the wars. Gilles, as king-of-arms of the march of Berry, thus set himself the task of journeying through all eight heraldic marches of France, recording and enregistering the names, crests, arms and cries of the nobility. As many nobles did not know what coats they bore, this was a work which entailed considerable research. A form of heraldic visitation such as this was one means of recording mens' arms.[45] Another, according to

40. See Armstrong, 'La Toison d'Or et la Loi des Armes', pp. 71-7; also *supra*, pp. 42-3.

41. Prost, op. cit., p. 199; BN, MS fr. 5867, fo. 6v: 'ainsy que jadis faisoient faire les Rommains consulles a leurs chevaliers et gens escrips pour aller aux conquestes et battailles pour le bien commun.' Henry V's alleged refusal to turn back on the eve of Agincourt once he had put on his coat-of-arms is quite consistent with such notions. See Huizinga, *Men and Ideas*, pp. 202-3. A sixteenth-century heraldic treatise endorsed these views when discussing the representation of nobles upon their tombs. The effigies of nobles were to show them wearing their coat-of-arms only if they had served their prince in a 'bataille mortelle' at which he was present in person (BR, MS 21551-69, fo. 27r). La Marche, *Mémoires*, ii, p. 271 claimed that Toison d'Or King-of-arms had told him that only if a man had died in battle were his banner, standard and pennon to be laid over his burial place. This was done for Cornille, bastard of Burgundy, in 1452.

42. The refusal of all members of the Luxembourg family to unfurl their banners or display their coats-of-arms against Louis XI at the battle of Montlhéry (July 1465) might illustrate the implications of doing so as far as the collective honour of the family was concerned: see Haynin, op. cit., i, pp. 61-2.

43. Le Bouvier, op. cit., p. 40.

44. Ibid., p. 40. Consciousness of the desolation caused by the war in France led Hugues de Lannoy (d.1456), according to the composer of his epitaph, to examine his conscience and to ponder 'de son salut aux lieux desoles de France plusieurs fois' during his retirement from the world in the collegiate church of St Pierre at Lille (BL, Add. MS 15,469, fo. 80r).

45. Le Bouvier, op. cit., pp. 39-40. Knowledge of the public display of coats-of-arms in churches, chapels and manor houses is clearly apparent among those who gave evidence to the inquiry into the bearing of the same arms by Sir Richard Scrope and Sir Robert Grovesnor in 1386. See *The Controversy between Sir Richard Scrope and Sir Robert Grovesnor*, ed. N.H. Nicolas (London 1832), i, pp. 91-3 (abbot of Selby's deposition), 94-5 (abbot of Jervaulx), 95-6 (abbot of St Agatha's, Richmondshire), 96 (abbot of Byland), 98-9 (subprior of Warter), 99-101 (priors of Lanercost and

Anthoine de la Salle in 1459, was to cry a tournament, or *pardon d'armes*.[46] This
had been done during the marriage celebrations of Margaret of Anjou at Nancy
in 1445, when René of Anjou had proclaimed that all 'who jousted at the said
behourt should be obliged to bear their natural hatchments (*haichemens*) on their
helms'. Their shields and the mantlings of their helms were to be blazoned with
their arms. This was done so that crests and coats-of-arms, 'forgotten through
their ignorance' should be recognised and remembered by 'young and
inexperienced noblemen'.[47] Anthoine de la Salle was therefore sought out by
nobles who did not know their arms, or were uncertain about the precise nature
of their coats. One suspects that this also provided an opportunity for the kings-
of-arms and heralds to swell their incomes by granting or approving arms. All
participants had to be nobles of four quarters and their arms were proof of this.
The tournament could thus serve to delineate the ranks of *noblesse* and ensure
that ancestral arms were duly recorded, respected and perpetuated.

To qualify for participation in a joust or *tournoi*, a man had thus to present his
blason or coat of arms, displaying the four quarters of his nobility. At the jousts
of the *Arbre d'Or* in 1468, each contestant was obliged to present his coat of
arms, through a herald, to the pursuivant of the *Arbre d'Or*.[48] His shield was
hung on the golden tree as a token that he had challenged the knight who was
guarding it. Much ingenious invention accompanied the appearance of
challengers in the lists. Horses were hung with silver bells, their coverings
embroidered with love-knots, interwoven letters and other conceits. Each
contestant, however, bore what Olivier de la Marche referred to as his *devise*
during the courses run with the lance.[49] These emblems or badges – such as the
barbican of Anthoine, *grand bâtard* of Burgundy, or the cockleshells of Claude de
Vaudrey, lord of l'Aigle – had assumed a much greater significance by the later
fifteenth century. Like a crest, they were more easily recognisable in combat
than the elaborately quartered coats of arms, with their numerous subdivisions,
which fifteenth-century noble houses bore.[50] Perhaps Anthoine de la Salle's
lament that coats of arms were no longer borne in war may be explained by the
fact that the shield was no longer carried in battle,[51] and that coats had become

---

Newburgh). The prior of Lanercost claimed that the house possessed banners bearing the arms of
those Scropes who were buried in their church (pp. 99-100). The heralds do not appear to have
played any part at this date in the enquiry. A form of heraldic visitation, however, is known in a
sixteenth-century copy recording the arms of Northern families between *c.* 1480 and 1500: see *A
Visitation of the North of England, c. 1480-1500*, ed. P. Hunter Blair (Surtees Society, cxliv, 1930).
  46. BN, MS fr. 5867, fos. 22r-23r.
  47. Ibid., fo. 22v; 'et ce fist il [René] pour aux josnes et simples gentilz hommes recorder leurs
haichemens et blasons darmes par leurs simplesses oublyez ...' René's order is interesting in that it
implies that there should be no distinction between arms borne in the tournament and in war.
  48. La Marche, *Mémoires*, iii, p. 134.
  49. Ibid., iii, pp. 152-69.
  50. See e.g. the coat of arms of Richard Neville, earl of Warwick (d. 1471): A.R. Wagner,
'Heraldry', *Medieval England*, ed. A.L. Poole, i (Oxford, 1958), fig. 90, p. 369.
  51. See *infra*, p. 105.

so much more difficult to recognise. Simpler methods of identification were needed, and the *devise*, or personal badge, was to some extent a reversion to the bolder heraldic signs of an earlier period. The alleged decline in the bearing of arms of war and peace at noble funerals in the second half of the century also suggests that the distinction between the two forms was now obsolete. The *devise* was no longer associated only with the tournament. Two further reasons for the neglect of such customs were advanced by the author of Louis de Bruges' chivalric miscellany: they had, he wrote, engendered jealousies between nobles, anxious to outdo their peers in the lavish funerary display of arms, horses and accoutrements.[52] Secondly, many men of great wealth and estate could not show four quarters of nobility because they could not claim four noble ancestors in the direct line of their descent.[53] The entry of rich *anoblis* into the ranks of the Flemish nobility may thus have exerted some pressure which led to the discarding of old customs and a re-definition of the nature of *noblesse*.

One cannot discount the influence of changes in taste and fashion on the ways in which the later medieval nobility used heraldic and other emblems in peace and war. The prevailing vogue for the *impresa* in Italy, the badge or cognisance in England, and the *devise* in France and the Low Countries, may partly derive from the contemporary taste for allegory.[54] Emblems were chosen because they symbolised certain ideal qualities or desirable attributes. Whatever the precise reasons behind their assumption, it can be shown that the badge or *devise* began to replace the coat of arms in warfare at a time when changes in military organisation and practice were also taking place. With the rise of standing armies in France (1445) and Burgundy (1470), a tendency towards the substitution of standards and ensigns for banners and pennons has been detected by Professor Contamine.[55] Banners and pennons bore hereditary coats of arms; standards and ensigns displayed personal badges, *devises* and mottoes. This tendency, Professor Contamine argues, can be related to a merging of distinctions between nobles and professional captains in the French standing army, and to the desire of the French crown to demonstrate that military command no longer depended upon social status or birthright.[56] It

52. BN, MS fr. 1280, fo. 133r-v. A desire to prevent envy and hatred between nobles led Philip the Good to command that the shields hung on Philippe de Lalaing's *Perron Fée* at Bruges in 1463 were not to be in order of rank (BL, MS Lansdowne 285, fo. 65r).

53. BN, MS fr. 1280, fo. 133r: many men 'qui se monstrent de grant estat ne sauroient armoier des quatre lignes les cierges denviron la biere parcequilz ne sont venus ... de tele noblesse.' For the entry of *anoblis* into the Flemish and Burgundian *noblesse*, see *supra*, pp. 20-1.

54. For examples, see Hill and Pollard, op. cit., pp. 7-14; E. Wind, *Pagan Mysteries in the Renaissance* (London 1967), pp. 73-8, 108-12; F.P. Barnard, *Edward IV's French Expedition of 1475. The Leaders and their Badges* (London 1925), fos. 1r-12v [sic]; J. von. Radowitz, *Die Devisen und Motto des späteren Mittelalters* (Stuttgart 1850), pp. 20-39; C.F. Menestrier, *Origine des Armoiries* (Paris 1680), pp. 2-19, 48-9 and *Traité des Tournois, Joustes, Carrousels et autres spectacles publics* (Lyon 1669), pp. 148-50, 271.

55. Contamine, *Guerre, Etat et Société*, pp. 675-6. For the use of standards bearing *devises* in the Burgundian army before 1470, see Haynin, op. cit., i, pp. 61-2, where those carried at Montlhéry in 1465 are described.

56. Contamine, *Guerre, Etat et Société*, p. 676; *infra*, pp. 147-8.

must also be related to the less theoretical considerations which have already been discussed.[57] When badges of the kind worn in the tournament were adopted in warfare, the distinction between 'arms of peace' and 'arms of war' lapsed. Among the booty captured by the Swiss from the Burgundians between 1474 and 1477 are standards bearing *devises* and mottoes, such as *Plus que vous* ('More than you'), with the letters *A* and *E* joined by a love-knot, or with the Flemish motto, *Euw plaisy* ('At your pleasure').[58] These would not have been out of place at a tournament. Above all, the standards of Charles the Bold's standing companies of *ordonnance*, with their St Andrew's cross, flints and steels, and the motto *Je lay emprins* ('I have undertaken it') demonstrate that clearly recognisable emblems were preferred to the complexities of the ducal coat of arms.[59] The distribution of liveries, collars and badges must have accustomed men to recognise a lord by his *devise*.[60] Emblems displayed in the tournament were now borne as badges upon standards in the thick of battle. Huizinga was in this sense right when he observed a 'close connexion between warfare and the tournament' even at the end of the Middle Ages.

There was furthermore no distinction between those who fought in the 'serious' business of war during the fifteenth century and those who frequented tournaments. Jacques de Lalaing, *le bon chevalier*, served Philip the Good in his wars as well as achieving an international reputation as a knight-errant and jouster. The regulations which he drew up for his *pas d'armes* of the *Fontaine des Pleurs* in 1449 stipulated that if he was called away from Châlon-sur-Saône (where the jousts were to take place) by a summons to war, the *pas d'armes* should be held 'in a place near to the field of battle'.[61] He was killed by a cannon-shot at the siege of Poucques, near Ghent, in July 1453.[62] Between that date and August 1483 no less than seven members of the Lalaing family died in battle.[63] Jacques was not the only paragon of chivalry among them. Simon de Lalaing, who died in 1476, had taken part in eight battles on land and sea. He was also, declared his epitaph, a 'great jouster and tourneyer'.[64] In 1483, his son Josse was killed at a siege outside Utrecht by two hand-gun shots, while he was

57. See *supra*, pp. 96-7.
58. See Deuchler, op. cit., nos. 179, 194; C. Brusten, 'Les emblèmes de l'armée bourguignonne sous Charles le Téméraire', *Jahrbuch des Bernischen Historischen Museum in Bern*, xxxvii-xxxviii (1957-8), pp. 118-32.
59. Ibid., pp. 120-6. The use of St Andrew's cross on these standards as a symbol of ducal sovereignty is perhaps paralleled by the juxtaposition of a St George's cross – one of the English royal emblems – with the badges of Tudor nobles on their standards. For illustrations see *The Heralds' Exhibition Catalogue*, plates XXIX, XXIV, p. 64. These standards and badges date from *c.* 1513-32: see *Banners, Standards and Badges from a Tudor Manuscript in the College of Arms*, ed. Lord Howard de Walden (London 1934), pp. 12-36.
60. See Barnard, op. cit., fos. 1r-4r [sic]; Wagner, 'Heraldry', pp. 357-9.
61. Planche, art. cit., p. 104.
62. La Marche, *Mémoires*, ii, pp. 309-10; Planche, art. cit., p. 122; *infra*, pp. 132, 137.
63. Brassart, op. cit., p. 24.
64. BR, MS II.1156, fo. 268r. He died 'sans reproche' having performed deeds of arms 'au pied et a cheval en liches closes', on 10 May 1476.

overseeing the setting up of a bombard. His epitaph equated deeds of arms in war with those performed in the tournament. He was 'in many great offices' and was a 'captain of 100 lances'.[65] It could not be argued that the realities of 'modern' warfare were of no concern to these noblemen.[66] By 1465 Louis de Bruges, ardent devotee of the tournament, had chosen a bombard as his emblem, with the motto *Plus est en vous* ('More is in you').[67] Adaptation by the nobility to the new techniques of warfare ensured that their traditional military rôle, and its concomitant style of life, was perpetuated. The distinction between participants in 'real' and 'sham' warfare was not yet made quite as sharply as has been imagined. In the achievement of honour, prowess and renown, the tournament still held a central and unchallenged place.

65. Ibid. fo. 268v. He was captured at Nancy in 1477 but served Mary of Burgundy and Maximilian until his death on 5 August 1483.
66. *Pace* Planche, art. cit., p. 122.
67. Van Praet, op. cit., p. 186; cf. Planche, art. cit., p. 122.

CHAPTER FOUR

The Techniques of War

i. Cavalry and infantry

Some of the ideas which lay behind chivalric literature, ritual and behaviour in the fifteenth century have now been examined. To assess the place and function of the mounted knight in the conduct of war, however, one must embark upon a discussion of technical questions because, in the history of warfare, techniques are all-important.[1] The impact of technical change on the three major arms – cavalry, infantry and artillery – was undoubtedly great in the later Middle Ages. Knightly warfare demanded the use of mounted men, yet the time-honoured cavalry of feudalism was threatened in the thirteenth and fourteenth centuries by new infantry tactics devised by the English, the Flemings and the Swiss. Longbowmen and pikemen, when matched against mounted knights at Courtrai (1302), Bannockburn (1314), Morgarten (1315), Laupen (1339), or Crécy (1346) had demonstrated the murderous effects of missile fire and pike-phalanxes on bodies of horsemen.[2] Arrows broke up their formations, killed, wounded or maddened their valuable mounts, and could penetrate their mail and rudimentary plate armour. Pikes formed an impenetrable hedge, a defensive and immovable wall. 'Knightly warfare,' it has been concluded, 'was probably already nearly a century out of date by the time of Agincourt',[3] and 'the supremacy of feudal cavalry is long gone by; it had ended at Crécy and Laupen and Aljubarotta, if not at Courtrai and Bannockburn.'[4] The dismounting of cavalry to fight at Poitiers and Agincourt had not solved the problem; unless a more effective rôle could be found for it in fifteenth-century warfare its future was clearly in jeopardy. Military historians, seeing no new function emerging, have tended to take refuge in the argument that the survival of heavy cavalry in European armies must have been dictated by other than purely military reasons. 'Elegant anachronism,' writes Professor Howard, 'was

---

1. P. Pieri, 'Sur les dimensions de l'histoire militaire', *Annales*, xviii (1963), p. 629.
2. C.W.C. Oman, *A History of the Art of War in the Middle Ages* (London 1924), pp. 426-7; Verbruggen, op. cit., pp. 99-100, 164-83.
3. Keegan, op. cit., p. 317.
4. Oman, op. cit., ii, p. 426.

to remain a characteristic of European cavalry for many a century yet.'[5]

The historian is thus presented with a paradox: heavy cavalry had outlived its usefulness, yet it still provided the core and the most prestigious arm of every major fifteenth-century army, including the new standing armies of France, Burgundy, Brittany, Venice and Milan.[6] In Italy, although infantry had a part to play, 'it is true that both in terms of numbers and particularly in terms of prestige, heavy cavalry did tend to predominate';[7] in France, the *compagnies d'ordonnance* of 1445 were nothing if not groups of heavy cavalry, supported by mounted archers;[8] in Burgundy, Charles the Bold's *ordonnances* of 1471 and 1473 followed the French model;[9] at Milan the *Ordine del'esercito ducale sforzesco* created a force of *lanze* between 1472 and 1474 which reflected a similar predominance of heavy cavalry.[10] It is not easy to explain this phenomenon, given the various ends for which the armies were raised, the differing military needs and forms of organisation of European monarchies, principalities and city-states. Nevertheless, the nucleus of the fighting army in the fifteenth century was provided by an apparently out-moded, inefficient, yet highly expensive fighting force.

The prejudice and innate conservatism of the nobility have often been cited as an explanation. M. Claude Gaier, for example, has argued that 'the social prejudices of the feudal class' lay at the root of the problem.[11] The rise of heavy cavalry is seen as the expression of a caste spirit, quite unrelated to pragmatic considerations, with which the nobility might emphasise their rank and status. This prejudice – if it existed at all – was clearly not widespread. Members of the Flemish and Burgundian nobility often dismounted and stood among the archers in battle, just as the English had done at Crécy.[12] In his account of the battle of Montlhéry (1465), Philippe de Commynes wrote:

> My lord Philippe de Lalaing dismounted, because among the Burgundians at that time the most honoured were those who dismounted with the archers, and they always put many men of substance there, so that the common soldiers might be encouraged, and fight better. They had learnt this from the English ...[13]

5. M. Howard, *War in European History* (Oxford 1976), p. 16.
6. Mallett, op. cit., pp. 146-7; P. Contamine, *Azincourt* (Paris 1964), pp. 21-6.
7. Mallett, op. cit., pp. 146, 151: '... the fact remained ... that heavy cavalry was an inflexible component of all fifteenth-century armies.'
8. Contamine, *Guerre, Etat et Société*, pp. 278-90.
9. Vaughan, *Charles the Bold*, pp. 206-10. For a copy of the 1473 edict see BL, Add. MS 36,619.
10. Contamine, *Azincourt*, p. 25.
11. C. Gaier, 'La cavalerie lourde en Europe occidentale du xiie au xvie siècle', *Revue internationale d'Histoire Militaire*, xxxi (1971), p. 386.
12. See J.E. Morris, 'The archers at Crécy', *EHR*, xii (1897), pp. 427-36.
13. Commynes, op. cit., i, p. 23: 'Messire Philippes de Lalain s'estoit mis à pied, car entre les Bourguygnons lors s'estoyent les plus honnoréz que ceulx qui descendoyent avecques les archiers, et tousjours se y en mectoit grant quantité de gens de bien, affin que le peuple en fust plus asseuré, et combattre myeulx, et tenoient cela des Angloys ...'.

He could have added that this also made the possibility of flight from the field less feasible, as Richard Neville, earl of Warwick, demonstrated at Towton in 1461, when he killed his horse and fought on foot.[14] At Agincourt the veteran knight Sir Thomas Erpingham was set over the archers and the first volley of arrows was released against the French at his signal.[15] A Burgundian battle-order drawn up in the army of John the Fearless outside Barsailles in September 1417 describes a similar practice. The duke's war-council advised him that 'all the archers and crossbowmen ... should be mustered under two small standards in two wings in front of the vanguard ... led by two notable and valiant *gentils hommes* who shall have command of the said standards and archers ...'[16] Contempt for the non-noble, as expressed against their *bourgeois*, artisan and peasant enemies during the Burgundian wars with Ghent and Liège, should not be used as an index of every nobility's attitude towards the baser elements in their own armies.[17] Neither English nor French nobles had been unwilling to dismount to fight at Poitiers or Agincourt, and there is little evidence for prejudice against humbly-born men-at-arms in fourteenth- and fifteenth-century armies. The profession of arms could itself ennoble a man, and there was no obstacle placed in the way of an able campaigner.[18]

It has been maintained that an aversion to new military techniques lay behind the survival of heavy cavalry, that a 'passion for single combat' produced widespread resistance to military innovation and invention,[19] and that new and more lethal weapons (such as firearms) were resisted on moral grounds. The same arguments assumed that, in their desire to perpetuate 'chivalrous' warfare, the later medieval nobility refused to make use of such weapons or to adapt themselves to the changing techniques of warfare, but there is no evidence to support this view.[20] On the contrary, English, French and Burgundian nobles took a lively interest in artillery and the development of new infantry weapons. Their willingness to fight in groups and in combination with other arms, rather than as individuals in search of single combat, suggests a flexibility and a readiness to accept technological change. As long ago as 1908, Sir Charles Oman put forward the idea that the importance of cavalry forces was enhanced

14. See P. Warner, *British Battlefields: the North* (London 1975), p. 55; *British Battlefields: the South* (London 1975), p. 90. According to a newsletter written by Margaret of York to Isabella of Burgundy soon after Barnet (1471), Warwick was killed as he tried to save himself by fleeing on horseback before Edward IV could reach him: *Analectes historiques*, ed. M. Gachard (Brussels 1856), p. 142.

15. C. Hibbert, *Agincourt* (London 1964), pp. 113-14, for this stage of the battle.

16. BN, MS. fr. 1278, fo. 58v, printed Lannoy, op. cit., pp. 478-9: 'Que touz archiers et arbalestriers de ceste presente armee ... se mectront soubz deux petiz estandars en deux helles devant ladicte avangarde ... conduiz par deux notables et vaillans gentilz hommes qui auroient le gouvernement desdiz estandars et gens de trait ...'.

17. See La Marche, *Mémoires*, ii, pp. 244, 270-71.

18. *Le Jouvencel*, ii, p. 80.

19. Keegan, op. cit., pp. 316-17.

20. For an extreme statement of the view see J.U. Nef, *War and Human Progress, c. 1494-c. 1640* (London 1950), p. 32; *infra*, pp. 144, 162.

towards the end of the fifteenth century both in their own right and 'in combination with missile-bearing infantry and artillery'.[21] Historians have not developed his hypothesis, but concentrated rather on the rise and sophistication of artillery and infantry tactics at the expense of the armoured horseman. In fact, the continued, even increased, importance of cavalry on the battlefield does not seem to have resulted from external pressures, but from changes in its organisation, deployment and equipment which increased its suitability for the conditions of fifteenth-century warfare.

Throughout his long history of European deployment the heavy cavalryman's function has been as much psychological as physical, and it was essentially this aspect of his rôle which was strengthened in the course of the fifteenth century. Pitted against foot-soldiers, heavy cavalry relied largely upon the 'shock' principle for its effect. The effect of a cavalry charge on infantry's morale was generally greater than its physical impact.[22] Its object was to induce fear, panic and flight among a dismounted enemy, and it was an essentially 'hit or miss' weapon.[23] General J.F.C. Fuller saw medieval cavalry as a 'shock group' and drew an analogy between the fully-armoured man-at-arms and the modern tank, emphasising the superiority of protected to unprotected offensive power.[24] Without iron discipline and nerves of steel, no infantry could withstand an assault of heavy cavalry, especially when it had already suffered from the damaging and demoralising effects of archery fire. The temptation to break ranks and flee was clearly very strong, and the English and Burgundian practice of placing the archers in the van, with men-at-arms among them on foot and behind them on horse, may have had a coercive as well as an exhortatory aim.[25] However, the mounted man-at-arms, matched against enemy cavalry, could engage in single combat with a picked adversary, or fight as a member of a group, lending aid to his comrades and being aided by them in turn. In both cases, the incentive to spare lives in the hope of ransom was strong, while no such constraint existed when the enemy consisted of archers, crossbowmen or pikemen. Modes of behaviour in battle were thus directly determined by the composition of the enemy's army. Cavalry *versus* infantry and cavalry *versus* cavalry were very different exercises.

Much has been made of the undisciplined nature of the feudal armies of the twelfth and thirteenth centuries. The desire of mounted knights for single combat, and their resistance to attempts at control and direction, have become

21. Oman, op. cit., ii, p. 428.
22. Keegan, op. cit., p. 96.
23. See Denholm-Young, 'The tournament in the thirteenth century', pp. 260-1: '... with heavy cavalry it was hit or miss; you could not manipulate a spear for more than one shot in one course.'
24. J.F.C. Fuller, *Armament and History* (London 1946), p. 23. A similar view had been propounded earlier: see J.G. Mann, 'Notes on armour of the Maximilian period and the Italian Wars', *Archaeologia*, lxxix (1929), p. 219: '... the armoured horseman ... still had his uses ... armour gave him something of the invulnerability of the modern tank, and the force and impact of his charge was tremendous.'
25. Commynes, op. cit., i, p. 23; BN, MS fr. 1278, fo. 59r.

historiographical commonplaces.[26] However, the work of Professor Verbruggen and Dr Smail has demonstrated that these men habitually fought in groups of ten to forty mounted knights, known as *acies, conrois* or *bannières*. These were grouped in turn into larger units or squadrons, which then formed three or more *batailles*. These mounted troops kept close order, endured enemy attack without retaliating, charged in line and were aided by a body kept in reserve which might decide the issue – as, for example, at the victory of the duke of Brabant over the duke of Guelders at Worringen in 1288.[27] Lessons learnt at the tournament, where participants were grouped together in the *mêlée* under the banners of lords and knights banneret,[28] and the strong personal bonds between lords, vassals and kinsmen, gave military and social cohesion to these armies.[29] Nevertheless, the full 'shock' and weight of the heavy cavalry charge was not developed in this period, and the ability to follow up a charge, or 'charge home', and then to regroup, was not yet cultivated. Discipline in the Roman sense was unknown and a battle might dissolve into a series of hand-to-hand encounters, where the taking of prisoners took precedence over the destruction of the enemy.[30] Only when his line had been pierced and broken by knights armed with sword and lance, was single combat feasible. Before that, the group (*conroi, bannière*) was of decisive importance, because the enemy was unlikely to break ranks unless his opponents were advancing in a tight, densely-organised battle order. Fear provided a further incentive to group together: degradation and dishonour followed the display of cowardice in battle, and men were more likely to fight better surrounded and aided by a small band of comrades than alone and isolated in the face of the enemy.[31] Until the later thirteenth century such tactics proved successful when the terrain was favourable to cavalry combat. After that date, the innovations in infantry tactics associated with English archers, Scottish spearmen and Swiss halberdiers and pikemen posed a threat to the mounted man-at-arms which was not effectively met until the fifteenth century. If cavalry forces were to develop a new rôle, the problem of their extreme vulnerability to arrows, crossbow bolts and pikes had first to be solved. Without adequate protection against their destructive effects, its offensive power was impotent.

Personal protection in battle was offered, in the first instance, by armour which was expressly designed to resist the two forms of offensive weapon borne by infantry – missiles and pikes – as well as the swords, lances and maces of an

26. See, e.g., Keegan, op. cit., pp. 316-17.
27. Verbruggen, 'La tactique militaire', pp. 164-5, 166-8; 'L'art militaire', pp. 488-90; R.C. Smail, *Crusading Warfare (1097-1193)* (Cambridge, 2nd ed. 1976), pp. 124-7, 128-9; for Worringen, see E. de Dynter, *Chronique des ducs de Brabant*, ed. P. de Ram (Brussels 1854-7), ii, p. 721.
28. Verbruggen, 'L'art militaire', pp. 488-9.
29. Verbruggen, 'La tactique militaire', p. 168; 'L'art militaire', pp. 488-9.
30. Verbruggen, 'L'art militaire', p. 180.
31. It is a little surprising that this aspect of military psychology should be applied only to modern, and not to medieval, warfare in Keegan, op. cit., pp. 310-11, 316-17.

enemy's cavalry. The problem faced by the mounted man-at-arms was to some extent similar to that which confronted his successors in the 1914-18 war. The need to neutralise the effects of missiles led to the design of the tank, that 'bullet-proof horse', and the fully-armoured cavalryman of the fifteenth century had also sought to render both himself and his mount invulnerable to archery fire.[32] A marked improvement in the degree of resistance offered by armour to the arrow and crossbow bolt was gradually achieved. By the first decade of the fourteenth century the limitations of the *hauberk* and other mail defences had been decisively demonstrated. Arrows could penetrate and break the inter-linked rings of a coat of mail and there was little chance of their glancing off its surface or of shattering upon impact. Writing of the weapons of the Turks in his *Voyage d'Oultremer* of 1432, Bertrandon de la Broquière told Philip the Good that they had 'arrows which I think would pierce a coat of mail'.[33] The terrible effects of missile fire upon men armed only in mail are borne out by grisly archaeological evidence from the grave-pits on the battlefield at Wisby, in Gotland, where a Danish royal army massacred a levy of Swedish peasants and townsmen on 27 July 1361.[34] Excavations revealed that at least 125 men suffered fatal head wounds from crossbow bolts and arrows which had fallen vertically upon their inadequate hoods of mail.[35] It was the desire for protection against such acute physical damage that led to the introduction and development of full plate armour (*harnois blanc* or 'white' armour) in the second half of the fourteenth century.

The evolution from mail to plate was common to all countries of Western Europe, although climatic considerations retarded the adoption of full 'white' armour in Spain and Italy. With the rise of plate after about 1350, the helm and the shield went out of use.[36] The heavy helm was replaced by the visored bascinet, then by the sallet and armet.[37] These were much lighter and less cumbersome helmets, the weight of which was borne less by the head and more by the *gorget* (throat-guard). The shield became redundant once the man-at-arms was encased in a complete suit of plate. This could not have been achieved without changes in metal-working processes. A certain sophistication in manufacturing techniques is apparent by about 1400, when higher-quality iron and steel were produced by new carburising processes and the use of the blast-furnace.[38] In the course of the fifteenth century, steel with a high carbon constitutent was used for the best armour, and the outer surfaces of the plates

32. Fuller, op. cit., pp. 24, 137. See plate 19.

33. *Le Voyage d'Outremer de Bertrandon de la Broquière*, ed. C. Shefer (Paris 1892), p. 227.

34. See B. Thordeman, *Armour from the Battle of Wisby, 1361* (Stockholm 1939), i, pp. 160-5.

35. Ibid., i, pp. 185-7, 190. Many arrow-heads were found lodged inside the crania of the dead.

36. See G. Laking, *A Record of European Arms and Armour through Seven Centuries* (London 1920), ii, pp. 99-100; Blair, op. cit., p. 182.

37. Ibid., pp. 67-73. See plates 16, 17, 18.

38. See G.W. Henger, 'The metallography and chemical analysis of iron-base samples dating from Antiquity to modern times', *Bulletin of the Historical Metallurgy Group*, iv (1970), pp. 49-52.

Plate 14. Great helm for the tilt (English, *c*. 1515). London, Wallace Collection.

Plate 15. Jousting helm (Italian, late fifteenth century). Paris, Musée de l'Armée.

were subjected to various hardening treatments, of which 'quenching', while the metal was still white-hot,[39] was the most effective. Improvements in the tensile strength of armour plates, and the increased skill with which they were shaped to offer the maximum resistance to missiles, have led to the conclusion that by the end of the century 'everything concerned with the defensive qualities and constructional details of armour had been discovered and carried to a high pitch of perfection'.[40] No further development was possible without an intolerable increase in the weight of the armour.

The demands made upon armour were threefold: the achievement of maximum protection, resistance to missile-penetration and protection that was

39. Ibid., p. 52; Table III *infra*. The samples used in these metallurgical tests were armour plates dating from *c.* 1400-*c.* 1550. See also A.R. Williams, 'Medieval Metalworking: armour plate and the advance of metallurgy', *The Chartered Mechanical Engineer* (September 1978), pp. 109-14.

40. C.J. Ffoulkes, *The Armourer and his Craft from the xith to the xvith century* (London 1912), p. 12. For technical analysis of tensile strength and other properties of surviving armours, see Table III *infra* and A.R. Williams, 'Metallographic examination of 16th-century armour', *Bulletin of the Historical Metallurgy Group*, vi (1972), pp. 15-23; P. Jones, 'The target', in R. Hardy, *Longbow: a Social and Military History* (Cambridge 1976), pp. 204-8.

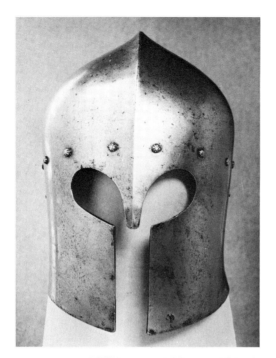

Plate 16. Sallets (Italian, mid-fifteenth century). London, Wallace Collection.

Plate 17. Sallets (German, mid-fifteenth century). London, Wallace Collection.

compatible with mobility. These were difficult conditions to achieve and reconcile. A balance between power of attack and power of defence could be established by thickening the plates of an armour, but this impeded mobility.[41] Maximum protection did not yet mean that armour was ever wholly invulnerable and foolproof – it perhaps came nearer to this condition than ever

41. Blair, op. cit., p. 191; Ffoulkes, op. cit., pp. 10-12.

before. Glancing surfaces were presented to all types of offensive weapons, and
weak points, such as the armpits and groin, were more effectively covered. Such
was the armourer's skill that some mid-fifteenth-century Italian armours
display such devices as stop-ribs, where the upper edge of a plate is turned over
to form a ridge which would deflect blows away from the groin when a man's
leg was bent in the saddle.[42] Reinforcing pieces were introduced to protect vital
areas such as the chest, the sword-arm and the left side, which was always most
vulnerable to an enemy's lance. Suits made for the Italian *condottieri*
Bartolommeo Colleone (d. 1475) and Roberto di San Severino both have
specially shaped reinforcing plates which are larger on the left shoulder and
bridle-arm, with high wings to protect the neck and deflect an opponent's blows
away from the head.[43]

A desire for physical protection by less material means is evident from the
inscriptions engraved on surviving armours, such as the invocations *Ave Maria*
and *Ave Domine* on the pauldrons (shoulder-defences) of a Milanese field-
armour of about 1440-50.[44] Armour of both an earlier and a later date bears
many such talismanic inscriptions. The commonest phrase is the protective
text: 'Jesus autem transiens per medium illorum ibat' (Luke 4:30) found on a
North Italian armour of about 1390 and on Italian and German armour of the
period 1500-20, engraved on breast or back-plates and sometimes accompanied
by etched representations of patron saints.[45] This reference to Christ's escape
from a hostile crowd at Nazareth was peculiarly appropriate to the predicament
of the man-at-arms, especially when fighting against heavy odds. The Virgin is
invoked on a Milanese breast-plate of about 1510 by the prayer 'Mater Dei
Memento Mei' and by the appeal 'Hilf Mir Maria' on a cuirass made at
Innsbruck at the same date.[46] Saints such as SS Barbara, George, Catherine
and Christopher were portrayed beside such inscriptions largely for their
efficacy in enhancing the defensive properties of the armour. St Sebastian's
popularity among the military classes stemmed not only from his career as an
officer in the Praetorian guard, but because he miraculously survived his
execution by archers under the emperor Diocletian.[47] There could be no more

42. See J.G. Mann, 'A further account of armour preserved in the Sanctuary of the Madonna
delle Grazie near Mantua', *Archaeologia*, lxxxvii (1937), p. 329 and pl. cxxiii; Blair, op. cit., fig. 219.

43. Ffoulkes, op. cit., pp. 4-5; Mann, 'A further account of armour preserved in the Sanctuary of
the Madonna delle Grazie', p. 325 and plate cxxx.

44. Oswald, Graf Trapp and J.G. Mann, *The Armoury of the Castle of Churburg* (London 1929),
p. 48, no. 20. The words 'JHS' and 'Avant' are also punched on the armour (now in the Scott
Collection, Glasgow Museum).

45. Ibid., pp. 19, 22 where the inscription runs along a brass border on the plates and bascinet of
the armour of *c.* 1390; Mann, 'Notes on the armour of the Maximilian period', plates lxx, fig. 1,
lxxvi, fig. 2.

46. Ibid., plate lxix, fig. a; Blair, op. cit., figs. 254-5.

47. Mann, 'Notes on armour of the Maximilian period', pp. 227-8. For a good example of SS
Sebastian and Barbara on an Italian armour and war saddle of *c.* 1500, see Trapp and Mann,
op. cit., pp. 103-4, no. 69 and plate xliv. See also *infra*, plate 24.

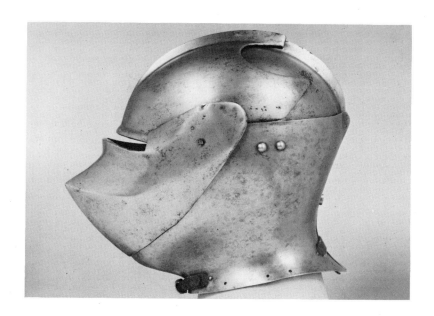

Plate 18. Armets (Italian, mid-fifteenth century). London, Wallace Collection.

relevant choice of patron among those who went into battle in the later Middle
Ages and early Renaissance.

The second quality demanded in a 'white' armour was an ability to
withstand penetration by missiles, and these fell into three categories in the
fifteenth century: longbow arrows (*trait*), crossbow bolts or quarrels (*viretons*)
and handgun shots.[48] In his fascinating comparison of the tactics and weapons
of Christians and infidels (1432), Bertrandon de la Broquière stressed the
superiority of the long-bow and crossbow over the short bows of the Turks. He
told Philip the Good:

> The archery fire of the Turks ... is not fierce, although they have strong bows.
> They are short ... and their arrows are also short and slender, and the arrowhead
> is lodged in the shaft in such a way that it cannot withstand a strong blow ... Their
> archers do not fire as often as ours, nor from such a long range ... For this reason, I
> say that a light white armour or brigandine seems to me the best.[49]

In a further memorandum, written in 1439, Bertrandon argued that in a
Christian army, ranged in battle order against the heathen,

> ... a large part of the archers and crossbowmen should be sown among the men-
> at-arms, because the Turks are all archers ... and they could fire right into the said
> *bataille* if it was not for resistance by, and fear of, the archers and crossbowmen of
> the Christians ... stationed among the men-at-arms or a little in front if
> necessary ... because the Christian archers and crossbowmen fire further; they
> can each have shot at least two or three arrows into the *bataille* of the Turks before
> the Turkish arrows can reach the Christian army ...[50]

The effects of such archery fire on the lightly-armed infidels, carrying small
shields and *targes*, and wearing only mail hoods beneath their turbans, was,
thought Bertrandon, likely to be devastating.[51] Its probable effect on the heavily
armed cavalry of Western Christendom remains to be assessed. Much must
depend on technical questions, such as the range, rate of fire and angle of strike
of arrows and crossbow bolts. Recent experiments have suggested that, used
against plate armour, 'it is unlikely that arrows of the long bodkin type would

---

48. See Hardy, op. cit., pp. 201-4, 204-8; A.R. Williams, 'Some firing tests with simulated 15th-
century handguns', *Journal of the Arms and Armour Society*, viii (1974), pp. 114-20; *infra*, pp. 134-8.

49. *Voyage d'Outremer*, p. 227: 'le traict des Turcz ... n'est point fort, combien qu'il y ait de fors
arcz. Ilz sont courtz ... et leur traict est court aussi et deliéet se boute le fer dedans le bois et ne
pourroit souffrir grant coup ... Et ne tirent point leurs archiers à beaucoup près que font les
nostres ... Pour ceste cause, je dis que le blanc harnois legier ou brigandines me samble le millieur.'

50. *Ibid.*, p. 271: 'une grande partie d'archiers et de gens de traict doivent estre entrelardez entre
les gens de bataille pour ce que les Turcz sont tous archiers ... et pourroyent tirer dedans la dite
bataille si n'estoit pas la resistance et dobte du traict des archiers et crennequiniers des chrestiens
qui seront ... parmy les gens d'armes ou ung pou devant si mestier est ... pour ce que les archiers et
crennequiniers chrestiens tirent plus loing: et porroient avoir tiré deux ou trois flesches et traicts au
moins dedans la bataille des Turcz avant que les flesches des Turcz puissent venir dedans la bataille
des chrestiens ...'.

51. *Ibid.*, p. 269.

penetrate completely'.[52] To pierce a plate effectively, an arrow would have had to strike its target at an angle of ninety degrees, at a range of well under 200 yards. Ricochet, and the shattering of arrows upon impact, would take place when the angle of strike was more oblique.[53] To release a sufficiently dense horizontal volley of arrows against a moving target at a relatively short range was not always possible in battle. The effects of high wind, poor visibility, lack of discipline and sheer panic upon a group of archers facing a charge of heavy cavalry are, moreover, imponderable. However, if armour was proof against the longbow by the end of the fourteenth century, its resistance to other missiles is not so easy to establish. What seems certain is that the improved steel crossbows of the fifteenth century had a more effective penetrating power, over a longer range, than did the longbow. A range of about 500 yards, as opposed to the 250 or so for the longbow, has been suggested, and the bolts fired by the windlass-drawn crossbow, or *crennequin*, 'were probably capable of piercing armour'.[54] Yet this would again depend upon the angle of strike and the defensive properties of the armour. It was against the crossbow bolt that armour was put to the test when undergoing proof. The statutes of the guild of armourers at Angers in 1448 describe two methods of proof – by the windlass-drawn crossbow, and by the hand-drawn crossbow or longbow.[55] The best armours were proved by the first method, and this was presumably the severest test. In 1441, Philip the Good bought 465 crossbow bolts with which to assay armour, and in 1455 Guillaume Fillastre, bishop of Toul, paid two cross-bowmen from Brussels for breaking sixteen bolts against body armour supplied to the episcopal troops.[56] To possess an armour stamped with a double armourer's mark, tested by crossbow fire at point-blank range, was clearly the best material guarantee against sudden death in warfare.

The heavy cavalry of fifteenth-century Europe was beset by another threat – that delivered by weapons effective in close combat, rather than in distant visitation from archers. The push of the common pike was paralleled by the thrust of the noble lance. As the Scottish *schiltrons* and the Swiss phalanxes had shown, the use of densely-packed groups of pikemen, in attack as well as defence, could be extremely damaging to heavy cavalry.[57] The Burgundian veteran Jean de Wavrin endorsed this lesson when he wrote of the four or five

52. P. Jones in Hardy, op. cit., p. 207.

53. Ibid., pp. 206-7, with illustrations of sections showing arrow perforations at 45, 60 and 90 degrees.

54. A.R. Williams, 'Metallographic examination of 16th-century armour', p. 15. Most of the arrows retrieved from the grave-pits at Wisby were apparently crossbow bolts: Thordeman, op. cit., i, pp. 160, 190.

55. Ffoulkes, op. cit., pp. 64-5, 180; *Ordonnances des Rois de France*, 22 vols (Paris 1723-1846), xx, pp. 156-8.

56. Gaier, *L'Industrie et le Commerce des Armes*, pp. 279-80. There is no surviving later medieval evidence for proof of armour by firearms. For proof marks, see Mann, 'A further account of the armour preserved in the Sanctuary of the Madonna della Grazie', pp. 330-2.

57. *Supra*, pp. 100-1, 104.

thousand Flemish pikemen who were in Charles the Bold's camp outside Amiens in March 1471:

> ... each had a sallet, jack, sword and pike or long lance with a slender shaft, and a long sharp spear-head, cutting on three sides. They were on foot and are called pikemen because they know better than anyone how to handle pikes. The Flemings had recruited them in the villages of their country ... These pikes make very useful poles for placing a spike between two archers against the fearful effects of cavalry trying to break their ranks, for there is no horse which, if struck in the chest with a pike, will not unfailingly die. These pikemen can also approach and attack cavalry from the side and pierce them right through, nor is there any armour however good that they cannot pierce or break.[58]

Wavrin's account is in many ways a *locus classicus* for historians who stress the uselessness of heavy cavalry when pitted against resolute infantry. He admits the 'fearful effects' of a cavalry charge, but alludes to the practice of placing spikes, or sharpened stakes, between the archers, as the English had done at Agincourt. The use of pikes for this purpose presupposes a combination of pikemen and archers against heavy cavalry which, given sufficient discipline and organisation, might be thought invincible. Yet the innovations which had been made in defensive armament since 1415 appear to have passed the aged Wavrin by. Horse armour had become very much more effective by 1450, and the need for protection from the pike, as well as from archery fire, had given the warhorse as much defence as was compatible with mobility. The plate defences for the chest (*peytral*), neck (*crinet*) and flanks (*crupper*) afforded some protection from both the arrow-volley and the pike-hedge.[59] If the pikeman-and-archer formation could first be broken up by archery or gun fire, as it was at Oudenaarde, Ghent and Gavere by Philip the Good's army in the war of 1452-3,[60] then its demoralised survivors might break ranks and flee before the onrush of charging cavalry.

Those knights, unlike their opponents, bore a 'noble' weapon – the lance – and sought occasions to engage with similarly armed enemies. To counteract

---

58. J. de Wavrin, *Receuil des croniques* (RS London 1864-91), vi, pp. 625-6: '... ayans chascun sallade, jacques, espee, picque ou des longues lanches a menu fust, a long fer et agu, trenchant de trois costez. Ceulx cy estoient de pie et les nommoit on *picquenaires* pource quilz scavoient lusage des picques plus que nulz autres; si les avoient Flamens cueillies parmy les villages de leur pays ... Ces picques sont bastons moult convenables pour mettre une picque entre deux archiers contre le fouldroieux effort des chevaulz quy vouldroient [entrer] dedens eulz, car il nest pas cheval, sil est attaint dune picque en la poitrine, quil ne doie morir sans remede; et si scevent ces picquenaires desmarchier et attaindre chevaulz de coste et yceulz perchier tout oultre; mesmement nest si bon harnas de guerre quilz ne perchassent ou faulsassent, ainsi le scevent ilz bransler et empaindre.'

59. Hardy, op. cit., pp. 84-5, 127; Keegan, op. cit., pp. 94, 95-6; Ffoulkes, 'Some aspects of the craft of the armourer', *Archaeologia*, lxxix (1929), p. 19 and fig. 19 for an unsuccessful attempt of 1480 to produce a complete leg-harness for a horse. See also Blair, op. cit., pp. 184-7 for a survey of the development of horse-armour. The earliest complete surviving horse-armour (*c.* 1450) is in the City Museum, Vienna (Blair, op. cit., fig. 65); there is a fine specimen made at Landshut in *c.* 1475-85 in the Wallace Collection, London (A. 21): see *Wallace Collection Catalogues*, i, pp. 9-15; see plate 19.

60. See La Marche, *Mémoires*, ii, pp. 235, 321; *Le Jouvencel*, ii, p. 203; *infra*, pp. 157, 160-1.

the offensive effects of the lance, plate armour had undergone further developments. Glancing surfaces, fluting, rippling and the addition of ridges and channels in order to deflect the lance head away from vulnerable or exposed parts were introduced.[61] To knock a mounted opponent out of his saddle was clearly the major aim of the man-at-arms, and many visual representations of the technique of handling the lance have survived. Yet it has been left to the antiquarian scholars of arms and armour to discover what the handling of the lance involved.[62] Historians have been curiously unaware of the importance of changes which were taking place in the techniques of fighting with the lance and, consequently, in the use of cavalry during the fourteenth and fifteenth centuries.

In his eye-witness account of the battle of Montlhéry (16 July 1465) Philippe de Commynes spoke of the state of the army led by Charles, count of Charolais, against Louis XI of France during the War of the Public Weal.[63] Commynes' bias should not be disregarded, given his subsequent defection from the ranks of Charles' army to the service of the king in 1472, but that does not undermine the significance of his assessment of Charolais' troops. He noted the poor order of the archers, out of wind through forced marching, and then devoted a passage to a criticism of the rank-and file cavalry:

> ... the said count marched in great haste, without allowing his archers and infantry to get their breath back. The king's men crossed over the hedge [which divided the two armies] in two groups, all composed of men-at-arms; and when they were close enough to put their lances into their lance-rests (*gecter les lances en l'arrest*) the Burgundian men-at-arms broke through their own archers and rode over them, without letting them fire a volley, although they were the flower and hope of their army, for I do not believe that there were fifty out of the twelve hundred men-at-arms or thereabouts who were there who would have known how to couch a lance in the lance-rest. They had only four hundred wearing breast-plates, and hardly an armed servant because of the long peace, and because this house of Burgundy did not keep paid troops so that the people were relieved of taxes ...[64]

The experience of Crécy – when the French nobles rode over their Genoese crossbowmen – was thus repeated at Montlhéry. Commynes' views on the value

61. See Ffoulkes, 'Some aspects of the craft of the armourer', p. 18.
62. See especially the major contribution by F. Buttin, 'La lance et l'arrêt de cuirasse', *Archaeologia*, xcix (1965), pp. 77-114.
63. Commynes, op. cit., i, pp. 26-9.
64. Ibid., i, p. 27: 'ledict conte marcha tout d'une boutée, sans donner allaine à ses archiers et gens de pied. Ceulx du roy passèrent ceste haye par deux boutz, tous hommes d'armes; et comme ilz furont si près que gecter les lances en l'arrest, les hommes d'armes bourguygnons rompirent les archiers et passèrent par dessus, sans leur donner loysir de tirer ung coup de flesche, qui estoit la fleur et esperance de leur armée, car je ne croy pas que de douze cens hommes d'armes ou envyron qu'ilz estoient, qu'il en y eust cinquante qui eussent sceu coucher une lance en l'arrest. Il n'y en avoit pas quatre cens arméz de cuyrasses, et sy n'avoyent pas ung seul serviteur armé à cause de la longue paix, et que en ceste maison ne tenoit nulles gens de soulde pour soullager le peuple de tailles.'

Plate 19. Armour for man and horse (South German, *c.* 1475-85). London, Wallace Collection.

of archers and on the reasons for the allegedly poor condition of the Burgundian army are debatable, but his remarks about the inability of the cavalry to do what was expected of them in the field deserve notice. It was their apparent inability to *jeter les lances en l'arrêt* that evoked Commynes' scorn. The phrase appears frequently in literary sources, from the later fourteenth century

onwards, and is common coinage by the mid-fifteenth century in the works of
Monstrelet, Anthoine de La Salle and Olivier de la Marche.[65] With the
development and refinement of plate armour during the fourteenth century,
techniques of fighting with the lance were bound to undergo changes. Complete
and more effective defensive armour meant that the force of penetration and

65. Buttin, art. cit., pp. 110-14 for citations.

weight of impact of the mounted man-at-arms had to be proportionately increased. The technique of couching the lance, that is of holding it beneath the right armpit in close combat, introduced during the twelfth century, was no longer so effective against a fully-armoured heavy cavalryman when moving at speed.[66] The mail *hauberks* and rudimentary cuirasses of the twelfth and thirteenth centuries had not provided a sufficiently rigid support for a weapon which had now become much heavier. Some device was needed to hold the lance firm at the moment of impact, to absorb recoil, prevent it from splintering into fragments and to keep a man's arm from being broken by the force of collision with his opponent. The weighty and cumbersome weapon had to be lowered, aimed and balanced while the warhorse was spurred into a gallop. A lance could weigh as much as 18 kilograms by the early sixteenth century, with its metal tip and circular hand-guard (*vamplate*).[67] An answer to the problem was found in the device known as the *arrêt de cuirasse*.[68] The breastplate now served as a support for the weight of the lance which was held on a prong attached to its right-hand side. This would also serve as a fulcrum on which to balance the weapon during a charge. It is found represented on the effigy of Walter von Hohenklingen (d. 1386) now at Zurich and documentary references appear from 1390 onwards.[69] The *arrêt* was in widespread use by 1420.

By enabling a mounted man to lower his lance from vertical to horizontal while moving at speed, aiming it accurately, and counteracting the inevitable tendency for the heavy steel-tipped weapon to dip forward and fall out of his grip, the lance-rest contributed to the process whereby heavy cavalry gained a new lease of life in the fifteenth century. Sixteenth-century cavalry manifestly did not dismount to fight.[70] The introduction of such technical innovations in the use of the lance had served to make the mounted man into a form of living projectile whose force of impact against both horse and foot was greater than it had ever been. Technological determinism can of course be taken too far but, combined with other factors working in its favour, the security and efficiency of heavy cavalry can only have been enhanced by these technical changes. It was now possible to 'charge home', piercing the ranks of enemy cavalry by sheer force of impact.[71] To couch a lance in the lance-rest, while moving to engage the enemy, was clearly the prime quality expected by contemporaries of a man-at-arms. Commynes' criticism reflects the criteria of his time, yet his prejudices may have played some part in his dismissal of Burgundian military prowess. He must have known that these men had taken part in Philip the Good's wars against Ghent and Liège, and hardly lacked experience in warfare.[72] If one of his purposes in the *Mémoires* was to justify his own conduct and denigrate that of

66. Ibid., pp. 93-4, plate I.
67. Ibid., p. 108.
68. Ibid., pp. 102-5; Blair, op. cit., p. 61; *infra*, plate 20.
69. Ibid., p. 61; for an early example, see Trapp and Mann, op. cit., pp. 19, 22.
70. See *infra*, pp. 128, 171.
71. See Buttin, art. cit., p. 113; cf. Smail, op. cit., pp. 113-15.
72. See *infra*, pp. 157, 160-1.

Charles the Bold, his assertions need not be taken at their face value. What they do suggest is that by the second half of the fifteenth century it was generally assumed that a mounted man-at-arms would be trained in deploying the lance rather than the sword, and in bearing the weight and heat of armour.

To make protection compatible with the need for mobility in battle, armour had to possess a certain degree of articulation, and it could not be intolerably heavy. These, too, were difficult conditions to fulfil. By the mid-fifteenth century, however, the introduction of a cuirass consisting of two separate pieces, joined by a sliding rivet, enabled the lance to be put into the *arrêt* without difficulty.[73] The vexéd question of the weight of armour has led historians to argue that a full 'white' armour greatly reduced a man's mobility and endurance. Yet a comparison between the weights of armour and of more modern kinds of military equipment (see Table I) suggests the contrary.[74] Modern analyses have suggested that 'contrary to popular myth [suits of plate armour] did not reduce mobility'.[75] A field armour might weigh 50-60 pounds in 1450, while jousting-armour could be as heavy as 90-100 pounds (see Tables I and II).[76] It seems that a man was less hampered by plate than by mail, because of the latter's uneven distribution over the body, most of the weight being borne by the shoulders.

More severe were the discomforts and difficulties occasioned by the heat of armour and its lack of ventilation. The removal of pieces of plate in battle, such as the bevor (protecting the chin and throat) was not unknown, so that a captain might not only breathe better, but issue commands. The sallet and its attached bevor was a useful and popular head-defence, but the rigid fixing of the bevor to the top of the cuirass made movement of the head from side to side impossible.[77] Charles the Bold sustained the wound in the neck which was to be visible for the rest of his life as a result of a missing bevor at Montlhéry.[78] Speech, hearing and respiration could only be impaired by attempts to protect face and head, and some of the deaths in battle of the period were caused by a raised visor or other discarded item of armour. According to La Marche, Cornelius, bastard of Burgundy, was killed on a hot day at Rupelmonde in June 1452 by a pike-thrust in the face as he was apparently not wearing a bevor beneath his sallet.[79] The death of Sir Philip Sidney at Zutphen in 1586, allegedly through lack of

73. See Ffoulkes, op. cit., pp. 5, 52-3; Mann, 'Notes on the evolution of plate armour in Germany in the 14th and 15th centuries', *Archaeologia*, lxxiv (1934), pp. 79-80.

74. See *infra*, Tables I, II and figures cited by Ffoulkes, op. cit., p. 119 and Blair, op. cit., p. 191.

75. Williams, 'Metallographic examination of 16th-century armour', p. 15.

76. See Tables I, II. A German half-armour for the joust, without leg-harness, weighs 90 lbs (dated 1500-1520) and is now in the Wallace Collection, London (A. 23): see *Wallace Collection Catalogues*, i, pp. 17-20, plates 6, 7. One reason for the exaggeration of the weight of armour may be that more pieces of jousting armour have survived than of pieces made for war.

77. Ffoulkes, op. cit., p. 105; Blair, op. cit., pp. 86-8, 191; Ffoulkes, 'Some aspects of the craft of the armourer', p. 24. See plates 18, 19.

78. Commynes, op. cit., i, p. 30. See *supra*, p. 78.

79. La Marche, *Mémoires*, ii, p. 270. The Burgundian nobles had previously complained of the heat and refused to march on foot 'en pesantes armes' (ibid., ii, p. 252).

another essential piece of armour, was not without precedent.

Practical demands for protection in war, however, were not always incompatible with aesthetic considerations. A choice of distinct styles of armour was offered to the fifteenth-century man-at-arms. Italian armourers vied with their German contemporaries to meet the needs of the military class. A divergence of Italian (especially Milanese) and German styles began to appear after 1440. Sir James Mann outlined the contrast between them when he observed that German 'Gothic' armour was characterised by 'finials and cuspings, attenuated lines and pierced borders in harmony with the Northern architecture of the time',[80] while the products of the Missaglia and Negroni in Italy, on the other hand, display a 'rounded outline and plain surfaces ... quite at home in the paintings of the early Renaissance'.[81] A cultural difference is also reflected here – the emergence of Italian sallets which imitate the graceful lines of the Ancient Greek 'Corinthian' helmet between 1445 and 1470 suggests conscious allusion to antique models,[82] while the extreme spikiness of a South German armour made for Sigismund, archduke of Austria in about 1470, reflects the late Gothic invention which is also found in the sculpture and architectural decoration of the period.[83] Yet this stylistic homogeneity in the fine and applied arts – which clearly affected scholars such as Wölfflin and Huizinga profoundly – may not be solely the result of aesthetic divergence. Climatic differences between Northern and Southern Europe may have determined a patron's choice of armour, just as glass was preferred to fresco in the churches of the North. A marked preference for lighter and better ventilated Italian products in Spain might suggest a desire for personal defence more fitted to Mediterranean heat.[84] To move 'without hindrance by armour' was a technique cultivated by the Turks and the Moors, and for the Christians who fought them – Venetian *condottieri* and Castilian *hidalgos* – a common acquaintance with the rigours of campaigning in intense heat may have led to a convergence of opinion about the merits of different armours.[85] The choice

80. Mann, 'Notes on the evolution of plate armour', p. 81. See plate 19.

81. Ibid., pp. 81-2.

82. See plate 16 and *Wallace Collection Catalogues*, i, pp. 96, 98 (A.75, A.78), plate 55. A.75 was probably in the armoury of the Venetian arsenal, as it bears a mark representing the lion of St Mark. Similar helmets were found among a collection of armour discovered in 1840 at the Hospitaller castle of Chalcis, near Thebes, which was captured by the Turks from the Venetians in 1470: see C.J. Ffoulkes, 'On Italian armour from Chalcis in the Ethnological Museum at Athens', *Archaeologia*, lxii (1910), pp. 381-90, esp. plate LII, nos. 7, 11; 'Armour from the Rotunda, Woolwich, transferred to the Armouries of the Tower, 1927', *Archaeologia*, lxxviii (1928), pp. 61-72 for sallets and armets from another Hospitaller stronghold at Rhodes, abandoned by them to the Turks in 1523.

83. For a description see Blair, op. cit., pp. 34-5. The suit is now in the Waffensammlung, Vienna (A.62). See also *An Exhibition of Armour of Kings and Captains from the National Collections of Austria* (Tower of London, London 1949), no. 7, plates I, V.

84. Mann, 'Notes on the armour worn in Spain from the 10th to the 15th century', *Archaeologia*, lxxxiii (1933), pp. 286, 294.

85. See *Voyage d'Outremer*, pp. 20-1, 269, 270; Mallett, op. cit., p. 152; Mann, 'Notes on the armour worn in Spain', pp. 293-4. For a representation of the battle at Puig (1237) between

between Italian and German styles might also have been partly determined by the kinds of warfare most likely to be encountered in a given area. Aesthetic reasons apart, the degree of protection offered by the smooth, rounded plates of Italian armour made it especially effective against sword-strokes and lance-thrusts. The enormous winged pauldrons of Italian suits suggest that their makers may have had defence against heavy cavalry particularly in mind, while many surviving German and Austrian armours gave the best protection against arrows and crossbow bolts. The long-tailed sallet, favoured among English, French and Burgundian men-at-arms in the second half of the fifteenth century, perhaps proved its worth against vertical archery fire better than the Italian armet.[86]

As there was no 'highly-trained infantry' for the heavily armoured *condottiere* and his men to encounter in Italy,[87] it would hardly be surprising if Italian armourers did not design their products with archers or pikemen in mind. *Condottieri* warfare relied upon heavy cavalry, and the hail of missiles or wall of pikes was not a technique cultivated by Italian captains. The fluted and rippled surfaces of a German armour presented a difficult target for archers, while the bald, smooth plates of the Italian were probably of greater value in mounted warfare. Towards the end of the century, styles of armour began to converge, and a compromise between 'Gothic' and 'Classical' forms was achieved.[88] Milanese armour was increasingly imported into the German principalities, and *vice versa*, so that a coalescence of styles was rendered possible and the so-called 'Maximilian' armour resulted. This reconciled the fluted plates of the North with the rounded forms of the South, and these globose and inelegant products of the armourers' craft became universal among those who fought the Italian wars of 1494-1559.[89] The heavy cavalryman had become heavier than ever before, and it was the crippling weight of armour, now designed to resist firearms, that was to lead to its ultimate disappearance.

By the second quarter of the fifteenth century it was clear that the mounted man-at-arms was not, and could not be self-sufficient. The greater weight of horse armour meant that horses tired more easily and a supply of spare mounts had to be readily available for him during a battle. In the armies of the dukes of Burgundy a scale of wages for men-at-arms with three horses and two horses

Christians and Moors, showing the latter without any form of plate armour, see C.M. Kauffmann, 'The altar-piece of St George from Valencia', *Victoria and Albert Yearbook*, ii (1970), pp. 65-100. The altar-piece is dated *c*. 1410-20 and was commissioned by a confraternity of archers dedicated to St George in Valencia.

86. See Mann, 'Notes on the evolution of plate armour', pp. 81-2, plate xxvi, fig. 1; but see Ffoulkes, 'Some aspects of the craft of the armourer', p. 25 for some of the disadvantages of the sallet. See plates 17, 18.

87. Mallett, op. cit., p. 148.

88. Mann, 'Notes on the evolution of plate armour', p. 89.

89. Mann, 'Notes on armour of the Maximilian period', p. 220; *Wallace Collection Catalogues*, i, plates 9-11. See also *infra*, plate 20.

each was established, and in 1465-6 the company led against Liège by Adolf of
Cleves, lord of Ravenstein, consisted of 223 heavy cavalrymen, of whom 105
possessed three, and 81 maintained two, armoured horses.[90]. According to
Charles the Bold's military ordinances of 1471 and 1473, each man-at-arms
should have three 'good horses' and this had also been the practice in Charles
VII's companies of *ordonnance* in the later 1440s.[91] Some possessed four horses,
one for carrying baggage and equipment, the rest for war. The sources of
warhorses in the fifteenth century have not been investigated as thoroughly as
they have been for the fourteenth century. The demise of the old feudal right
of *restaur*, or indemnity paid by lords to their vassals to replace lost warhorses,
deprives the historian of a valuable source of evidence.[92] Yet the purchase and
breeding of horses strong enough to bear the greater weights imposed upon
them in battle is documented by the military ordinances issued in Burgundy in
1473 and in France in 1484. Charles the Bold ordered that one of the three
warhorses maintained by each man-at-arms should be 'sufficient to charge and
break lances' and the French ordinance stipulated that

> ... five or six horse merchants ... shall be held to come and bring into this kingdom
> horses from Spain, Apulia, Germany and other places, to provide the *gens de guerre*
> of the said *ordonnances* with them, at their costs. After they have brought them, they
> shall not sell them to anyone except the said *gens de guerre*, giving them always first
> refusal ...[93]

Horses of the large hunter type, capable of carrying their own armour as well as
their riders, and of enduring the rigours of combat, were clearly a special breed,
not readily available in France. Between 1448 and 1450 Jacques Coeur's agents
were therefore buying warhorses in Sicily,[94] but a source of supply nearer home
was the Carthusian monastery of Notre-Dame-de-Berthoud, in the Dauphiné,
which had a stud farm of fifty mares[95] and, with other monastic houses of the
Dauphiné, had apparently been supplying horses bred for war during the
previous century.[96] The fairs in Champagne and at Avignon also served as
occasions on which the best warhorses were selected by the nobility of France

90. ADN, B. 2058, fo. 222r.
91. BL, Add. MS 36,619, fo. 9r; Vaughan, *Charles the Bold*, pp. 206-10; Contamine, *Guerre, Etat et Société*, pp. 658, 659.
92. Used to good effect by V. Chomel, 'Chevaux de bataille et roncins en Dauphiné au xive siècle', *Cahiers d'Histoire*, vii (1962), pp. 5-23.
93. BL, Add. MS 36,619, fo. 9r; Contamine, *Guerre, Etat et Société*, p. 663: 'cinq ou six marchans de chevaulx qui (...) seront tenuz venir et amener en ce reaulme des chevaulx d'Espaigne, de Poille, d'Alemaigne et d'autres lieux, pour en fournir les gens de guerre desdictes ordonnances, a leurs despens. Et apres qu'ilz les auront amenez, ilz ne les pourrint vendre a autres que ausd. gens de guerre que premierement ilz n'en soient refusans et fournys.'
94. C. Marinesco, 'Jacques Coeur', *Comptes Rendues de l'Académie des Inscriptions et Belles-Lettres* (Jan.-Mar. 1959), pp. 138-9.
95. Chomel, art. cit., p. 16.
96. Ibid., pp. 16-17.

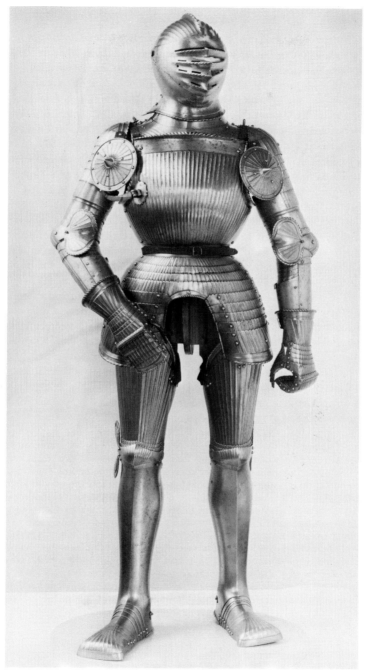

Plate 20. Field armour (German, early sixteenth century). London, Wallace Collection.

and Burgundy.[97] Demand for such mounts might easily outrun supply, especially if casualties in battle were high. At Termonde in May 1452, Jacques de Lalaing had five horses killed under him, one while he rescued his brother Philippe from the press of the Ghenters' pikes.[98] Such casualties clearly underlined the need for an expensive reservoir of spare horses.

The organisation of fifteenth-century armies into composite units known as 'lances', of between three and six men each, including mounted archers, is perhaps made more comprehensible by the tactical needs of the individual man-at-arms as well as by the administrative requirements of those responsible for recruiting and paying him. It has been argued that the French 'lance', of six men, was devised more for disciplinary and administrative reasons than for technical ones. The unit 'formed a group with uncertain, variable contours, of which the utility was more disciplinary than tactical' and these divisions had, writes Professor Contamine, 'above all an administrative purpose: on the field of battle, the groupings were different; the men-at-arms fought on one side, the archers on another.'[99] This may well have been true for the French companies of *ordonnance* after 1445, but, as we have already seen, it was not always so in English and Burgundian armies. The practice of dismounting among the archers, or of using them to provide cover for cavalry movements, was common, and the Burgundian *lance* of 1473 could clearly be a tactical, as well as an administrative reality. Each *lance* comprised a heavily armoured man-at-arms, with a mounted page and *coustillier* (armed servant); three mounted archers; a crossbowman, culverineer (handgunner) and a pikeman to fight on foot.[100] Some members of these nine-man detachments were clearly intended to fight together as a support group for the mounted man-at-arms. In the ordinance, the duke commanded his captains that they should,

> ... take a detachment of their men-at-arms to exercise in the fields, sometimes fully armed, sometimes partly armed, to train them in charging with the lance, keeping them in close order during a charge, and charging boldly, defending their ensigns, retreating on command and rallying to aid each other ... and the way in which to withstand (*soustenir*) a charge. Similarly, with the archers, all mounted, to familiarise them with dismounting and firing their bows, making them learn the manner of attaching and bridling their horses together, and getting them to walk after them ... by attaching the reins of three archers' horses to the saddle-bow of the page of the man-at-arms to whose *lance* they belong. Furthermore, to march boldly forward, to fire without breaking ranks, and to make the pikemen advance in close order in front of the said archers and, at a signal from them, to kneel while holding their pikes as low as the height of a horse's hind quarters so that the archers can fire over the said pikemen as if over a wall; and that if the ... pikemen

97. Ibid., p. 19.
98. La Marche, *Mémoires*, ii, p. 249.
99. Contamine, *Guerre, Etat et Société*, p. 482.
100. BL, Add. MS 36,619, fos. 5r-10v; Vaughan, *Charles the Bold*, pp. 206-10.

see their enemies in disorder they will be more ready to charge them effectively as they shall be ordered ...[101]

A combination of cavalry, mounted infantry and pikemen is here prescribed, with the man-at-arm's page playing a vital rôle in the preservation of a supply of horses for the unit. Pikemen and archers could form a defensive wall or screen behind which the mounted men-at-arms could form up and regroup. Jacques du Clercq, writing in the second half of the fifteenth century, endorsed the essential unity of the *lance* in his assertion that '... each *lance* contained one man-at-arms armed with ... all that is necessary for a fully-armed man ... He had three costly horses, one for himself, another for his page who carried his lance, the third for his servant ... and two mounted archers.'[102] The rôle of this support group, which rode behind a man-at-arms, could be crucial in battle. Jacques de Lalaing owed his life to a mounted servant at Oudenaarde in July 1452, who rescued him after he had been trapped by the Ghenters' pikes.[103] At the battle of Gavere the following year mutual aid was given by the *lances*, even to the duke himself, whose horse was wounded in the *mêlée*.[104] The prodigal expenditure on horses merely contributed to the rising costs of war for the man-at-arms. In Italy, a tendency for enemies to strike at valuable mounts has been discerned after 1450, although this had previously been thought unchivalrous.[105] No such constraints bound the archers and pikemen of Northern Europe during the Hundred Years War, or the wars of the dukes of Burgundy against the Flemings and the Swiss.

The cost of armour, horses and military equipment had risen dramatically since the mid-fourteenth century. Even then, a noble in the Dauphiné who had

101. '... meynent aucuneffoiz partie de leurs hommes darmes jouer aux champs armez aucuneffoiz du hault de la piece suelement une autreffoiz de toutes pieces, pour eulx essayer a courre la lance eulx tenir en la courant jointz et serrez, et aussy courre vivement, garder leurs enseignes, eulx departir sil leur est ordonne, et eulx ralyer en secourant lun lautre par commandement ... et la maniere de soustenir une charge. Et pareillement les archiers atout leurs chevaulx pour les accoustumer a descendre a pie et tirer de larc. En les faisant aprendre la maniere detachier et a brider leurs chevaulx ensemble et les faire marchier aprez eulx defront derriere leur doz en atachant les chevaulx de iij archiers a bridez aux cornetz de larcon de la selle derriere le cheval du paige de lomme darmes a qui ilz sont. En oultre de marchier vivement de front, de tirer sans eulx rompre et de faire marchier les piquenaires en front serrez devant lesdis archiers et a ung signe deulx mettre a ung genoul en tenant leurs piques bassees de la haulteur des ars des chevaulx afin que les archiers puissent tirer par dessus lesdis piquenaires comme par dessus ung mur et que se lesdis piquenaires veioient leurs ennemis mettre en desarroy ilz fussent plus prestz a leur courre sus par bonne maniere ainsy quil leur seroit ordonne ...'. BL, Add. MS 36,619, fos. 30v-32v; Vaughan, *Charles the Bold*, pp. 209-10. See also *infra*, pp. 154-5.

102. J. du Clercq, *Mémoires*, ed. F.A.T. de Reiffenberg (Brussels 1835), i, p. 376. Cf plate 28.

103. La Marche, *Mémoires*, ii, pp. 239-40. The importance of non-combatant écuyers serving with the Knights Templar in the twelfth century is emphasised by Smail, op. cit., pp. 108-9. There was clearly an organisation similar in many respects to the later *lance* in these crusading armies.

104. La Marche, *Mémoires*, ii, p. 269.

105. Mallett, op. cit., pp. 149, 206. Ibid., 148-53 for an excellent account of the nature and development of the Italian *lance*.

Plate 21. Coronal for a lance to be used in jousts 'of peace' (fifteenth century). Paris, Musée de l'Armée.

an annual income of less than 100 florins could not afford to go to war on a good warhorse.[106] Some nobles were simply unable to bear the loss of their horses in war without compensation from their lord. In the French companies of *ordonnance* a good warhorse could cost the equivalent of at least six months' wages or, at most, 26 months' wages between 1441 and 1459.[107] A complete suit of 'white' armour cost about three months' wages between 1460 and 1494.[108] The incentive to preserve one's capital investment, especially in a period marked by scarcity of bullion and poor liquidity, was evidently great, and this was accentuated by the fact that both armour and horses were now regarded as the personal property of the captain, rather than as an issue from a lord or sovereign.[109] In return for the receipt of equipment from a captain, the members of a *lance* served him as a group which possessed a certain inner cohesion. This

106. Chomel, art. cit., p. 15. For similar figures demonstrating the high cost of warhorses among the Flemish nobility in 1297 and 1302, see Verbruggen, op. cit., pp. 26-8.

107. Contamine, *Guerre, Etat et Société*, p. 662.

108. Ibid., pp. 658-63, especially the table on p. 662. For comparisons with the Low Countries, see Gaier, op. cit., pp. 344-5.

109. Contamine, *Guerre, Etat et Société*, p. 664: 'la monarchie … n'entreprit pas de financer elle-même l'équipment de l'ensemble de ses troupes permanentes.'

was particularly the case in English and Burgundian armies, while French heavy cavalry appear to have remained aloof – often to their cost – from the archers with whom they were coupled for fiscal, administrative and disciplinary purposes. To extend Fuller's analogy a little further, the fifteenth-century *lance* could indeed be compared with the modern tank, with a support unit as well as a crew, its composition changing as tactical needs changed. No man was an island in the sea of battle – and both a kingdom and a duchy might allegedly be lost for the lack of a horse.

Without cavalry, a fifteenth-century army was unlikely to achieve a decisive victory on the field of battle. To pursue an enemy, whether in the hope of ransom or in an attempt at annihilation, was scarcely possible without mounted units.[110] Although the issue of a battle might be decided by archers or pikemen, a retreat could only be cut off effectively or followed up by cavalry. A plentiful supply of fresh horses was a *sine qua non* for military success. The last battles of Charles the Bold at Grandson (2 March 1476), Morat (22 June 1476) and Nancy (5 January 1477) exemplify the value of cavalry. At Grandson, the tiny number of Burgundian casualties and the precipitate, though safe, withdrawal of Charles' army, were due largely to the complete absence of cavalry among the Swiss who attacked him.[111] At Morat, on the other hand, the Burgundian rout was followed up by a pursuit conducted by mounted nobles including the young duke René II of Lorraine and his allies.[112] At Nancy, the Burgundians not only found their retreat cut off by Campobasso's Italian cavalry, but were pursued and in some cases captured and put to ransom by the nobles of the opposing allied force.[113] Olivier de la Marche owed his survival to the fact that the Burgundians were facing an army which was not composed only of Swiss, who took no prisoners.[114] At Nancy, the Swiss were serving merely as mercenaries in the pay of René and his allies, and without the cavalry contingents brought by the bishops of Basle and Strasbourg and by Sigismund, archduke of Austria and count of Tirol, the victory might not have been decisive.[115] To see Burgundian power meeting its end solely through defeat at the hands of urban leagues and Swiss infantry is to distort the pattern of military events between 1474 and 1477.[116] Charles the Bold was resisted by a

110. For examples, see C. Brusten, *L'armée bourguignonne de 1465 à 1468* (Brussels 1953), pp. 164-6. The practice of feigned retreats or withdrawals to entice the enemy out of his position was also a technique cultivated by Burgundian cavalry in the wars against Ghent and Liège (ibid., p. 164, Brustem and Ruppelmonde; p. 165, Gavere).

111. Vaughan, *Charles the Bold*, pp. 376-7 for an account of the battle.

112. Ibid., pp. 388-91; L.-E. Roulet, 'Le Duc René à la Bataille de Morat', *Cinq-Centième Anniversaire de la Bataille de Nancy (1477). Actes du colloque ... à l'Université de Nancy II* (Nancy 1979), pp. 424-6.

113. Vaughan, *Charles the Bold*, pp. 430-1.

114. Ibid., pp. 429-30; La Marche, *Mémoires*, ii, pp. 241-2.

115. Vaughan, *Charles the Bold*, p. 428; F. Rapp, 'Strasbourg et Charles le Hardi: l'ampleur et le prix de l'effort militaire', *Anniversaire de la Bataille de Nancy*, pp. 403-5, 412-13.

116. Cf. Vaughan, *Charles the Bold*, p. 311.

combination of infantry and cavalry forces, in which the nobility of Alsace, Lorraine and Tirol served beside others from the German empire against the house of Burgundy. The Swiss did not single-handedly deliver the final crushing blow because they could not do so without mounted troops supplied, not only by the towns, but by the nobility.

The paradox with which these pages began has perhaps lost some of its force. Heavy cavalry was not the obsolescent arm that military historians have often decried, eking out an irrelevant existence for social reasons unconnected with the art of war. In 1494, over one half of Charles VIII's army which began the Italian campaigns was composed of heavy cavalry.[117] The *gendarmerie* of nobles, all mounted and fully armed, was to be the only truly permanent element in French royal armies for most of the sixteenth century.[118] In 1549, Raymond, sire de Fourquevaux, urged Francis I to incorporate the mounted *gendarmerie* into his infantry 'legions', to serve as a disciplined force 'established to stand firm, and not to rush here and there'.[119] Yet by then their days were numbered. The rise of companies of light horse, and the increasing sophistication of hand firearms and field artillery, posed a far graver threat to the mounted man-at-arms than had English longbows or Swiss pikes. There was certainly a place for him in the conduct of war during the second half of the fifteenth century, however. Many of the pitched battles of the time were fought by cavalry forces sent to relieve a besieged place,[120] and the pressures upon governments to bring wars to a speedy and decisive conclusion, rather than perpetuate a deadlock through the laying of sieges, worked in favour of heavy cavalry.[121] A disciplined, organised body with great power of offensive 'shock' was, when used aright and in favourable conditions, the equal of any force pitted against it. Governments – especially insecure later medieval governments – did not usually spend money, painfully gathered from taxation and loans, to underwrite forces which had outlived their usefulness. 'The most dangerous arms in the world,' wrote Jean de Bueil in *Le Jouvencel*, 'are those of horse and lance, because there is no means of stopping them.'[122] Heavy cavalry could carry all before it through the momentum and impact of a properly-conducted charge and the resolute pursuit of a fleeing enemy. The lords of battle could rule the field in the fifteenth century as they had rarely done before.

117. See F. Lot, *Recherches sur les effectifs des armées françaises des Guerres d'Italie aux Guerres de Réligion, 1494-1562* (Paris 1962), pp. 15-16; Mallett, op. cit., p. 238.
118. See F. Michaud, 'Les institutions militaires des guerres d'Italie aux guerres de réligion', *Rev. Hist.*, ccccxxiii (1977), p. 35.
119. *The 'Instructions sur le faict de la guerre' of Raymond de Beccarie de Pavie, sieur de Fourquevaux*, ed. G. Dickinson (London 1954), fo. 24r; *infra*, pp. 152-3.
120. See *infra*, p. 171.
121. Mallett, op. cit., pp. 177-80 for an account of one such battle (Caravaggio 1448).
122. *Le Jouvencel*, ii, p. 100. Cf. the similar remarks of sixteenth-century writers upon the value of heavy cavalry: C. Gaier, 'L'opinion des chefs de guerre français du xvie siècle sur les progrès de l'art militaire', *Revue internationale d'histoire militaire*, xxix (1970), pp. 731-2.

ii. The impact of firearms

The threats posed to the military superiority of the nobility in the first half of the fifteenth century had been met and contained by improved methods of defence. In the course of the following century, however, the technology of weapons advanced to such an extent that there were many who would have agreed with Cervantes when he wrote,

> Blessed be those happy ages that were strangers to the dreadful fury of these devilish instruments of artillery, whose inventor I am satisfied is now in Hell, receiving the reward of his cursed invention, which is the cause that very often a cowardly base hand takes away the life of the bravest gentleman; and that in the midst of that vigour and resolution which animates and inflames the bold, a chance bullet (shot perhaps by one who fled, and was frightened by the very flash the mischievous piece gave, when it went off) coming nobody knows how, or from where, in a moment puts a period to the brave designs and the life of one that deserved to have survived many years ...[1]

Don Quixote's lament for the passing of those 'happy ages' which knew no firearms was a commentary upon the changes which had transformed the conduct of war in the sixteenth century. War had become impersonal and mechanical. 'The indiscriminate death dealt by shot and ball,' observed Professor Hale, 'ruined war as a finishing school for knightly character'.[2] It is normally assumed that the introduction of the arquebus in the sixteenth century lay at the root of Cervantes' complaint, but the beginnings of the process whereby the knightly ideal was undermined might profitably be sought at an earlier date. I shall therefore attempt to examine the impact of firearms upon the practice of war and upon chivalrous ideals during the fifteenth century.

The first effective small-arms charged with gunpowder had developed in the fourteenth century largely as a result of the introduction of effective siege guns: offensive techniques provoked a defensive reaction. The patterns of attack and defence in siege warfare had remained largely static during the early Middle Ages. In the early fourteenth century, the advantage still tended to lie with the defenders of a fortified place, who relied upon the height and thickness of their walls and their ability to withstand starvation and undermining by the enemy. In attack, little movement was made to improve the siege engines and catapaults described by the Roman theorist Vegetius. It is well known that by

---

1. M. de Cervantes Saavedra, *Don Quixote*, ed. H. Bohn (London 1925), i, p. 402. For similar views, see also Blaise de Monluc, *Commentaires* (SHF, Paris, 1864), i, pp. 49-50 (drafted 1570-1, first published 1592).

2. J.R. Hale, 'Fifteenth and sixteenth century public opinion and war', *Past and Present*, xxii (1962), p. 23.

the late fourteenth and early fifteenth centuries techniques permitting the manufacture of large cannon of vast calibre had been developed.[3] The effectiveness of this new artillery has, however, been disputed. The liability of these guns to fracture and burst, to roll off their carriages, to become bogged down and to provoke crippling transport problems has often been pointed out. In the context of Italian Renaissance warfare it has been argued that 'artillery had little effect on the fortunes of campaigns as a whole or on the balance of power';[4] firearms exerted 'no serious influence on the issue of battles before the late fifteenth century', and 'gunpowder ... revolutionised the conduct, but not the outcome, of wars'.[5] Similarly, discussing Henry V's bombardment of Harfleur in 1415, J.H. Wylie remarked: 'It would be a mistake to suppose that much change had been introduced into siege methods by the introduction of gunpowder';[6] Oman was confident that 'we may almost say that the triumph of artillery only commences in the middle years of the fifteenth century'.[7] Such conclusions can be tested against evidence which survives from France and the Burgundian lands, and which is especially plentiful for English Gascony during the last phase of the Hundred Years' War.

In this much-contested area of South-West France, for example, the constant state of war or truce between areas in English and French obedience gave rise to a kind of arms race. At Bordeaux, the capital of English Gascony, the probable effectiveness of the communal artillery in the 1420s can be assessed by comparing the ballistic force of its cannon, for which detailed figures survive, with others derived from the accounts and inventories of other European towns. In August 1420, reference was made in the registers of the town council to a large cannon, which would throw a stone weighing seven hundredweight (784 pounds).[8] Later in that year, the town gunfounder was commissioned to make another cannon, which would fire stones of five hundredweight (560 pounds), or five-and-a-quarter hundredweight (588 pounds).[9] The contrast with the lighter pieces recorded at Nuremberg in 1427, firing projectiles weighing 200 pounds, and at Munich in the 1450s, which fired projectiles weighing 392, 224 and 25

3. For recent surveys, see C.M. Cipolla, *Guns and Sails* (London 1965), pp. 21-30; J-F. Finò, *Forteresses de la France Médiévale* (Paris 1967), pp. 273-98; B.J. St. J. O'Neil, *Castles and Cannon* (Oxford 1960), pp. xiii-xvii, 1-21; for older, but still valuable accounts, see T.F. Tout, 'Firearms in England in the fourteenth century', *EHR*, xxvi (1911), pp. 666-88; R.C. Clephan, 'The ordnance of the fourteenth and fifteenth centuries', *Archaeological Journal*, lxviii (1911), pp. 49-64, 98-125.

4. J.R. Hale, 'Gunpowder and the Renaissance', *From Renaissance to Counter-Reformation*, ed. C.H. Carter (London 1966), p. 114.

5. Nef, op. cit., p. 29; Hale, 'Gunpowder and the Renaissance', p. 115.

6. J.H. Wylie, *The Reign of Henry V* (Cambridge 1919), ii, p. 33.

7. Oman, op. cit., ii, p. 226.

8. *Archives Municipales de Bordeaux* [henceforth *AMB*], ed. H. Barckhausen, iv (Bordeaux, 1883), p. 426. In December 1453 a Mons gunfounder supplied Philip the Good of Burgundy with a bombard 17 feet long, weighing 7,764 lbs: ADN, B.2012, fo. 342r.

9. *AMB*, iv, p. 478 (14 Dec. 1420).

pounds, is striking and the earlier Bordeaux guns leave little doubt about the potential damage they could inflict.[10]

With the introduction and development of artillery, sieges and siege-craft became more complex. Broadly speaking, the use of guns meant that sieges could be brought to a conclusion much more quickly. In Gascony, as in other regions of France, castles and fortified towns studded the frontiers. To reduce an area successfully it was essential for the invader to take such strongholds, because they would serve to hold down the surrounding area and provided a secure centre from which raids could be conducted and an entire region occupied. If a frontier outpost was not taken, the risk of a rear-guard action was high. The castles and fortified towns of Gascony also commanded routes of communication and supply, especially when they were sited, like Fronsac, Beynac, Domme, or Clermont-Dessus, on the rivers. For the defender, the stubborn resistance of his forts meant that the enemy's manpower would be immobilised and absorbed for many months. In the autumn and winter of 1442, for instance, the refusal of the English garrison at La Réole on the Garonne to surrender saved Bordeaux from being besieged by the French.[11] The English garrisons knew that they could both disperse and delay the concentration of French forces at the decisive point – Bordeaux – by holding out for as long as they could. With the introduction of effective siege guns, the advantages of attack over defence now became apparent. The speedy recovery of seven strongpoints from the French between April 1420 and October 1421 by the troops of Bordeaux owed much of its success to the communal artillery.[12] The guns were carried from siege to siege by water, thereby reducing the difficulties and chronic delays of overland carriage.[13] These were also experienced by Philip the Good of Burgundy during his war with Ghent in 1452-3. Such was the weight of a great bombard which he borrowed from the town of Mons that all the bridges between Mons and Lille had to be strengthened with iron supports for its passage. During the journey, the gun fell into a ditch, and took two days to be extricated by men using lifting equipment specially constructed for the purpose.[14] Yet the internal waterways of West Flanders served the Burgundians well during the Ghent war, just as the rivers of South-West France helped the English. In mid-campaign, the 'great bombard of Courtrai' was sent

10. See Clephan, art. cit., pp. 102-4. For the provision of guns in English towns, see e.g. Royal Commission on Historic Monuments, *The City of York. Volume II. The Defences* (London 1972), p. 19.

11. See Thomas Beckington, *Official Correspondence*, ed. G. Williams (RS London 1872), ii, pp. 213, 238; AN, JJ. 182, no. 1; Leseur op. cit., i, p. 22. Fortunately for the defenders, a 'grete gunne' which the French had before the castle of La Réole was fractured on 29 October and the siege ended on 7 December: see Beckington, op. cit., pp. 219, 247-8; PRO, E.364/84, E.101/650, no. 285 (8 December 1442).

12. *AMB*, iv, pp. 363-596.

13. Ibid., iv, pp. 434, 520. See PRO, E.101/189/12, fos. 40v, 61v for the use of river transport for artillery at the siege of Marmande by the English in March 1428.

14. ADN, B.2012, fo. 247v (3-4 May 1453).

by water to the siege of Schendelbeke, and gunstones came to the siege of Poucques by barge from Bruges.[15] In Gascony, however, English superiority in the use of siege artillery was seriously challenged by the French after 1437. The measures taken by the English administration in Gascony to meet the attacks of 1437-8, 1442-3 and 1449-53 reflect the extent to which the situation had changed.[16]

There is a good deal of evidence for extensive use of cannon by the French armies launched against English Gascony after about 1439. Towns such as Montréal-du-Gers, which gave their loyalty to Charles VII, offered their metallurgical and technical resources to the royal cause. They supplied raw materials to the master of the king's artillery and received culverins (light cannon) from the dauphin in return.[17] Not only did the companies of *ordonnance* gain the help of the royal siege-train, but the great magnates of the South-West were now able to maintain their own cannon. In 1450, Gaston IV, count of Foix, marched through the English area of Labourt with seven 'great culverins of metal', before returning to Béarn to refresh his troops and repair, restock and refurbish his artillery.[18] Similarly, in 1443, Charles II, lord of Albret was negotiating with the town council of Montréal-du-Gers for the provision of four hundredweight of metal with which to cast bombards and cannon.[19] In the Burgundian lands, too, noble families such as the Lannoy kept their own guns, and in the course of the Ghent war, the *échevins* of Lille gave a gift of wine to 'the cannoneers of my lord of Lannoy' for inspecting the town's artillery and advising them on the mounting of two *veuglaires*, or light cannon.[20]

It is often difficult to ascertain precisely where the hand of the gunner was responsible for the speedy conclusion of a siege or for the dilapidation of town and castle walls. But in at least two cases, the evidence from English Gascony seems quite specific. In a grant by letters patent by Henry VI on 22 March 1437, the castle of Castelnau-de-Cernès, which had been recently recaptured from the French, was assigned to a loyal supporter of the English.[21] It was said that the place had been 'broken down during the said siege by cannon and engines, and a great part of the walls of the same thrown to the ground, so that it was in no way defensible against the king's enemies'.[22] Similarly, in July 1453,

15. ADN, B.2012, fo. 217v, 219r (24 June, 4 July 1453).

16. For an account of these campaigns *see Histoire de Bordeaux*, iii, ed. Y. Renouard (Bordeaux 1965), pp. 505-21; also M.G.A. Vale, 'The last years of English Gascony, 1451-1453', *TRHS*, 5th series, xix (1969), pp. 119-38.

17. See 'Comptes des consuls de Montréal-du-Gers', ed. A. Breuils, *AHG*, xxix, p. 126; xxxii, pp. 4, 9, 33. The Flemish towns performed a similar service for the dukes of Burgundy: see ADN, B.2012, fos. 347v, 350r-352v, 217v-219r, 223r (1453) for the supply of guns and munitions during the war with Ghent.

18. Leseur, op. cit., i, pp. 99, 106-7.

19. *Archives Historiques de la Gironde* [henceforth *AHG*], ii, pp. 33, 35, 43.

20. AML, MS 16.194, fo. 37v (6 June 1453).

21. PRO, C.61/127, m.9.

22. Ibid., m. 9.

the manner in which the French entered the town of Castillon was said to be 'through the breaches made by the artillery', and by means of a collapsed tower.[23] To meet such threats to fortifications which had previously been considered impregnable a number of measures could be taken. At the seigneurial castle of Blanquefort, near Bordeaux, modifications were made between 1380 and 1420 to existing structures. Gun-emplacements were built in the outer concentric wall and a specially strengthened tower, to provide flanking fire, was added to the more exposed portion of the defences.[24] At Bordeaux in the summer of 1442, when preparations were being made to meet an expected French invading force, earthworks described as *boulevards* were thrown up before the principal gates of the city,[25] and they were stocked with defensive artillery. A similar concentration on the outer defences of a fortress or town – barbicans and *boulevards* – is found in the repairs which were in progress at Langon, St Macaire and Bordeaux from 1432 to 1434.[26] At Dax, Guissen and Cadillac, in 1449 and 1451, the French encountered heavy resistance from such outer works constructed by the defenders.[27] As far as it is possible to generalise from surviving architectural and documentary evidence, there was as yet little attempt to build permanent stone defences designed to resist and house artillery in this area. At Cadillac, for instance, the communal accounts for 1449-51 include payments to carpenters and labourers for constructing palissades of timber and for moving earth from the ditches to build earthwork *boulevards* in front of two of the town's principal gates.[28] In Gascony, it is only at the seigneurial castle of Bonaguil, rebuilt by the Roquefeuil family from 1445 onwards, that an approach towards greater sophistication was made.[29]

The administration at Bordeaux had always provided defensive artillery for

23. BN, MS Duchesne 108, fos. 35v, 40r, 41r.

24. See L. Drouyn, *La Guienne Militaire* (Bordeaux/Paris 1865), pp. 53-65, plate 72. The town of Cadillac was employing masons to install gunports in the walls in 1438 and 1442: Archives Communales de Cadillac, E.-Suppl. 589, C.C.2, fos. 23r, 44r, 58r.

25. See J. Bernard and F. Gîteau, 'Compte du trésorier de la ville de Bordeaux pour 1442 (février-août)', *Bulletin philologique et historique*, 1961 (1963), p. 200. For the etymology of *boulevard* (a fortification made of earth and timber) from German *bolwerk*, Dutch *bolwerc*, first recorded in French in 1435, see C. Bloch and W. von Wartburg, *Dictionnaire Etymologique de la Langue Française*, i (Paris, 1932), p. 93.

26. See PRO, E.101/191/5, 191/7, nos. 7, 8. In January 1446, John Clement, lieutenant of Sir Edward Hull, constable of Bordeaux, was paid for going with carpenters to Bourg and surveying the construction of 'the walls of the Bollewerk' there: see PRO, E.364/84. For three 'bolvers de bois' at the Burgundian castle of Le Crotoy in May 1469, see BN, MS fr. 26,092, no. 810. For references to 'bolvers' built at Burgundian fortifications in 1465-6, see ADN, B.2058, fos. 251r-254r.

27. Leseur, op. cit., i, pp. 5-14. See also ibid., ii, p. 24, where the French encountered fierce opposition from the 'portal du boulevert que les Angloys avoient tous jours jusques alors tres bien ... defendu' at Cadillac in 1451. For the construction of boulevards at Cadillac, see Archives Communales de Cadillac, E.-Suppl. 589, C.C.2, fos. 93r-95v. (For the use of Breton labourers and provision of gunports, see ibid., fos. 93v, 96r, 98v.)

28. Ibid., fos. 98v, 99r, 101r.

29. See R. Ritter, *Châteaux, donjons et places fortes* (Paris 1953), pp. 131-3; P. Lauzun, *Le Château de Bonaguil* (Agen, 1897), passim.

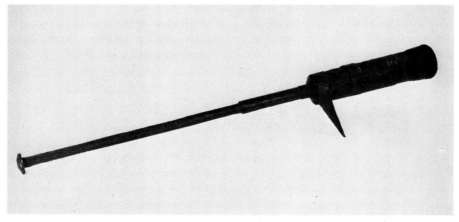

Plate 22. Hand culverin (fifteenth century). Paris, Musée de l'Armée.

the garrisons which lay in the path of armies invading English Gascony. From
Easter 1437 to Easter 1438, for instance, when the French were converging on
Bordeaux, the constable of the city disbursed at least 224 pounds of gunpowder
at 7½d and 8d sterling per pound.[30] This figure represents a significant fall in
price since the early years of the fifteenth century, when gunpowder stood at 1s
a pound.[31] Between March and December 1437, two cannon were sent by the
constable to the frontier of war.[32] One of these had three detachable breech-
blocks or 'chambers' for loading. However, the culverin was the defensive
firearm most commonly purchased by the constable at this time: eleven of these
were dispatched. His accounts suggest that these were probably handguns, for
large steel crossbows cost twice as much, and cranking devices for the crossbow
were the same price.[33] References to *couleuvrines enfustées en bastons* in an account
of 1431 seem to indicate that the culverin, at least in its smaller calibres, was a
portable firearm.[34] The inventory of the artillery found in the castle of Rouen on
the death of John, duke of Bedford, in 1435 also lists many 'small culverins',
including no less than 29 which were said to be *ad manum*.[35] Tripods and other

30. PRO., E.101/192/9, nos. 14, 27 (1 October 1437, 18 April 1438).
31. See PRO, E.101/404/6, m. 1 (privy wardrobe account, 5 November 1399 - 5 November
1401). (Gunpowder also cost 1s. sterling in March 1415: see *AMB*, iv, p. 123.)
32. PRO, E.101/192/9, no. 28.
33. Ibid., nos. 14, 28; E.101/193/15, no. 24. For *couleuvrine* (Medieval Latin *colubrina*), from
Latin *colubra, colobra*, a serpent, see Bloch and Wartburg, op. cit., i, p. 183. See plate 22.
34. See Napoleon III and Favé, *Etudes sur le passé et l'avenir de l'artillerie* (Paris 1846-71), iii, pp.
134-5; Clephan, art. cit., p. 93. For references to handguns in fourteenth-century England, see
Tout, art. cit., pp. 678-87.
35. See Stevenson, op. cit., ii, p. 567. They were distinguished in the inventory from the *magnae
colubrinae*, of which the smallest fired a leadshot weighing ⅓ lb.

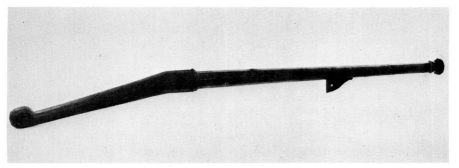

Plate 23. Hacquebuts (late fifteenth century). Paris, Musée de l'Armée.

stands for these small guns were also listed. A distinction was made between gunpowder intended for culverins and for cannon – the former being twice as expensive. These guns fired leadshot, and, with their long wooden stocks, could be mounted on battlements or parapets for use against the personnel of a besieging force.[36] Small handguns which fired leadshot (*plombées*) were found among the Burgundian artillery in the 1420s, and were distinguished in the receiver-general's accounts from the *veuglaires* and other light cannon firing stone balls.[37] Although still outnumbered by the crossbow in such sources, the increasingly frequent occurrence of such entries suggests that a cheap manual firearm, possessing some degree of accuracy and effectiveness, had been devised. The arquebus, or match-lock musket, did not finally oust the crossbow

36. Ibid., ii, pp. 567-8. For a description of the earliest culverins, appearing in the late fourteenth century, see Finò, op. cit., pp. 278-9; for illustrations, see ibid., fig. 71 (*bâton à feu*, an early fifteenth-century handgun); B. Gille, *Les ingénieurs de la Renaissance* (Paris 1964), p. 53 (illustration from the *Bellifortis* of Konrad Keyser, *c*.1400).

37. ADN, B.1933, fos. 170v-171r (1425-6).

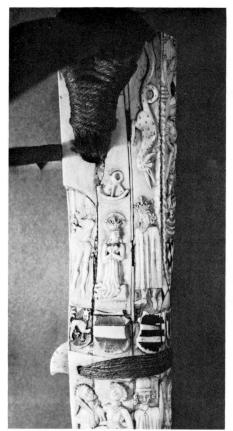

Plate 24. Crossbow (German, *c.* 145070). The carved stock shows scenes from the lives of military saints, including St George. London, Wallace Collection.

from French armies until 1567, but the introduction of the handgun meant that it now had a potentially dangerous rival.[38]

From the second quarter of the fifteenth century examples of death or mutilation by gunfire in Northern Europe and Italy became more numerous. There were others besides Thomas Montagu, earl of Salisbury who owed their deaths to artillery fire.[39] In November 1442, John Payntour, an English esquire,

38. For handgunners in Italian armies from *c.* 1440, see Mallett, op. cit., pp. 156-8. See plate 23.

39. Salisbury was apparently killed by a stone cannon ball fired from a bombard. The ball shattered as it hit a window and the earl was mortally wounded in the head by a fragment (24 October 1428): see Thomas Basin, *Histoire de Charles VII*, ed. C. Samaran, i (Paris 1933), pp. 118, 120. Thomas Fitzalan, earl of Arundel, was reputedly killed by a culverin shot at Beauvais in 1434: see Napoleon III and Favé, op. cit., ii, p. 101.

was killed by a culverin shot at La Réole.[40] Four years previously, Don Pedro, brother of the king of Castile, had been decapitated by a gunshot during the siege of the castle of Capuana at Naples.[41] The death of Prégent de Coëtivy, lord of Rais, admiral of France and bibliophile, was due to a cannon shot while he was directing trenching operations at the siege of Cherbourg in August 1450. With him perished Tudal le Bourgeois, *bailli* of Troyes, who was killed by a culverin.[42] Others were fortunate to escape death, although they were badly wounded by gunfire. In April 1422, one Michael Bouyer, esquire, was languishing in prison at Meaux, 'gravely ill and mutilated in one of his legs by a cannon shot, in such a way that he cannot aid himself'.[43] In August 1451, at the siege of Bayonne by the French, Bernard de Béarn was struck in the leg by a culverin ball, but recovered, it was said, through the skill of his surgeons.[44] On the same occasion, a French esquire called Philippe Charrapon lost one of his feet through being hit by a cannon shot, but apparently lived on as a war pensioner.[45] The *bon chevalier*, Jacques de Lalaing was killed by a cannon shot in June 1453.[46] It was becoming obvious that the gun could not only batter down fortifications, but could kill, and kill selectively from afar.

Yet the crossbow had done exactly that since the twelfth century, so that it is perhaps hardly surprising that there was no 'chorus of disapproval' directed at the gun during the fifteenth century.[47] Its alleged association with the devil did not deter Christian princes from using it.[48] The risk of death at the hands of a 'cowardly', plebeian crossbowman was merely augmented by that of death by gunfire. Yet the greater range and penetrating power of the culverin and handgun was coming to be acknowledged. Pope Pius II could write that 'no armour can withstand the blow of this torment, and even oaks are penetrated by it'.[49] Recent scientific tests using simulated models have demonstrated that later fifteenth-century handguns were reasonably accurate and could penetrate

40. Beckington, op. cit., pp. 223, 228.
41. See J. Nève, *Antoine de la Salle: sa vie et ses ouvrages* (Paris/Brussels 1903), pp. 40, 226-31.
42. For references by French and Burgundian chroniclers to wounding and death by gunfire after 1450, see Chartier, op. cit., ii, pp. 231-2; La Marche, *Mémoires*, ii, p. 307 (wound from a culverin at Schendelbeke during the Ghent war, June 1453); p. 321 (death by cannon-shot at Gavere, July 1453); Haynin, op. cit., i, p. 67 (wound from a *serpentine* at Montlhéry, July 1465); pp. 75-6 (three deaths, one case of concussion, by gunfire at Montlhéry). In the sixteenth century Blaise de Monluc survived seven wounds from gunfire, but lost three of his four sons in battle, killed by arquebus shots: *Blaise de Monluc. The Habsburg-Valois Wars and the French Wars of Religion*, ed. I. Roy (London 1971), pp. 14, 31, 41.
43. *Choix de pièces inédites*, ii, p. 86.
44. Gilles le Bouvier, Berry Herald, *Chronique*, in *Histoire de Charles VII*, ed. D. Godefroy (Paris 1661), p. 464.
45. BN, MS fr. 32,511, fo. 146r.
46. Basin, op. cit., ii, p. 212; Chastellain, op. cit., ii, pp. 360-4; *supra*, pp. 98-9. Bayart met a similar end in 1522: see *L'histoire du gentil seigneur de Bayart*, pp. 412-13.
47. See Hale, 'Gunpowder and the Renaissance', p. 134.
48. Described as 'Instrumento illo bellico sive diabolico quod vulgariter dicitur gonne' in John Mirfield's treatise of 1390: BL, MS. Harl. 3261, fo. 69r.
49. Cit. G.L. Tomasi, *Ritratto del Condottiero* (Turin 1967), p. 234.

armour plate at a range of at least twenty yards, using wet-mixed gunpowder and steel bullets. Over longer ranges, firing lead bullets, they were much more erratic, owing to decreased muzzle velocity, but progressive lengthening of the barrel compensated for this defect.[50] Death was thus meted out indiscriminately by an unseen hand, which sheltered behind the smoke created by its cowardly weapon. There is some evidence of social prejudice against the operators of such weapons in the fifteenth century. At Naples in 1438 Anthoine de la Salle commented that Don Pedro had been killed by men who were 'only artisans by trade'.[51] But this notion does not appear to have penetrated North of the Alps. La Salle's account is, moreover, slightly ambiguous in its attitude to the gunners concerned. The soldier who brought Don Pedro's severed head to the Angevins within the castle of Capuana was given a reward of six ducats by Isabella of Lorraine, René of Anjou's queen.[52] The story was also used by La Salle to demonstrate that sacrilege does not pay. The besiegers had mounted some of their artillery in a church, and thus had their just deserts.[53] There seems to be no evidence from France or Burgundy at this time that captured gunners were executed or maltreated in the manner which was allegedly common in Italy.[54] In the chronicles, the potentially dangerous and socially disruptive implications of using the culverin and handgun were simply not considered.

The increasing accuracy and range of the culverin was paralleled by improvements in the larger siege cannon. In English Gascony, the leisurely pace of siege warfare was quickened, as it was in Normandy and the Burgundian lands, by Charles VII's artillery under the Bureau brothers. During the summer and autumn of 1346, for instance, Henry of Grosmont, earl of Derby, had spent four months besieging Aiguillon.[55] In August 1442, Charles VII took Dax, after an artillery bombardment, in three weeks, and St Sever fell in less than a month.[56] At Bourg, in June 1451, the town surrendered in under six days, after the heavy artillery of the French had been brought up, without firing a shot.[57] Castillon capitulated to them in July 1453 after a bombardment by the siege

50. See Williams, 'Firing tests', pp. 114-20, especially conclusions on p. 119. The arquebus was fully effective against armour by the mid-sixteenth century: Gaier, 'L'opinion des chefs de guerre', pp. 732-3.
51. Nève, op. cit., p. 228.
52. Ibid., p. 231.
53. Ibid., pp. 231-2.
54. See Tomasi, op. cit., pp. 234-5, but for opposing evidence cf Hale, 'Gunpowder and the Renaissance', p. 125. Handgun men captured in Italian battles in the 1440s 'were usually executed on the spot: this was a tribute to their effectiveness rather than a sign of abhorrence for their unchivalrous weapon': Mallett, op. cit., p. 157. See plate 25.
55. E.C. Lodge, *Gascony under English Rule* (London 1926), p. 82; K. Fowler, *The King's Lieutenant: Henry of Grosmont, first duke of Lancaster* (London 1969), pp. 213-14.
56. Beckington, op. cit., ii, pp. 187, 196, 213-14; PRO, E.364/84, m. 5; Leseur, op. cit., i, pp. 28-41.
57. Enguerrand de Monstrelet, *Chroniques*, ed. J-A. Buchon (Paris 1826-7), xii, p. 93.

Plate 25. Cristoforo da Preda: Galeazzo Maria Sforza praying for victory, from a Book of Hours of 1477-80. This miniature shows both cavalry and infantry in action, including handgunners. London, Wallace Collection, M.342.

guns.[58] At Cadillac, a section of the town walls was rapidly demolished by the French guns.[59] It is not surprising that inhabitants of many towns preferred to come to terms. Moreover, it was often in the best interests of the besiegers to withhold their siege artillery and press for an agreement to surrender, as the French did at Bergerac in June 1451.[60] By withholding their guns, they gained not only an undamaged fortress but, under the laws of war, the sum total of all heavy artillery which could not be carried out on horseback or foot by the defeated garrison.[61] In July 1453 Roger, Lord Camoys, told the Three Estates of the Bordelais that Charles VII possessed 'marvellous artillery'.[62] Such scanty evidence as is found in other sources seems to bear out his words.

Throughout the campaigns of 1449-53 in Normandy and Gascony, however, little approach was made towards the development of field artillery. There was no part for it to play in a war of attrition conducted almost entirely by means of siege. Technical improvements were introduced into Charles VII's siege guns under the pressure of events. During the conquest of Normandy, between August 1449 and February 1450, the Genoese Louis Giribault, the king's gunner, was experimenting with a design for a new gun-carriage.[63] A model of the carriage was sent to the king during the campaign. The object of the experiment was to create a gun-carriage which was not drawn by horses. The siege-train might then be drawn by other means, but whether that required oxen or men is not clear. Perhaps the detrimental effects of requisitioning horses from those who lived in the path of armies of reconquest might be somewhat mitigated.[64] If horses were less in demand, other 'necessaries' for the artillery were not. The abbot and monks of St-André-le-Gouffier, near Falaise, were recompensed for the loss of timber felled in their woods by the king's artillerymen for the siege of Falaise.[65] Others were paid for their services. On 24 May 1450, sixteen local masons were paid by Robin Fontaine, *commis* for the payment of pioneers and siege-works at Bayeux, for making gunstones to be fired by the king's cannon and bombards during the siege.[66] They had worked

---

58. Leseur, op. cit., ii, p. 19; BN, MS Duchesne 108, fos. 35r-42r; MS fr. 18,442, fos. 46r, 47v (24-29 July 1453). The town was said to have capitulated on 20 July, three days after the battle in which Talbot was killed.

59. Leseur, op. cit., ii, pp. 21-5. The *grosses couleuvrines* of the French were trained so as to 'batre tout du long de ce pan de mur'. See also Drouyn, op. cit., pp. 258-9.

60. See *Ordonnances des rois de France*, xiv (Paris 1786), p. 109; Chartier, op. cit., ii, pp. 268-77.

61. Ibid., ii, p. 273.

62. BN, MS Duchesne 108 fo. 31v.

63. G. du Fresne de Beaucourt, 'Recueil de pièces pour servir de Preuves à la Chronique de Mathieu d'Escouchy', Escouchy, op. cit., iii, pp. 381-2.

64. For requisitioning horses and carters for the Guyenne expedition of 1453, see Contamine, *Guerre, Etat et Société*, p. 311. Charles the Bold was requisitioning carts for his artillery from the Flemings during his campaigns against René II of Lorraine and the Swiss: ADN. B. 17,723 (November 1476).

65. Beaucourt, op. cit., p. 390.

66. BL, Additional Charter 4066 (24 May 1450). See Chartier, op. cit., ii, pp. 204-11 for an account of the siege and surrender of Bayeux. During the siege, which lasted 'fifteen or sixteen days' many men were killed by bowshots and culverin fire (ibid., p. 205).

for sixteen weeks on their task. Three months later, Cherbourg fell after a bombardment by guns mounted in batteries on the sea-shore. These were covered with greased skins at high tide and, according to the chroniclers, the powder with which they were charged remained dry. Nevertheless three bombards and one cannon were fractured during the bombardment, and the town surrendered by agreement.[67]

The later stages of the Hundred Years' War (1442-53) did not nurture any species of artillery beside the bombard, the mortar and the culverin. Even on the field of Castillon (17 July 1453) where the heavy and light guns of the French demonstrated the murderous effects of enfilading on infantry advancing in close order, no field guns were used. Siege guns and culverins were placed in an earthwork camp dug by the French pioneers. Talbot's dismounted men-at-arms and foot, who were attempting to storm the camp, were mown down by the hail of gunfire. There is no need, as some have done, to look for deep-seated strategic principles behind this 'curiously defensive step'.[68] It had become normal practice by the 1440s for besiegers to construct a field fortification or entrenched park for their artillery out of the range of the defenders' guns, from which trenches might be dug as far as the battery positions.[69] The principle had been put to the test at Dax in 1442,[70] at Mauléon and Guissen in 1449. During the siege of Guissen, near Bayonne, Gaston IV of Foix prepared a large fortified earthwork with which to repel an Anglo-Gascon relieving force. It was defended by 'great culverins of metal ... and great serpentines'.[71] At the second taking of Dax in 1451, according to Guillaume Leseur, it was possible to 'go safely from one extremity of the siege to the other' by way of the network of supply trenches dug by pioneers during the night.[72] The principles of cross-fire and its terrible effects were already appreciated, and the distribution of arrow-loops and gun-ports in Gascon and other strongholds suggests that it had been applied to their defence. At Mauléon and Guissen in 1449 the defenders seem to have enfiladed the French from their outworks. At Guissen the English had 'a strong fort which they had built and fortified at the foot of their castle', and met the French assault with fire which was 'so vigorous and accurate where they saw the press of our men that they galled them with it'.[73] The culverin and the earthwork

67. Ibid., ii, pp. 232-3. Frequent firing tests were made on large guns, in the hope of avoiding fractures. Philip the Good regularly had new cannon assayed in his presence, and was especially interested in a large gun made for him by Master Hubrecht, cannoneer of Bruges in 1425-6. It was tested in the fields outside Bruges, approved by the duke and housed in a special hut erected in the courtyard of the ducal *hôtel* there: ADN, B.1933, fos. 169r-169v.

68. A.H. Burne, *The Agincourt War* (London 1956), p. 334.

69. See Napoleon III and Favé, op. cit., ii, pp. 97-100. For Italian examples of field fortifications from 1440, see Mallett, op. cit., pp. 158-9.

70. Leseur, op. cit., i, pp. 11-12.

71. Ibid., i, p. 85. For the siege of Mauléon, see ibid., i. p. 52.

72. Ibid., i, p. 119; Napoleon III and Favé, op. cit., ii, pp. 97-8 for other instances.

73. Leseur, op. cit., i, p. 73. This fort was clearly similar to the *boulevards* constructed elsewhere in Gascony: see *supra*, pp. 133-4.

boulevard, it could be argued, represented the first positive reaction to the great improvements which had been made in the techniques of attack. Town and castle walls bristled with defensive artillery and experiments which were to result in the development of the permanent angle bastion and gun platform had already begun in France by the 1440s.[74]

In theory, as well as in practice, soldiers were putting their minds to the problem of the most effective use of artillery. No objections were raised to the cannon, least of all by the Church, which gave gunners a patron saint, St Barbara.[75] There was no room in fifteenth-century France for a Cervantes to deliver a tirade against 'those devilish instruments'. The gun, like the standing army, had come to stay. Jean de Bueil was able to advocate the siting of a besieger's camp before a beleaguered fortress on the model of the fortified entrenchments dug at Mauléon, Guissen, Cherbourg, Dax and Castillon fifteen years before.[76] Trenches, he wrote, were to be dug from one part of the siege to another, covered by hoardings. Ease of contact and movement between the units of the encircling force could thus be ensured. The gunners themselves were to be shielded by wooden mantlets. From the trenches, the enemies' gun-ports and arrow-loops could be effectively damaged, while the besiegers were sheltered from their artillery fire.[77] According to the accounts of the Norman and Gascon campaigns of 1449-53 by Jean Chartier, Gilles le Bouvier and Mathieu d'Escouchy, the French seem to have gone about their task of reducing strong-points in just this manner.[78] Louis XI put the principle into practice in reverse when resisting the forces of Charles of Charolais who was besieging Paris in August and September 1465.[79] A trench was dug from the city at a crucial point towards the besieging army's positions. A *boulevard* of earth and wood was thrown up at the furthest extremity of the trench and the royal artillery opened fire on the troops of Duke Jean of Calabria from this vantage point. Commynes, in an engaging passage, wrote of the panic inspired in the

74. For contemporary Italian developments, see J.R. Hale, 'The early development of the Bastion: an Italian Chronology, *c*.1450-*c*.1534', *Europe in the Late Middle Ages*, ed. J.R. Hale, J.R.L. Highfield and B. Smalley (London 1965), pp. 466-94.
75. See J.R. Hale, 'War and public opinion in Renaissance Italy', *Italian Renaissance Studies*, ed. E.F. Jacob (London 1960), p. 102; for St Barbara and her patronage of gunners, see *Bibliotheca Hagiographica Latina* (Brussels 1898-9), pp. 142-6; S. Peine, *St Barbara, die Schützheiliger der Bergleute und der Artillerie und ihre Darstellung in der Kunst* (Freiberg 1896), pp. 10-14.
76. *Le Jouvencel*, i, pp. 164-9.
77. Ibid., ii, p. 41. Charles of Charolais had several culverins equipped with shields (*pavaix*) to protect the gunners during the War of the Public Weal: ADN, B. 2056, no. 64, 160 (6 July 1465).
78. See e.g. Chartier, op. cit., ii, pp. 237-8: '... c'estoit merveilleuse chose a veoir les boulevers, approuchemens, fossez, trenchees et mines que les dessus dits Jean et Gaspard Bureau faisoient faire devant les villes et chasteaux qui furent assiegez durant icelle guerre ...' He thought that all the places taken by agreement to surrender could easily have been taken by assault.
79. Commynes, op. cit., i, pp. 60-1. The guns used by Charolais included bombards, mortars, *courtaulx, serpentines*, and culverins. The *serpentines* were cast in bronze and fired lead shot: some had been captured from Louis XI at Montlhéry: ADN, B. 2056, nos. 64,150-1; 64,160; 64,168; 64,182; 64,186-7; 64,198; 64,207 (July-August 1465).

besieging army, especially when two cannon balls were shot into the upper room where Charles was dining. One of his servants was killed instantly, and the count, fearing the worst, uncharacteristically retired to the ground floor and 'decided not to budge'.[80] The principle of contravallation by the defender, as well as circumvallation by the besieger, was obviously appreciated at this time. Although such outworks were generally in earth, the notion of a castle or fortified town as an inert, defensive mass was on the wane.

If we are to believe the chroniclers, and an expert like Jean de Bueil, the combination of heavy and light artillery in siege-craft was also understood by the 1450s. The *Jouvencel*, in its chapter on sieges, gave the following advice:

> When your bombards have begun to fire, make sure that the *veuglaires* and light artillery fire as much as possible after each bombard shot, so that those within have no chance to make *boulevards* nor to repair the damage which the bombard will have done to them.[81]

Guillaume Leseur, writing of the siege of Dax in 1451, gives an instance of the practice, when the French culverins picked off the defenders who were trying to repair breaches in their walls made by the heavier guns.[82] Jean de Bueil considered the older system of circumvallation – by building separate *bastilles*, as the English had done at Orléans in 1428 – to be both ineffective and outdated.[83] The direction of siege-works was to be left to the technicians, he went on – above all, to the masters of the artillery. They were competent to advise not only on the deployment and laying of the guns, but on the placing of shields and hoardings to protect the besiegers and gunners, as well as the digging of trenches and hauling of the cannon. The cannoneers – a distinct class – were to advise on the number of bombards, gunstones and gunpowder necessary for laying siege. 'It's their trade,' wrote Jean de Bueil, and referred the aspiring siege engineer, tantalisingly, to 'the book of the master of the artillery.'[84]

In the regrettable absence of evidence for the nature and organisation of Charles VII's artillery at the end of the Hundred Years War, one is forced to argue from sources of a rather later date. An inventory of Louis XI's artillery drawn up in August 1463, gives a total of 9 bombards and 32 smaller guns in and around Paris.[85] It would have been surprising if Charles VII's siege-train had been much smaller than his son's. The Bureau brothers were reputed to have founded 16 bombards for the siege of Harfleur alone in 1449.[86] Gaspard

80. Commynes, op. cit., i, p. 61.
81. *Le Jouvencel*, ii, p. 41.
82. Leseur, op. cit., i, pp. 119-20.
83. *Le Jouvencel*, ii, p. 44.
84. Ibid., ii, pp. 45, 52. This has not been discovered.
85. BN, MS fr. 20,492, fos. 16r-16v.
86. See G. du Fresne de Beaucourt, *Histoire de Charles VII*, v (Paris 1890), pp. 25-6; Chartier, op. cit., ii, p. 178. Conditions at the siege were made exceptionally difficult by the bitterly cold weather (December 1449).

Bureau, knight, *maître de l'artillerie*, went on to serve Louis XI in the same capacity.[87] His skill was too valuable for a king to lose. Around him was his *bande* of 30 cannoneers, a keeper of the artillery, a master-carter and a *maître artilleur*.[88] This permanent personnel may have served with him in the last campaigns of the Hundred Years War. It was to these men that Jean de Bueil could delegate the responsibility of laying siege. But the *maître de l'artillerie* was a nobleman, although his nobility may have been recently acquired. The conduct and direction of war was not to be left entirely in the hands of technicians and artisans. It was to the Quercynois family of Genouillac that the mastership of the artillery was to be given.[89] The French nobility thus displayed a marked capacity for adaptation to the changing techniques of war.

A similar acceptance of the gun is to be found in the art and literature of the fifteenth century. An English verse paraphrase of Vegetius, written between 1457 and 1460, referred disparagingly to the older forms of siege engines:

... but now it is unwiste,
Al this aray, and bumbardys thei cary,
And gunne and serpentyn that wil not vary,
Fouler, covey, crappaude and colueryne
And other soortis moo then. VIII. or IXne.[90]

In both naval warfare and sieges, the author had no illusions as to the value of fire-arms. They could destroy a besieger's siege-works and dismast a ship.[91] Their appearance in illuminated manuscripts is a commonplace by the middle of the century. In a magnificent copy of Froissart's *Chronicles*, made for Anthoine, *grand bâtard* of Burgundy in about 1468, the Burgundian artillery of the time is faithfully depicted.[92] Philip van Artevelde is shown, somewhat anachronistically, attacking at Ghent in 1381 with two field guns mounted on their wheeled carriages by means of trunnions.[93] Bertrand du Guesclin besieges Bourbourg with a large bombard on a wheeled carriage similar to those shown in use by the Turks at Constantinople in a manuscript of 1455.[94] The artist of

87. P. Contamine, 'L'Artillerie royale française à la vieille des guerres d'Italie', *Annales de Bretagne*, lxxi (1964), pp. 258-60. For an account rendered by Bureau in 1469 for his expenses in office, see BN, MS fr. nouv. acq. 21,156, no. 58.

88. Ibid., no. 58; BN, *Pièces originales* 3051, no. 67,943 (November 1458).

89. See F. Vindry, *Dictionnaire de l'Etat Major français au xvie siècle*, i (Paris 1901), pp. 401-2; ii, p. 205; *infra*, pp. 162-3. Genouillac's salary was 1,500 *livres tournois* p.a. in 1491; the total personnel with him numbered 157: R. Gandilhou, 'Le personnel de L'Artillerie royale en 1491 d'après un compte inédit', *Annales du Midi*, liv-lv (1942-3), pp. 102-7.

90. *Knyghthode and Bataile*, ed. R. Dyboski and A.M. Arend (EETS, London 1935), ll. 148-52.

91. Ibid., ll. 2544-52, 2854-60.

92. See A. Lindner, *Der Breslauer Froissart* (Berlin 1912); for illustrations of surviving pieces captured by the Swiss from the Burgundians between 1474 and 1477, see Deuchler, op. cit., figs. 161-78a, pp. 167-82.

93. Lindner, op. cit., plate 1.

94. Ibid., plate 24; BN, MS fr. 9087 fo. 207v (*Voyage d'Outremer*), reproduced in S. Runciman, *The Fall of Constantinople, 1453* (Cambridge 1965), plate I.

the Froissart manuscript even incorporates the gun into the borders of his pages. A centaur is shown playfully firing a handgun.[95] The 'devilish instrument' was being domesticated and tamed. Men were curiously endeared to the gun by the end of the Hundred Years War. Siege guns achieved a certain individuality. There was no standardisation of calibre and each gun was given a name. It was not only Pope Pius II who could christen his cannon with names such as *Enea, Silvia* and *Vittoria*.[96] In 1463, Louis XI had two bombards called *Jason* and *Medea*, and their Burgundian rivals were named *Artois, Ath* and *La Bergière*.[97] Others were called *La plus du monde, Paris, La Dauphine, La Realle, Londres, Montereau* and *St Pol*.[98] Some of Louis' cannon bore the name of Charles VII's captains – *La Hire, Barbazin, Flavy* and *Boniface*.[99] The English had guns called *Bedford, Robin Clement, Brisebarre* and *Herr Johan* in the castle of Rouen in 1435.[100] Christine de Pisan could even include a gun called *Seneca* in her chapter on siege-craft in the *Faits d'armes*.[101] Each gun was an individual, and demanded careful treatment from its operators. The projectiles which it fired had to be specially made for each gun, so that a siege gun in the fifteenth century still possessed a personality of its own.

Just as Italian Renaissance artists were to attempt to domesticate and even beautify the gun, so fifteenth-century Englishmen, Frenchmen and Burgundians made it acceptable to a chivalrous society. By 1445, Anthoine, *grand bâtard* of Burgundy, had chosen a wooden barbican with gun-ports as his emblem.[102] By 1465, Louis de Bruges, lord of La Gruthuyse, had selected a bombard, with the motto *Plus est en vous*.[103] The *imprese* of the Este and Montefeltro were thus paralleled and anticipated in Northern Europe during

95. Lindner, op. cit., plate 5. Handguns are frequently shown in action in the battle scenes from Swiss chronicles of the later fifteenth century: see J. Zemp, *Die Schweizerischen Bilderchroniken* (Zurich 1897), plates 11, 18, 19 (*c*. 1480-5). For the use of handguns at the battle of Vercelli (1476) between the Burgundians and Galeazzo Maria Sforza of Milan, see London, Wallace Collection M. 342: miniature of Galeazzo Maria, praying for victory (1477) and M.A. Jacobsen, 'A Sforza Miniature by Cristoforo da Preda', *Burlington Magazine*, cxvi (1974), pp. 91-6. Also *supra*, plate 25.

96. Hale, 'Gunpowder and the Renaissance', p. 131. (The pope's names were Aeneas Silvius Piccolomini.)

97. BN, MS fr. 20,492, fo. 16r; ADN, B. 1056, nos. 64,186-7; 64,209 (June and August 1465).

98. BN, MS fr. 20,492, fo, 16r. *La plus du Monde* was evidently the motto of Pierre de Brézé, *grand sénéchal* of Normandy under Charles VII: see *Oeuvres complètes du Roi René*, ed. H. de Quatrebarbes (Angers 1846), iii, p. 127. The bombard was probably named after Brezé and perhaps brought to Paris from Normandy, as other guns in the 1463 inventory had been.

99. BN, MS fr. 20,492, fo. 16r. La Hire = Etienne de Vignolles, *dit* La Hire (*c*.1390-1443); Barbazan = Arnaud-Guillaume, lord of Barbazan (*c*.1431); Flavy = Guillaume de Flavy, captain of Compiègne (d.1449); Boniface = Boniface de Valpergue (*fl.* 1438-46).

100. Stevenson, op. cit., ii, p. 566.

101. Coopland, art. cit., p. 179 observes that the writer(s) of *Le Jouvencel* did not include these names when annexing passages from Christine de Pisan.

102. See Lindner, op. cit., plates 5, 6, 9, 10, 23, 28.

103. See P. Durrieu, *La Miniature Flamande au temps de la cour de Bourgogne* (Paris/Brussels 1921), plates LII, LXII (MS of *Le Jouvencel* executed for Louis de Bruges, BN, MS fr. 191, fo. 1). See also Van Praet, op. cit., *passim*. The Hôtel Gruthuyse at Bruges has a number of carvings of this motto and device.

the fifteenth century.[104] The harsh reality of war and of the gun's bite and sting, recalled in the names *couleuvrine, serpentine* and *faucon*, was being smothered under a cloak of illusion. The gun had come to stay, and its influence on the final campaigns of the Hundred Years War was not derisory. If it had 'no serious influence on the issues of battles before the late fifteenth century' this was only because there were so few battles in which it could play a part, while its influence on Charles the Bold's battles would have been greater if he had been a better general.[105] Had it not been for the French siege guns, however, the outcome of the campaigns which effectively ended the Hundred Years War, and of Charles VIII's Italian expedition of 1494-5, might have been very different.[106] The challenge which they offered to traditional methods of siege-craft and fortification led to the creation of new techniques of both attack and defence. In the realm of ideas, the gun was accepted without serious reservations, just as former innovations had been accepted, and the chivalrous class adjusted to its effects without serious difficulty. Yet it was not until the last quarter of the sixteenth century that the arquebus and the pistol finally drove the lance from the battlefield.[107]

104. See Wind, op. cit., figs. 71, 81, 82, pp. 108-12 for these emblems of bombshells and cannon balls.

105. See Vaughan, *Charles the Bold*, pp. 222-3, 376, 393. (His 400 guns at Morat were unfortunately pointing in the wrong direction.)

106. In 1494 Charles VIII had 36 siege cannon, properly mounted on gun-carriages, weighing less than the bombards of the 1450s and 60s. Since 1489 the French *bandes* of artillery had achieved considerable technical advance, reflected in the ease with which their weapons were transported and the speed with which they could be drawn up into battery positions: see Contamine, 'L'artillerie royale française', pp. 221, 251-3.

107. See Gaier, 'L'opinion des chefs de guerre', pp. 740-4.

CHAPTER FIVE

The Changing Face of War and Chivalry

In the late fifteenth and early sixteenth centuries the effects of the changes in warfare which have been discussed multiplied. Whereas the campaigns of the final stages of the Hundred Years War had consisted largely of siege warfare and Charles the Bold had failed to make effective use of artillery in his battles, in the course of the Italian wars (1494 to 1559) this potential was to be exploited with devastating effect. The impersonality of war increased, and it was intensified by the centralised organisation of newly-founded standing armies in France, Burgundy and some Italian states, by the greater numbers and degree of specialisation involved, and the disciplinary measures that were consequently necessary.[1] At the same time, wars against non-noble armies and the employment of mercenaries both eroded the conventions of *guerre nobiliaire* which had governed war-time behaviour for at least the previous two centuries. This chapter seeks to examine these changes and the response of the nobility to them.

During this transitional period new and old techniques were of course mingled in a constantly changing relationship. One of the earliest isolable forces was undoubtedly the creation of the French standing army in 1445-8. This was a permanent, professional body, in the direct employ of the crown, where rank no longer conferred automatic command.[2] From 1445 to 1560 the French royal army was led by professional captains who were no longer differentiated according to social rank by the administration – differences in the pay-scale (which had marked off the banneret from other nobles) were, for example, eliminated.[3] 'Efficiency in war had ceased to be the attribute of a class, and was becoming the attribute of a profession.'[4] In Burgundy, the old social hierarchy was reflected in the receiver-general's accounts for the duchy in 1465-6, when knights banneret were still paid twice as much as knights bachelor, with a

---

1. These problems are discussed by J.R. Hale in *The New Cambridge Modern History*, i (Cambridge 1957), chapter ix; ii (Cambridge 1958), chapter xvi. For a recent general account see Howard, op. cit., pp. 30-77, 54-60.

2. T. Courteaux in Vindry, op. cit., p. xiv.

3. See W.L. Wiley, *The Gentleman of Renaissance France* (Harvard 1954), p. 13 for a petition of 1560 by the second estate at the Estates-General that membership of the *compagnies d'ordonnance* should be confined to nobles.

4. Oman, op. cit., ii, p. 436.

similar relationship between esquires banneret and bachelor.[5] When Charles the Bold created his standing force of *compagnies d'ordonnance* in 1471 these distinctions were demolished, as they had been in France. The banners and pennons that had been a focal point for the groups that fought around them were replaced by standards, ensigns, cornets and *banneroles* (scroll-like plumes worn on the helmet) according to the nature of the unit rather than the social status of the commander.[6] Each captain (*conducteur*) of a Burgundian company of *ordonnance* was to bear an ensign; each commander of a squadron (*escadre*) a cornet; and each head of a *chambre* wore a *bannerole*. Charles the Bold's great military ordinance of 1473 laid down a method of numbering units in the standing army, stating:

> So that the men-at-arms may recognise their ensign better, my lord ordains that the ensigns should be of different colours, having various devices painted upon them. He also ordains that the commanders of every squadron in each company shall ... carry a cornet of the same colour and device as the captain, with large gold letters reading *C, CC, CCC, CCCC* according to the squadron. The *banneroles* which the heads of *chambres* shall wear on their sallets shall be of similar colours, with painted devices, as the squadron commanders' cornets, and shall be numbered I, II, III, IV respectively, inscribed beneath the *C* of the squadron ...[7]

For the first time in European history since the fall of the Roman empire, an army was subjected to a system of differentiation by insignia which had no connection with social status. The uniformity of these attributes facilitated organisation and recognition, factors whose importance increased with the growing specialisation of individual units. Renaissance armies were to adopt the same practice despite the collapse of the Burgundian dynasty in 1477.

Above all, the use of standards and ensigns provided an invaluable aid to discipline – an area where the size of the new standing armies had caused problems. This was highlighted in the remarks of Jean de Bueil, veteran of the Hundred Years War, to Louis XI in a council of war during the Burgundian invasion of 1471:

> War has become very different. In those days, when you had eight or ten thousand

---

5. ADN, B.2058, fo. 222r; Brusten, *L'Armée bourguignonne*, pp. 38-9.

6. BL, Add. MS 36,619, fos. 12v-13r; C. Brusten, 'Les emblèmes de l'armée bourguignonne sous Charles le Téméraire. Essai de classification', *Jahrbuch des bernischen historischen Museums in Bern*, xxxvii-xxxviii (1957-8), pp. 122-3.

7. 'Et afin que lesdis hommes darmes et archiers ayent meilleur congnoissance de leurs enseignes pour les suyr, monditseigneur ordonne que les conducteurs ayent et portent doresenavant enseignes de diverses couleurs ayans dedens enseignes diverses en painture. Il ordonne aussi que les chefs descadre ... portent cornettes de pareille couleur et de pareille enseigne en painture a lenseigne de leurdit conducteur, ayans grans lettres dor de *C, CC, CCC, CCCC* selonc lescadre. Les banneroles que les chefs de chambres portent sur leurs salades seroient de semblables couleurs, ayans enseignes en painture, que les cornettes des chefs descadre, et seroient nombrés I, II, III, IV, inscrits audessous du *C* descadre ...'. BL, Add. MS 36,619, fos. 12v-13r; Vaughan, *Charles the Bold*, p. 209. For illustrations of some of the insignia see Deuchler, op. cit., figs. 96, 99, 104.

men, you reckoned that a very large army; today, it is quite another matter. One has never seen a more numerous army than that of my lord of Burgundy, both in artillery and in munitions of all sorts; yours is also the finest which has ever been mustered in the kingdom. As for me, I am not accustomed to see so many troops together. How do you prevent disorder and confusion among such a mass?[8]

Part of the answer lay in the use of standards and ensigns. *Le Jouvencel* was similarly explicit on this point, stressing the importance of keeping all troops together under their own ensign and none other.[9] In the ordinances of war proclaimed by its hero for his army, every man-at-arms and archer was to fight only under the standard of his captain.[10] To prevent disorder, and especially disputes over billets, each quartermaster was to fix a little banner, bearing the captain's livery and device, on the lodgings of each company. This, thought the *Jouvencel*, would reduce the risk of 'hue and cry' among the troops.[11] That such ordinances were so frequently reissued suggests that the level of discipline among fifteenth-century standing armies was not high. The *Rozier des Guerres* (a late fifteenth-century military treatise) echoed the *Jouvencel*, commenting that 'there is nothing so profitable for achieving a victory than obeying the orders of the ensigns' because this kept troops together in close order.[12] Flags had become a means of disciplining and controlling the soldiery – the commissioned ranks of ensign and cornet of horse in later European armies stemmed from the authority which their bearers inevitably acquired.

The sense of corporate identity that was an essential adjunct to discipline was also promoted by the introduction of uniforms, often corresponding to the livery colours of the commander or captain.[13] In 1471 surcoats of blue and white (Charles the Bold's colours), with a red St Andrew's cross (the Burgundian emblem) were prescribed for the Burgundian army.[14] This perhaps reflects a greater degree of dependence on the commander-in-chief than was the case with the French *bandes* proposed by Raymond de Beccarie, Sire de Fourquevaux, in his *Instructions sur le faict de la Guerre* of 1549. These were to be dressed in the colour of their captains' ensigns, with a device or 'certain cognisances on their stockings, whereby one can distinguish the soldiers of one *bande* from another.'[15]

8. *Le Jouvencel*, i, p. cclxxxi: 'Mais, depuis son temps, la guerre est devenue bien différente. Pour lors, quand on avoit huit ou dix mille hommes, on comptait que c'était une très grande armée; aujourd'hui, c'est bien autre chose. On n'a jamais vu une armée plus nombreuse que celle de Monsieur de Bourgogne, tant d'artillerie, tant de munitions de toutes sortes; la vôtre est aussi la plus belle qui ait été assemblée dans le royaume. Pour moi, je ne suis accoutumé à voir tant de troupes ensemble. Comment gouverner tant de gens? Comment empêcher le trouble et la confusion dans une telle multitude?'

9. Ibid., i, pp. 159-60; ii, pp. 245-6.

10. Ibid., ii, p. 194.

11. Ibid., i, p. 179.

12. *Le Rozier des Guerres*, ed. A. d'Espagnet (Paris 1616), p. 75.

13. Vaughan, *Charles the Bold*, p. 206; *Instructions*, fos. 13v, 14r, 25r.

14. See *Mémoires pour servir à l'histoire de France et de Bourgogne*, ii (Paris 1729), p. 290.

15. *Instructions*, fo. 14v. The ensigns were to be differenced by 'quelque difference en facon, ou par quelques barres'.

Plate 26. The siege and battle of Pavia (1525). French, anonymous. Ashmolean Museum, Oxford.

By the mid-sixteenth century it was becoming more important to recognise one particular unit through the gun-smoke than to express the unity of an army under its sovereign.

The introduction of uniforms struck a singularly forceful blow at the military function of heralds.[16] They had little part to play in armies which no longer required the services of experts to recognise and identify an individual and his retinue by his coat-of-arms on the field. Even the ancient heraldic duty of carrying messages, challenges and summonses was gradually taken from them. As early as 1428, Philip the Good was employing trumpeters and minstrels to carry diplomatic messages, and there is fifteenth-century evidence to suggest that one employed a *trompette* if a herald or pursuivant was not available.[17] By the later years of the century, moreover, a reliance not upon officers of arms, but upon drummers, fifers and trumpeters as envoys and accredited representatives begins to emerge. In 1497, René II of Lorraine was using Swiss drummers (*tambourins*) as messengers,[18] and by the middle of the sixteenth century an English treatise on the conduct of war laid down that the players of drums and fifes 'shall be faithful, secret and ingenious, of able personage to use their instruments and the office of sundry languages; for oftentimes they be sent to parley with their enemies, to summon their forts or towns, to redeem and conduct prisoners, and divers other messages, which of necessity requireth language.'[19] These were precisely the qualities demanded of kings-of-arms, heralds and pursuivants in later medieval treatises.[20] In 1513, Bluemantle Pursuivant still summoned the town of Thérouanne to surrender,[21] but in Elizabeth I's campaigns in Portugal and the Netherlands, that function was performed by drummers and fifers.[22] Their non-combatant status, with its attendant immunity under the laws of arms, made them – as it had heralds before them – suitable diplomatic agents, and their elaborate uniforms may have owed something to the herald's tabard.

These drum and fife players were another facet of the apparatus of discipline attendant upon the new bodies of infantry. They seem to have originated with the use of Swiss and German mercenaries. Owing no allegiance beyond the cash nexus, these men had to be subjected to a rigorous disciplinary code, whose instruments were the drill sergeant and the drumhead tribunal. With the

---

16. See de Vaivre and Jequier, art. cit., p. xiv; P. Adam-Even, art. cit., pp. 24-6.

17. See J. Marix, *Histoire de la Musique et des Musiciens de la Cour de Bourgogne sous le règne de Philippe le Bon* (Strasbourg 1939), p. 57.

18. See P. Contamine, 'René II et les mercenaires de langue germanique: la guerre contre Robert de la Marck, seigneur de Sedan (1496)', *Anniversaire de la Bataille de Nancy*, pp. 384, 392.

19. Written by Ralph Smith: see H.G. Farmer, *The Rise and Development of Military Music* (London 1912), p. 31.

20. See A.R. Wagner, *Heralds and Heraldry*, pp. 41-6; Oxford, Bodleian Library, MS Rawlinson C. 399, fos. 76v, 77v, 79r-v; N. Upton, *De Studio Militari*, ed. F.P. Barnard, (Oxford 1931), pp. 1-3.

21. Cruickshank, op. cit., pp. 82-3.

22. C.G. Cruickshank, *Elizabeth's Army* (Oxford 1946), pp. 58, 301.

Swiss and the *Landsknechte* came the first attempts to raise a disciplined infantry which drilled to the beat of the drum.[23] The 'habits of order, obedience and uniform behaviour' were hardly innate and they had to be forcibly inculcated.[24] Drill was crucial, for the pike formations, with their handgunners and cross-bowmen, were to fulfil an offensive function, as well as a merely defensive one. Their squares or columns advanced to the tap of the drum, which gave a measured pace to these enormous bodies of massed infantry and kept them together. An early representation of a group of handgunners in the *Mittelalterliches Hausbuch* of about 1480, shows them on the march, led by a drummer and a fifer.[25] With the Swiss and German mercenaries came their drum and fife, which provided European regiments of foot with a means of keeping in step and transmitting commands, which long outlived the fifteenth century.

Fourquevaux wrote at some length about the value of the drum to military discipline. He visualised each of his reformed infantry legions of 1549 having two drummers and a fifer on their strength, as well as a provost marshal with the title of *conservateur de la discipline militaire*.[26] Francis I's infantry legions of 1534 had four drummers and four fifers each.[27] Fourquevaux thought that the Swiss were the inventors of the drum, but this was an inaccuracy, for the *tabour* or *tabourin* had certainly been well-known to medieval Europe.[28] A fresco, dated 1373, in the Palazzo Publico, Siena, for example, shows a company of Sienese infantry advancing at the battle of Val di Chiana (1363) to the sound of three pipes and three small tabors at their head,[29] but Northern Europe does not seem to have experienced the sight and sound of drums and fifes in its armies until the later fifteenth century. The medieval tabor was then increased in size to become the deep military side-drum.[30] Its functions were to prevent troops from straggling, to transmit orders on the march, and to prevent disorder in the ranks by keeping all the men together at the same pace.[31] Fourquevaux thought

---

23. Howard, op. cit., p. 32.

24. Keegan, op. cit., p. 319.

25. See A. Essenwein, *Mittelalterliches Hausbuch* (Frankfurt-am-Main, 1887), fos. 51v-52v. The manuscript was owned by the Goldast family of Constance; the authorship of the engravings is discussed in M. Lehrs, *Der Meister 'W.A.'* (Dresden 1895), pp. 24-37. See end-papers.

26. *Instructions*, fo. 13v. Each company was to be composed of 510 men. The Swiss mercenaries in French service under Charles VIII had two drums and two fifes for each company of 300 men: Contamine, *Guerre, Etat et Société*, p. 310, n. 202.

27. *Instructions*, p. lix.

28. See H.G. Farmer, *Military Music* (New York 1950), pp. 10-11. The tabor was of Arabic origin and was normally played in conjunction with the pipe from the twelfth century onwards. See A.H. Baines, 'Ancient and folk backgrounds', *Musical Instruments through the Ages*, ed. A.H. Baines (Harmondsworth 1961), pp. 225-6.

29. For a reproduction, see G. Trease, *The Condottieri* (London 1970), fig. 49.

30. See J. Blades, 'Orchestral instruments of percussion', *Musical Instruments*, pp. 335-6.

31. *Instructions*, fos. 16r-v, 20r; Farmer, *Rise and Development of Military Music*, pp. 17-21, 27-30: he claims that the march, as a 'strictly rhythmic piece of music', dates from the late fifteenth century (p. 21).

that trumpets might be used more effectively in battle to transmit commands, because their penetrating sound was more likely to be heard above the gunshots and the noise of the *mêlée*. Yet a musical treatise published in 1588 was quite explicit about the role of the drums in battle. Jean Thoinot (*dit* Arbeau) wrote in his *Orchésographie* that,

> The noise of all the said instruments serves as a signal and warning to the soldiers to strike camp, to advance, & to withdraw; and to give them the heart, boldness and courage to attack the enemy on sight; and to defend themselves manfully and vigorously. For soldiers can march in confusion and disorder, so that they would be in danger of being overthrown and defeated; hence our said French [captains] have taken steps to make the rank and files advance at certain measured paces ...[32]

Although he was writing towards the end of the sixteenth century, Arbeau was clearly referring to well-established conventions. He set out the *mesures* or patterns of drum-beats with helpful musical illustrations, demonstrating how the Swiss differed from the French in observing a different rhythm of *batterie*.[33] The drummers added elaborations to the basic rhythm of the drums, while the fifes were to 'fall in step with the sound of the *tambour*'.[34] Arbeau was quite sure about the nature and provenance of the fife – it was, he wrote, a small transverse flute, pierced with six holes 'which the Germans and the Swiss use'.[35] Its function was to incite men to battle, and to keep them cool and cheerful in the face of danger. The Phrygian mode was thought particularly suited to this purpose, and Greek and Roman precedents for the use of flutes in war were eagerly seized upon.[36] Exactly what the drums and fifes played in the later fifteenth century is not known, because their music had not yet been written down. The tunes of popular songs and dances were perhaps most likely to evoke some response from the troops, and the earliest known regimental marches,

32. J.T. Arbeau, *Orchésographie et traicté en forme de dialogue* (Langres, 1588), fos. 7v-8r: 'Le bruit de tous lesdits instruments sert de signes et advertissments aux soldats, pour desloger, marcher, se retirer, et à la remontre de l'ennemy leur donne coeur, hardiesse et courage d'assaillir, et de se deffendre virilement et vigoureusement. Or pourroient les gens de guerre marcher confusément et sans ordre, cause qu'ils seroient en péril d'estre renversées et deffaicts, pourquoy nosdicts françois ont advisé de faire marcher les rencs et jougs des escouades avec certaines mesures ...'.
33. Ibid., fos. 8r, 9v-14r, 15v.
34. Ibid., fos. 9v, 18r. Arbeau told his interrogator Capriol that in battle the drums were to beat lighter strokes mixed with 'coups de battons, frappez rudement' to simulate arquebus shots, then a quadruple dance-rhythm continually as the troops closed up (fo. 17r).
35. Ibid., fo. 17v. It produced a 'son aïgue' (ibid.). Drums and fifes were clearly not considered alien to chivalric ceremonial: as early as 1446 René of Anjou had 'tambours et fifres ... à cheval', who appeared at the *pas d'armes* at Saumur (Vulson de la Colombière, *Le Théâtre d'Honneur* (Paris 1648), ii, p. 166); the account of an Arthurian *pas d'armes* at Sandricourt by Orléans Herald, held in 1493, mentions a large number of *tambours de Suisses* and other instruments which 'sounded incessantly' (ibid., i, p. 83). For mounted fifers and drummers in the early sixteenth century, see the woodcuts of Hans Burgkmair in *The Triumph of Maximilian* (1512), reproduced in Farmer, *Military Music*, pp. 14-15.
36. Arbeau, op. cit., fo. 18r. The flutes were thought to keep the Greeks 'cool and firm' in battle.

such as those of the French *vieilles bandes*, were derived from them.[37]

The Swiss mercenaries who were responsible for the rise of drum and fife bands in the armies of Northern Europe were apparently first seen in France in August 1465. According to Commynes, Jean, duke of Calabria, brought 500 with him when he joined the rebel magnates of the Public Weal outside Paris. They were responsible for the others who have since come, he wrote, 'because they conducted themselves very bravely in all places in which they found themselves'.[38] Olivier de la Marche corroborated this and explained that the Swiss had no fear of cavalry because they were grouped into units of three – pikeman, handgunner (culverineer) and crossbowman – so that each man might aid his comrades.[39] A tactical combination of pikes and missiles, with the pikemen forming a protective hedge for the shot, was a marked improvement upon the earlier and more primitive techniques of the Swiss. In the fourteenth century, the armies which routed the Habsburgs at Morgarten, Laupen and Sempach had been composed of levies from the cantonal militias, relying mainly on the halberd, or axe-headed pike, which was swung in close combat. During the fifteenth century the densely packed pike phalanx emerged, which enabled massed infantry to keep opponents at a distance and presented a body rather like a moving porcupine which was impenetrable to cavalry.[40] The Burgundian wars of 1474-7 stimulated demand for mercenaries among the enemies of Charles the Bold. Louis XI concluded the first of a long series of French recruiting agreements in 1474, and in the sixteenth century the Swiss *bandes* were a normal part of French armies.[41] The cantons became recruiting agents for foreign powers, supplying corps of mercenaries armed with cross-bows and handguns, as well as the pike, to those prepared to pay for them. The Swiss professionals brought a flexible, though not entirely reliable, infantry force to the battlefields of Europe. However, they also brought with them some

37. See Farmer, *Military Music*, pp. 15-16, 24 and the somewhat colourless comments on soldiers' songs in Contamine, *Guerre, Etat et Société*, p. 527, n. 218. For the sixteenth- and seventeenth-century developments, see H.G. Farmer, 'Sixteenth and seventeenth-century military marches', *Journal of the Society for Army Historical Research*, xxviii (1950), pp. 49-53; 'The martial fife', ibid., xxiii (1945), pp. 66-71. By the early seventeenth century English critics were claiming that the 'aire of a whistle' distracted soldiers on the march and did not improve their order ('The martial fife', p. 67). Evidence for military music of earlier periods is slight, but cf. *infra* Appendix, for a poetic evocation of contemporary trumpet calls and drum rhythms. The fifteenth-century Burgundian composers Dufay (d.1474) and Busnois (d.1492) had already set Masses to the song *L'homme armé* which contain onomatopoeic effects of a similar, if less directly imitative kind.

38. Commynes, op. cit., i, p. 48, where Jean of Calabria's troops are described as 'presque la fleur de nostre ost'.

39. La Marche, *Mémoires*, iii, pp. 22-3. The unit of three was also adopted in the Burgundian military ordonnance of 1473: see BL, Add. MS 36,619, fos. 31v-32r; *supra*, p. 124.

40. Oman, op. cit., ii, pp. 73-115.

41. See V.G. Kiernan, 'Foreign mercenaries and absolute monarchy', *Crisis in Europe, 1550-1660*, ed. T.H. Aston (London 1965), pp. 125-6; Contamine, *Guerre, Etat et Société*, pp. 308-10. For the treaty with the cantons, see B. de Mandrot, *Les relations de Charles VII et de Louis XI avec les cantons suisses* (Zurich 1881), p. 123.

of the problems which had resulted in paid foreign service becoming such a dominant feature of the Swiss state.

The pool of surplus manpower from which mercenaries were drawn was partly the result of unemployment and internal disorder. Without foreign service the men who became mercenaries turned to brigandage and private war in the cantons.[42] By the 1470s migrant companies of mercenary *déracinés*, German *Landsknechte* as well as the Swiss, served wherever pay and booty were most easily and regularly to be found.[43] Both these incentives were closely bound up with more general questions of discipline. For the mercenaries, war was a purely business proposition, and the raising of a sufficiently large source of liquid capital with which to pay them became an overriding concern to contemporary governments.[44] In 1512, there were 18,470 *Landsknechte* in the French royal army, and by 1515 their number had swelled to 23,000.[45] The feeling in the sixteenth century that there was a paramount need for a native French infantry reflects the mercenaries' lack of discipline and its accompanying social problems. Francis I's military ordinance of 1534 was to a great extent the product of their behaviour.[46] Thus the rise of an infantry drawn wholly from the king's subjects was one consequence of the inability of governments to restrain and discipline their hired men. In the shorter term, however, various measures were adopted in an attempt to control looting and pillage.

The Swiss *bandes* were governed by laws about booty framed at Sempach in 1393 until the enormous quantities of plunder taken during the Burgundian wars required new ordinances to be drawn up.[47] The Masters of the Booty were responsible for the collective gains of the army and for sharing out the proceeds. After the battle of Morat (1476) they were required to register and describe the booty after collecting it together at a central point.[48] Although they were also given powers of confiscation to prevent disputes between rival claimants, the difficulties of enforcement proved insuperable.[49] Charles the Bold, in his

42. See L.E. Roulet, 'Le duc René à la bataille de Morat', *Anniversaire de la bataille de Nancy*, pp. 415-28.

43. Oman, op. cit., ii, pp. 104-15 over-emphasises the exclusiveness of the Swiss reliance on the pike. For their role in the Italian wars, see C. Kohler, *Les Suisses dans les Guerres d'Italie, 1506-12* (Paris 1897), esp. pp. 125-6; for changes in Swiss military organisation, see R. Sablonier, 'Etat et structures militaires dans la Confédération autour des années 1480', *Anniversaire de la bataille de Nancy*, pp. 429-47.

44. Howard, op. cit., p. 22. The changing nature of the French infantry forces, native and foreign, is stressed in Michaud, art. cit., pp. 35-6.

45. See A. Spont, 'Marignan et l'organisation militaire sous François I', *Revue des questions historiques*, n.s., xxii (1899), pp. 61, 65.

46. Ibid., p. 76.

47. See Deuchler, op. cit., pp. 40-1.

48. Vaughan, *Charles the Bold*, pp. 394-5; Deuchler, op. cit., pp. 29-31, 37-40. The Swiss seized the entire contents of the ducal treasury, chancery and chapel in Charles' camp at Grandson in March 1476.

49. Deuchler, op. cit., p. 40. There was a black market in booty, in which Masters of the Booty were often implicated, and much concealment of loot.

ordinances of 1473, attempted to combat the problem in his own forces by stipulating the fixed share of booty to be taken from each company by the captain, squadron commander and the head of each *chambre*, if (and only if) they had been present when the booty was won,[50] a regulation that may have owed something to Swiss practice. The collective sharing-out of booty to keep the troops together was also forcefully advocated by writers such as Bérard Stuart, lord of Aubigny.[51] He stressed the importance of allowing the whole army to seek booty after a pitched battle, so that companies would not dissolve into independent groups running after prisoners and loot. The threat posed by such attractions is underlined by Charles the Bold's orders in August 1466 for the arrest of all those men-at-arms who had deserted from his army on the pretext of guarding booty from the town of Dinant.[52]

Contemporary literature also reflects the problem: in *Le Petit Jean de Saintré* the king of France, haranguing his troops before the great battle with the Turks, exhorts them to be 'friends and brothers without jealousies, without disputes and without tumults, because companies are often broken in this way and sent to perdition and dishonour'.[53] *Le Jouvencel* emphasises the authority of captains over booty taken by their men.[54] A common soldier needed the captain's licence to ransom a prisoner, and it was the commander's task to 'mettre la compaignie à buttin' ('put the company to [seek] booty') at specific times, in the hope of preventing indiscriminate pillaging.[55] Nevertheless, shares were manifestly unequal in the army's hierarchy and the incentive for the common soldier to conceal booty and to kill (rather than take prisoners) grew as the prospect of lucrative plunder diminished.[56]

This process was inevitably hastened by the fact that the Swiss and German mercenaries did not as a rule take prisoners. These were encumbrances in the search for booty and, in any case, the opportunities for the capture and pursuit of prisoners became rarer as men fought in larger groups, kept apart by gunfire over longer ranges. A Swiss battle-order of 18 March 1476, for example, laid down that all Burgundians and their allies were to be killed, and no prisoners were taken at the battle of Morat that followed.[57] Their aim was victory, not honour, and the privileges of rank were simply ignored. Nobles were butchered along with the common soldiery, and anyone who recruited Swiss and German mercenaries for his army in effect indicated a readiness to wage war of a crueller

---

50. BL, Add. MS 36,619, fo. 26v.

51. Contamine, *Guerre, État et Société*, p. 525; 'The war literature of the late Middle Ages', *War, Literature and Politics*, pp. 116-18, 120; *Traité sur l'art de Guerre de Bérault Stuart*, ed. E. de Comminges (The Hague 1976), pp. 8-9. (The treatise was written in 1508.)

52. ADN, B. 18,842, nos. 29, 431-2.

53. *Le Petit Jean de Saintré*, p. 202.

54. *Le Jouvencel*, ii, pp. 215-16.

55. Ibid., ii, p. 216; cf. Cruickshank, *Elizabeth's Army*, pp. 301, art. 40, p. 302, art. 47.

56. La Marche seems to attribute his survival at Nancy to his capture by 'gentilz compaignons de guerre': *Mémoires*, iii, pp. 241-2. Had he fallen into the hands of the common soldiery his fate would have been very different.

57. See Vaughan, *Charles the Bold*, p. 393.

and more brutal kind. Thus between 1494 and 1512 the French with their Swiss troops, the Germans and the Spanish, brought to the Italian states a war of 'unheard-of cruelty and callousness'.[58] The habitual employment of such methods could only erode the chivalric ethic and increase the horror of war.

Ironically, the nature of the wars waged by the Burgundian nobility in the late fourteenth and fifteenth century reinforced this tendency.[59] *Guerre mortelle* (in which no lives were spared) had of course always been an option in medieval warfare. In so far as the *oriflamme* was unfurled (although in fact prisoners were taken), it was waged by the French at Crécy and Poitiers, and Henry V adopted its conventions when prisoners were killed at Agincourt.[60] The more savage episodes of the Wars of the Roses and the War of the Public Weal (1465) were merely strict applications of the laws of treason.[61] The ruthlessness of war to the death had remained exceptional, reserved for such rebels and traitors. Against the Flemings in 1383-4 and the towns of Ghent and Liège from 1451 to 1468, however, the Burgundian nobility fought against rebellious peasant and *bourgeois* enemies whom they regarded with profound contempt.[62] Their experiences in these punitive wars affected the later conduct of their wars with the Swiss, where quarter was not given, nor prisoners taken. According to the laws of arms, the Burgundians were fully justified in withholding from the rebels the privileges of ransom and humane treatment which these laws theoretically bestowed upon enemies.[63] At the same time their enemies' ruthless disregard for the conventions in which their own pitilessness was founded produced a climate in which the chivalric code seemed meaningless. In Philip the Good's war with Ghent of 1451-3, for example, Burgundian ideas of chivalry were conspicuous only by their absence.

A revolt which had begun with the imposition of a salt-tax on Ghent in January 1447 'exploded into a prolonged and disastrous war which involved the ducal government and the entire Burgundian state in a veritable struggle for survival'.[64] This was war to the death in which neither side expected quarter. Against the Ghenters were ranged the nobilities of Flanders, Brabant, Hainault, Holland, Zeeland and the duchy and *comté* of Burgundy. The receiver-general's account of 1453 recorded the response of the families of Ravenstein, Rolin, Lalaing, Croy, Boorsele, Hallewin, Berchem, Thoisy,

58. Hale, 'War and public opinion in Renaissance Italy', p. 112.
59. Contamine, *Guerre, Etat et Société*, pp. 196-8.
60. Keegan, op. cit., pp. 107-12; Keen, *The Laws of War*, pp. 104-6.
61. See Gachard, op. cit., p. 142 for Margaret of York's description of the death of Warwick at Barnet (April 1471); cf. *supra*, no. 38.
62. Gaier, 'La cavalerie lourde dans l'Europe occidentale', p. 390, where he points to an 'esprit de caste' among the nobility. See also P. Thomas, 'Mépris des nobles a l'égard de leurs inférieurs au xve siecle', *Revue du Nord*, xix (1933), pp. 230-2, for examples of Burgundian *hauteur* and contempt (although directed towards servants, rather than *bourgeois* or peasants); cf. *supra*, pp. 23-4.
63. Keen, *The Laws of War*, pp. 104-6; for a practical application of such notions, see e.g. M.G.A. Vale, 'Sir John Fastolf's "report" of 1435', *Nottingham Medieval Studies*, xvii (1973), pp. 78-84.
64. Vaughan, *Philip the Good*, pp. 304, 306-7.

Plate 27. Military camp or *laager* from the *Mittelalterliches Hausbuch*, fos 53r-v. Photo: Bodleian Library.

Luxembourg, Commines, Lannoy, L'Isle-Adam and many other 'noble vassals and loyal subjects' to the ducal summons to reduce the Ghenters to obedience.[65] They were paid a total of 87,870 francs for their services in garrisons and the field.[66] Olivier de la Marche best expresses the typical Burgundian attitude towards the Ghenters, one of extreme contempt and desire for revenge which turned to fury on the death of Cornelius, bastard of Burgundy, at Rupelmonde in June 1452. He died, wrote La Marche, at the hand of a 'cursed and disloyal villain' whose pike thrust felled him as he rode *chevalereusement* against the enemy.[67] His death was avenged by putting 3,000 Ghenters to the sword, and the duke's intense grief at the loss of his eldest illegitimate son made the Ghent war all the more pitiless.[68]

Describing the war, La Marche's prose fills with images redolent of the slaughter-yard. At Oudenaarde in April 1452, the Ghenters fled before the onrush of Burgundian cavalry and the 'archers and infantry cut their throats like sheep'.[69] As 'sheep fleeing before wolves' they were cut down by the cavalry, while the foot 'took and killed them without mercy and without ransom'.[70] The hard winter of 1452-3 was memorable for an increasingly cruel war. In March 1453 ducal letters were sent to the *bailli* of Hainault, ordering him to 'execute and put to death all the prisoners from Ghent'; Jacques de Lalaing was similarly ordered to put to death any prisoners held by himself or his men.[71] These ducal commands perhaps suggest an unwillingness among some nobles to be deprived of potentially valuable captives, but they were bound to submit to the rigours of *guerre mortelle*.

Like the subsequent conflict with Liège which both Philip the Good and Charles the Bold waged between 1465 and 1468, the Ghent war was one of 'fire and blood'. Jean Aubrion, *bourgeois* of Metz, thought that Philip's last expedition against Liège in 1467 was the most terrible campaign the duke had ever waged,[72] and the techniques of destruction learnt in the Ghent war were to serve his son well. The punitive nature of these brutal campaigns was amply demonstrated by the burning of villages, demolition of belfries (so that neighbouring settlements could not warn each other of a Burgundian

65. Ibid., p. 317 for the ducal summons of 31 March 1452. For a payment to Pélérin, pursuivant of the marshal of Burgundy, for taking letters from the 'mareschal es pays de Bourgogne a pluseurs nobles feaulx et subgez de monditseigneur ... pour eulx mettre sus et venir en ladicte armee' (20 January-3 March 1453), see ADN, B. 2012, fo. 159r.

66. ADN, B. 2012, fos. 425r-446v (2 December 1453). Quittances for these payments are found in B. 2011.

67. La Marche, *Mémoires*, ii, p. 270.

68. Ibid., ii, p. 271.

69. Ibid., ii, p. 244.

70. Ibid., ii, p. 244.

71. ADN B. 2012, fos. 198r, 205r; La Marche, *Mémoires*, ii, p. 298.

72. *Journal de Jehan Aubrion, Bourgeois de Metz, 1465-1512*, ed. L. Larchey (Metz 1857), p. 27. The *échevins* of Antwerp were ordered to write to their troops, who had been sent to Brabant, so that 'sans dissimulacion ilz feissent guerre aux Liegois de feu et de sang comme faire devroient et que autres faisoient' (16 October 1465): ADN, B. 2058, fo. 111v.

approach), mass hangings of the rebels, confiscation of their property and the imposition of blockades.[73] The rebels retaliated by burning down ducal wind- and water-mills, ransoming, killing and hanging peasants, and by causing a complete suspension of the machinery of justice in the *pays du Waas* during the winter of 1452-3.[74] The duke's intransigent harshness was mitigated only by the issue of pardons to the indigent poor.[75]

In his description of the Ghent war La Marche sees nothing incongruous in the juxtaposition of the increasingly impersonal and savage aspects of warfare which were undermining the ethic of chivalry and its formal and outward expressions. He writes with pride of the fine sight afforded by the Dutch nobles who joined the duke's army in June 1452, properly resplendent in their coats-of-arms, with banners and pennons displayed.[76] After a decisive battle at Gavere, the duke's banners, still unfurled, were carried with great ceremony from the field, while the victorious Burgundian army withdrew to its billets: '... it was a fine sight to see the brilliance of the ... arms worn by the noble princes and lords who bore banners.'[77] The banners of the Ghent trades were seized in retribution and borne before the duke by the archers of his guard after the proclamation of a final peace in June 1453.[78] The emphasis upon the chivalric signs of war is undeniable and highlights one aspect of the almost paradoxical developments that were taking place at this period. Similarly, despite the disincentives, the practice of ransoming continued well into the seventeenth century;[79] despite the loss of automatic prerogative, nobles were still found in positions of military command, and despite changes in technique and strategy the single combat – and, above all, the associated notion of individual honour – retained its importance.

73. See La Marche, *Mémoires*, ii, p. 289; ADN, B. 2012, fos. 154r, 182r (confiscations); fos. 182v, 204r (blockade); B. 4103, fo. 165v for payment to Geoffroi de Thoisy on 22 June 1453 for a 'galiotte armee de xc hommes et dune barge et ung brigandin armez chascun de xxx hommes estans soubz lui en armes sur mer audit maniere pour lempeschement des vivres qui peuent venir et arriver a ceulx de Gand, ennemis, rebelles et desobeissans ...'

74. ADN, B. 4103, fo. 148r (payment for 'deux molins a vent nouvellement assiz es ville et terroir de Chaestinghes ou lieu de Cazewele et ou polre de Namur ou monditseigneur avoit deux semblables molins qui es darrenieres guerres furent brulez par les rebelles de Gand'); f. 150r (three mills destroyed at Hulst); fos. 151v-152v, 155r (mills destroyed at Pettghien, Eekloo and Caprique); fos. 169r-v (remissions of *ferme* because the Ghenters had 'ars et brule les meilleures places ... et prins, pendu et ranconne la plusgrant partie des manans et habitans ...' and because 'len a aussi cesse de faire loy ... par quoy il na peu joyr desdictes fermes' in the lordship of Zeezele (2 October 1453): similar remissions on fos. 170r-171r. B. 17,674 contains a file of letters on the Ghent war, including remissions of rent and *ferme* so that houses, mills and churches might be repaired (1452-3).

75. La Marche, *Mémoires*, ii, pp. 273-4.

76. Ibid., ii, pp. 271-2.

77. Ibid., ii, p. 325.

78. Ibid., ii, pp. 331-2.

79. See Viscount Dillon, 'Ransom', *Archaeological Journal*, lxi (1904), pp. 102-19, where the last reference is to the ransom of Henry Verney in 1644. The subject warrants further investigation. Cf. also Barnie, op. cit., pp. 71-2, 95-6; Cruickshank, *Army Royal*, p. 123.

It is clear that, for all the changes in military practice, there were some elements of continuity. The contrast between highly disciplined permanent armies with a central organisation and the feudal units which preceded them has been exaggerated, and the picture distorted by over-stating the individualistic nature of the earlier forces.[80] Even the striking concern with discipline was not unprecedented, for this issue had taxed the Templars.[81] It has been argued that in fifteenth-century England, for example, the knight '... passed away with the French Wars and the Wars of the Roses, driven from his monopoly of the military profession by the yeoman archer, gunpowder, and the professional captain'.[82] Yet none of these were recent innovations,[83] and if the knight really passed away in the fifteenth century, he spent a long time a-dying. The evidence suggests rather, that the nobility in England and on the Continent adapted themselves to changes dictated by new techniques of war and military organisation.

In the sixteenth century the nobles of Francis I did not consider an infantry command dishonourable. Fourquevaux commanded 1,000 Gascon infantry in Italy in 1537; in 1548 he led the legion of infantry that brutally suppressed a rebellion over the levying of the *gabelle* in Guyenne and Languedoc.[84] Even Bayart, the flower of French chivalry, served for part of his career as an infantry captain,[85] and lesser men felt no compunction at leading troops armed with pike and arquebus rather than lance. Young nobles would sometimes serve as pikemen or archers in the sixteenth century before rising to positions of authority. The great Gaspard de Saulx-Tavannes, (who was to become one of the commanders in the French Wars of Religion), for example, began his career as an archer in Galiot de Genouillac's company during the Italian wars.[86] As captains of infantry, both French and English nobles trailed pikes,[87] while artillery, the newest arm of all, also had its noble officers. The service of Galiot de Genouillac, lord of Assier, as *grand maître de l'artillerie* between 1512 and 1546 set the seal of aristocratic approval on the art of gunnery.[88]

The emergence of the professional soldier, who might also be – and often was – a nobleman, as an ideal literary type reflects this trend,[89] but, again, this was not in itself new: nobles had become career soldiers, and professional soldiers

80. Howard, op. cit., p. 56; Keegan, op. cit., p. 321; Gaier, 'La cavalerie lourde en Europe occidentale', p. 395.

81. *La Règle du Temple*, nos. 159, 164, 574. (This text of the statutes dates from *c*.1257-65.)

82. Ferguson, op. cit., p. 3.

83. See Hewitt, op. cit., pp. 63-73, 94-5.

84. *Instructions*, p. xci.

85. See Contamine, *Guerre, Etat et Société*, p. 550; *L'histoire du gentil seigneur de Bayart*, pp. 138-40, 432.

86. Vindry, op. cit., i, p. 402; Wiley, op. cit., p. 167; *Instructions*, fo. 22v.

87. See Cruickshank, *Elizabeth's Army*, pp. 54-7; Michaud, art. cit., pp. 35-6.

88. Vindry, op. cit., i, p. 401; ii, p. 205.

89. For the idea that the profession of arms might ennoble any man, see *Le Jouvencel*, ii, p. 80.

ennobled, for a very long time.[90] The precise relationship between the representations of knightly conduct in literary forms (such as the romance) and actuality is open to debate, but some of the changes in fifteenth-century redactions of, for example, parts of the Arthurian cycle nevertheless reflect shifts of emphasis in contemporary values.[91] Brunor le Noir, *le chevalier sans peur* (who first appears in the *Palamède*)[92] introduces a combination of qualities which constitute a thoroughly professional and single-minded idea. A fifteenth-century description stresses his whole-hearted commitment to the profession of arms: he did not sing, dance, or hunt and disliked music; 'All his heart was in arms', he was no great lover and he was never afraid.[93] This picture would have fitted Charles the Bold admirably, and a parallel with Bayart has also been suggested.[94]

The ascetic and dedicated hero was of course no newcomer to the chivalric world (although the religious element is much less emphatic in the character of Brunor le Noir). In the mid-fourteenth century Geoffroi de Charny's writings were simply an expression of those stern martial qualities which had been revered by St Bernard and Ramon Lull long before the establishment of standing armies.[95] *Le Jouvencel* took up the theme, translated it into mid-fifteenth-century terms, and inveighed against *chevaliers de chambre* and the softness of contemporary knighthood.[96] Chivalry had had its moral reformers almost from the time of its inception,[97] and it was natural that fifteenth-century writers should try to remould traditional themes to accord with contemporary preoccupations and tastes. As we have seen, the didactic writings of Ghillebert de Lannoy, Diego de Valera, and their associates at the court of Burgundy expressed essentially similar concerns, but drew upon classical, rather than Arthurian *exempla*.[98]

This shift was obviously partly influenced by the contemporary humanist interest in classical texts. Their study of the Stoic philosophers made Roman military practices all the more relevant and appealing. Without their superhuman self-restraint and their willingness to submit to the authority of their generals, Roman armies would never have conquered the world. It was no coincidence that the classical triad among the Nine Worthies – Hector of Troy, Alexander the Great and Julius Caesar – should have attracted so much

90. For English evidence, see K.B. McFarlane, *The Nobility of Later Medieval England* (Oxford 1973), pp. 19-40.

91. Doutrepont, op. cit., pp. 1-27, 501-22.

92. Pickford, op. cit., p. 217.

93. Ibid., pp. 217-20, cit. BN, MS fr. 112.

94. Ibid., pp. 119-20. See *L'Histoire du gentil seigneur de Bayart*, ch. lxvi, pp. 423-8: 'Des vertues qui estoient au bon chevalier sans paour et sans reprouche.'

95. Cf. *supra*, pp. 31, 65-6.

96. *Le Jouvencel*, ii, p. 114. Blaise de Monluc adopted a similar tone in his *Commentaires*, op. cit., iii, p. 519.

97. See Keen, 'Huizinga, Kilgour and the Decline of Chivalry', pp. 3-7.

98. *Supra*, pp. 14-30.

attention in the fifteenth century.[99] To their ranks was added a fourteenth-century career soldier, Bertrand du Guesclin, and representations of the *Neuf Preux* as captains of the *ordonnance* riding in processions akin to Roman triumphs merely demonstrated the extent of this identification with classical models.[100] In his *Art of War* Machiavelli was building on well-laid foundations when he urged princes to adopt the military practices of the Ancients.[101]

Fourquevaux was among those who followed closely in Machiavelli's footsteps. His *Instructions sur le faict de la Guerre*, composed in 1549,[102] demonstrate three main concerns: the knowledge that a captain-general needed to wage war *à son honneur*, military discipline, and how the king of France might raise sufficient troops, in particular infantry, from within his own kingdom. His treatise is, like most of its kind, descriptive and prescriptive. If he has any ideal type, it is that of the Roman general who ensures the total and unswerving obedience of his troops by means of the strictest disciplinary code. Fourquevaux had already advocated the creation of a French native infantry, just as Machiavelli had urged the Florentine republic to reform its moribund militia.[103] It was perhaps inevitable that when seven new infantry corps were created in France in 1534 they should have been entitled 'legions' on what was thought to be the Roman model.[104] Fourquevaux's obsession with discipline, however, was not essentially different from that of Jean de Bueil in *Le Jouvencel*. He too was disturbed by the unnerving ease with which armies – particularly bands of infantry – could dissolve into packs of brigands and pillagers. The office of *prévôt des maréchaux* had been evolved to police the army by the late fourteenth century, and the savagely brutal code of punishment advocated by Fourquevaux was a logical extension of the *prévôt*'s jurisdiction over military crimes.[105] His argument was that if soldiers would not instinctively obey the ordinances of war, then they were to be coerced into doing so by exemplary punishments.

Fourquevaux's concentration upon infantry reflects both the course of his own career and the contemporary importance of that particular arm. The innovations brought by firearms and pike-formations ensured that the unit, not the individual, played the dominant part in battle.[106] When great masses of infantry moved over the battle-field in the first pike-and-musket encounters, the

99. See R.L. Wyss, 'Die neun Helden', *Zeitschrift für schweizerische Archaeologie und Kunstgeschichte*, xvii (1957), pp. 73-106.

100. Ibid., pp. 75-6, 82-4. BN, MS fr. 4985 has woodcuts showing the Nine Worthies in procession, dating from *c.* 1460-70: see P.A. Lemoisne, *Les Xylographies du xive et du xve siècle* (Paris-Brussels 1930), ii, fig. lxxiv, pp. 29-30.

101. N. Machiavelli, *The Art of War*, trans. P. Whitehorne (London 1905), pp. 63-5.

102. For Fourquevaux's career, see *Instructions*, pp. cx-cxvi.

103. Ibid., pp. xxxii-xxxiii; S. Anglo, *Machiavelli: a Dissection* (London 1969), pp. 21-2.

104. *Instructions*, pp. xxxiii, lix-lx.

105. See *Le Jouvencel*, ii, p. 194; J.H. Mitchell, *The Court of the Connétable* (New Haven 1947), pp. 9, 10. For the activities of the *prévôts* in the 1460s see H. Stein, *Charles de France* (Paris 1909), pp. 524-41, 578, 609.

106. *Supra*, pp. 151-6; Cruickshank, *Army Royal*, pp. 123-4.

knightly *mêlée* was a thing of the past. As their traditional knightly rôle in warfare diminished, and their position as potentially independent military forces within the kingdom dwindled, a compensatory interest in the procedures of single combat seems to have developed among the nobility.[107] Already in the fifteenth century there is evidence for a revival of interest in the *duel judiciaire*, or trial by battle, in the large number of copies of the *Gaige de Bataille* (setting out the necessary procedures) in newly-commissioned manuscript miscellanies.[108] The following century saw the rise of the duel fought over very widely-defined points of honour. This was not – unlike the *duel judiciaire* – a judicial process with a fixed place within a legal framework, but there was a clear link between the two forms, for the accusation and counter-accusation which had instigated the process of trial by battle were essentially responses to insults to the protagonists' honour.

In sixteenth-century France and Italy, the duel over points of honour, theoretically licensed by the state, was perhaps the most popular and enduring legacy of the laws of chivalry. In 1586, Hardouin de la Jaille published his *Formulaire des gaiges du bataille* which drew upon later medieval precedents and became a standard manual for duelling among the French nobility.[109] Any man who claimed nobility had a duty to avenge an insult to his honour, for to 'leave an affront unavenged is to leave one's honour in a state of desecration and is therefore equivalent to cowardice'.[110] The state was forced to tolerate the nobility's predilection for settling disputes by means of the duel. All noblemen carried swords, and used them to defend or avenge their honour. In 1547 and 1549, duels licensed by Francis I and Henri II took place over issues of outraged honour,[111] although they corresponded closely to private feuds, for both parties might be accompanied by kinsmen and armed retinues as well as their 'seconds'. Although opposed by his lawyers, such combats were supported by Francis I as the acknowledged fount of chivalry. In political terms the crown could not afford to alienate a bellicose nobility by withholding what they considered an inalienable right to submit disputes to the test of skill-at-arms in single combat. If warfare offered fewer opportunities of testing that skill, the duel at least provided a substitute.

The continued practice of some facets of the chivalric code was also reflected in the issue of formal challenges and defiance, sometimes stipulating a time and

107. See H. Morel, 'La fin du duel judiciaire en France et la naissance du point d'honneur', *Revue historique du droit français et étranger*, ive série, xlii (1964), pp. 590, 608; cf. *infra*, n. 121.

108. See e.g. Viscount Dillon, 'On a MS collection of ordinances of chivalry', pp. 29-70. There is much similar material in B.L. Lansdowne MS. 285 (Sir John Paston's Great Book); see also Anglo, 'Financial and Heraldic Records of the English Tournament', Appendix B. La Marche's treatise on trial by battle, which argues so forcibly against judicial combats, may reflect such a revival: see Prost, op. cit., pp. 1-54.

109. Prost, op. cit., pp. 135-91. See also F.R. Bryson, *The Point of Honour in Sixteenth-century Italy: an aspect of the life of the gentleman* (New York 1935), pp. 55-6.

110. Pitt-Rivers, art. cit., p. 26.

111. Morel, art. cit., pp. 580-2.

a place for combat, before a war or battle was commenced.[111a] Opportunities for single combat were sometimes artificially created in the course of war. Jean de Haynin described how after an initial exchange of gunfire, the two sides waited at Montlhéry, to see if any individuals wished to engage in feats of arms before the battle was joined.[112] In September 1475 Charles the Bold waited with his household troops 'in fine array' in the fields outside Neuss, 'to see if anyone came'.[113] At Ravenna, in 1512, both sides agreed to withhold their artillery until the cavalry had vied with each other.[114] 'Chivalrous' deeds in war were now increasingly confined to the interstices between combat (as at Barletta in 1503),[115] but there is no evidence that such occasions were treated with anything other than the highest seriousness.

The great interest in single combat and the use of the duel were products of a reaction to the impersonality and mechanisation of war, above all to the gun and the insistent beat of the drum,[116] which seems to have been responsible for an increased emphasis on personal bravery and individual achievement, and which continued to centre above all on the pursuit of honour. This notion was too deeply engrained in the minds of kings and captains to be eradicated by changing circumstances, and the élitist nature of the chivalric ethic also ensured that it was to some extent self-perpetuating.[117] In 1510 Jean de Margny, a minor Picard noble, composed a poem called *L'Adventurier*, recounting his exploits and expressing the ideas about war which were common among his class:

> Sur tout, honneur garder je doy,
> Et pour riens perdre ne le doy.
> Aucuneffois, pour le cercer,
> Ay mis ma vie en grant danger.
> Souvent voy, pour querir honneur,
> Que lon se met a deshonneur.
> Pour ce, devons nous bien penser
> Comment honneur pourrons trouver.[118]

111a. See *Lettres de Rois, Reines et autres Personnages des Cours de France et d'Angleterre*, ed. J.J. Champollion-Figeac (Paris 1839-47), iii, pp. 632-3 (formal challenge of René II of Lorraine to Charles the Bold, 1475); Dynter, op. cit., ii, pp. 632-3 (challenge of 1397); J. Glénisson, 'Notes d'histoire militaire, quelques lettres de défi du xive siècle', *BEC*, cvii (1947-8), pp. 235-54 (Italian examples). See ADN, B. 18,842, no. 29,389 for a formal letter of defiance sent to the bishop of Liège by ten Burgundian nobles as 'vassaux, serviteurs ou subges' of Philip the Good. They undertook to defend his 'corps, honneur, heritage et subges', and declared 'vous signiffions et pour noz honneurs faisons savoir attendre lesdictes deffiances par vous ainsi faictes, que nous ... vous greverons, ensemble voz pays et subges, alies et bien veuillans et vous ferons toute guerre de nous et des nostre.'
112. Haynin, op. cit., i, p. 58.
113. Vaughan, *Charles the Bold*, p. 323.
114. See Gaier, 'La cavalerie lourde en Europe occidentale', p. 394.
115. *Homo Ludens*, p. 110; Mallett, op. cit., p. 258.
116. Cf. *The Waning of the Middle Ages*, p. 97.
117. See La Marche in Prost, op. cit., pp. 43, 53.
118. J. de Margny, *L'Aventurier*, ed. J.R. de Chevannes (Paris 1938), p. 14, ll. 128-35.

Above all, I must defend [my] honour and never lose it for any reason whatsoever. I have sometimes put my life in great danger when seeking it. I often see that to gain honour one must submit to dishonour. So we should think very hard how we can best find honour.

The parallels with *Le Livre Messire Geoffroi de Charny*, written over one hundred and fifty years earlier, are remarkable:

Tu veulx a une chose traire
Qui est trop dure a parfaire
Ce est honneur.
Faire te convient grant labeur
Avant que tu as honneur
De ce mestier ...[119]

You want to reach something which is all too difficult to achieve: that is, honour. You will have to work very hard before you can gain honour from this profession [of arms] ...

The potency of the concept of honour, however illusory and unattainable, was clearly undiminished at the end of the Middle Ages. Charny and Margny – like Jacques de Lalaing, Jean de Bueil, Bayart or Blaise de Monluc – would have accepted that the acquisition of honour was paid for by the privations of a military calling. These hardships probably increased, especially for the privileged classes, in the course of the sixteenth century, and at the same time the notion of honour became a more intensely personal attribute and possession. Even in defeat it might remain intact: 'Tout est perdu fors l'honneur,' wrote Francis I after his defeat and capture at Pavia (1525), a view endorsed by Bayart's biographer.[120] Preference for an honourable death in battle or duel was a logical extension of the supremacy of the law of honour.[121] Ghillebert de Lannoy would not have felt himself a total stranger in this sixteenth-century company.[122]

Eager to secure the allegiance of the nobility and the knightly classes, princes and monarchs found it expedient to graft the powerful concept of personal honour on to that of loyalty to the sovereign. Writing on the use of banners, Olivier de la Marche demonstrated how the insignia borne in battle was no longer thought of as a sign of feudal independence, but inextricably bound up with obedience to a sovereign:

Every banneret displays the banner of his arms to show that he serves in person,

119. BR, MS 11,124-6, fo. 9r.
120. D. Seward, *Prince of the Renaissance* (London 1974), p. 136; *L'histoire du gentil seigneur de Bayart*, p. 427; cf. Monluc, op. cit., ii, pp. 517-18. See plate 26.
121. Bryson, op. cit., p. 13; Gaier, 'L'opinion des chefs de guerre', pp. 728-9.
122. Cf. *supra*, pp. 15-16.

and that he wishes to keep his faith and loyalty, desiring to live and die with his prince ...[123]

With a similar emphasis, the Burgundian military ordinances of 1473 had translated chivalric ideas into terms easily understood by a standing army. The captains were to,

> ... do the duty ... to which the love and obedience that they owe towards my said lord should principally move them, and for the exaltation of his house, and also *their own honour and renown, which is found in the way in which my said lord can, by means of their good service, achieve the defeat of his enemies* ...[124]

In this way chivalrous sentiments of honour and renown were welded on to concepts of service to the prince to produce what have been called 'national chivalries', pledged to serve him in war, diplomacy and administration.[125] The supra-national order of knighthood no longer exerted the magnetism that had drawn together men of many allegiances in a crusade against the infidel. Instead chivalry was exploited to focus purely secular allegiance upon the person of the prince. This was achieved primarily through the orders of chivalry, the dubbing of knights by the prince himself in war, and by an appeal to the nobility as servants of the state.[126]

Until national identities were more fully developed, appeals to mere patriotism were likely to fall upon barren soil, but the association between personal honour and service to a prince's just cause in war might exercise a profounder influence upon noble motivation. The lessons of a plethora of treatises upon the just war were reflected in Jean de Margny's assertion:

> Pour son prince on se doit armer
> Et combattre, se il est mestier.
> Chascun a son seigneur tenu
> Est a le servir en tout lieu ...[127]

123. 'Et pour ce desploie chascun banneret la bannière de ses armes, pour monstrer qu'il sert en personne, et qu'il veult tenir sa foy et loyaulté, comme il vault vivre et morir avec son prince et que faire le doit.' See e.g. La Marche, *Mémoires*, iv, p. 60, and Prost, op. cit., pp. 17, 53 for the regulation that confined duelling to the noble classes.

124. BL, Add. MS 36,619, fo. 32v (the italics are mine): '... faire leur devoir ... a quoy ... les doit principalement mouvoir lamour et obeissance quilz doivent avoir envers monditseigneur et a lexaltacion de sa maison et aussy leur propre honneur et renommee qui consistent en ce que monditseigneur par le moyen de leur bon service puist parvenir au reboutement de ses ennemiz ...'.

125. *Supra*, p. 9. This was merely an expression of the traditional rôle of the nobility adapted to fifteenth- and early sixteenth-century conditions. For the continuity of military and administrative service by the English nobility, see McFarlane, op. cit., pp. 161-2; see also Wright, art. cit., pp. 30-1.

126. *Supra*, pp. 9-10, 62; Keen, 'Chivalry, nobility and the man-at-arms', p. 45. The dubbing of knights had become a royal prerogative by 1520 in France: see Wiley, op. cit., p. 170. See also P. Contamine, 'Points de vue sur la chevalerie en France à la fin du Moyen Age', *Francia*, iv (1976), pp. 255-85 for knighthood in later medieval France.

127. Margny, op. cit., p. 91, ll.7-10.

One should take up arms for one's prince and fight if need be; everyone is bound to serve his lord anywhere ...

Such sentiments, rooted in loyalty to the sovereign, had been firmly planted in the cult of chivalry by the end of the fifteenth century. Although some nobles, like the Constable Bourbon, might still indulge in rebellious and treasonable acts,[128] they found themselves in an increasingly small minority. The fifteenth-century Italian *condottiere* has been described as 'gradually transformed into a relatively faithful, increasingly aristocratic and highly professional captain'.[129] Much the same could be said for the captains of the French standing army, although there was no social transformation within their ranks. Francis I's nobles saw themselves fulfilling their traditional rôle as they accompanied the king in battle and commanded his troops. Jannequin's brilliant musical evocation of the different sounds, moods and rhythms of the battle of Marignano (1515), written in 1528, encapsulates this relationship:

Nobles, sautez dans les arçons,
Frappez dedans, la lance au poing,
Donnez dedans, frappez dedans.
Soyez armé;
Chacun s'assaisonne.
La fleur de lys, fleur de haut prix
Le roi Francois
Y est en personne.[130]

Nobles, leap into the saddle, strike from within, lance in hand ... be ready; every man prepares himself [for battle]; The *fleur de lys*, that precious flower, king François is here in person.

The classes concerned to perpetuate chivalric ideals now stood in a much more tractable and dependent relationship to the monarchy than was formerly the case. The wars of the fifteenth century had taught chastening lessons. Of the English nobility after Bosworth the late K.B. McFarlane wrote, 'most men ... preferred almost anything to another civil war. So violently had their fathers untuned that string that the discord could still be heard well into the sixteenth century'.[131] A similar conclusion might be hazarded for the French nobility after 1494. Fourquevaux was convinced that there would be no danger of revolt in raising infantry legions in France. He pointed out that the nobles who had previously 'emboldened the people to rise' were dead, and their duchies and lordships annexed to the crown.[132] (He was thinking of the reversion of the

128. See A. Lebey, *Le Connétable de Bourbon, 1490-1527* (Paris 1904), pp. 150-67, 205-53.
129. Mallett, op. cit., p. 257.
130. See Spont, art. cit., pp. 76-7; *infra*, Appendix.
131. K.B. McFarlane, 'The Wars of the Roses', *Proceedings of the British Academy*, 1 (1964), p. 119.
132. *Instructions*, fo. 9v.

lands of Burgundy, Brittany, Bourbon and Alençon to the royal demesne.)[133] In these changed circumstances there could be no Public Weal, no revolt of the Constable. Fourquevaux was writing before 1562, of course, and took no account of religious issues, but his view probably accurately reflects the opinion of the French nobility during the Italian campaigns. By the end of the fifteenth century the fundamental principle of allegiance to a sovereign prince had been acknowledged, if not yet universally realised.

In *Le Jouvencel* Jean de Bueil had been adamant about the primacy of the public good. In his story, two nobles had been challenged to single combat, and the Jouvencel ordered them not to accept the challenge.[134] The reasons he gave are interesting:

> First, those who do so wish to seize another's possession. That is to say, his honour, to attribute to themselves a vainglory which is of little worth; and, by doing this, he serves no-one, he risks his body to deprive another of life or honour, which brings him little profit; while this occupies him, he neglects ... war, his king's service, and the public weal; and no-one should risk his body except in meritorious works ... these displeasing [feats of] arms that you wish to perform are not founded upon any just quarrel, neither [do they] serve God nor man, and the jealousy which is found there is worthless, for it stems from pride or some other vice ...[135]

In the event, the Jouvencel did permit the contestants to fight their single combat. It provided an excellent pretext for a lengthy discourse on the techniques of combat on horse and foot. Yet the grounds for his initial reaction were clear: such challenges were wasteful in terms of men and money, which should both be conserved for the common good.[136] For Jean de Bueil chivalry was a means to promote loyalty and obedience among the nobility, not to dissipate their energies on frivolous challenges. It was an austere view, but not without precedent.[137] (Interestingly, the Jouvencel had no objection to

133. See R.J. Knecht, *Francis I and Absolute Monarchy* (Historical Association, London 1969), p. 25.
134. *Le Jouvencel*, ii, pp. 99-111. (See also Kilgour, op. cit., pp. 330-1 for a rather different interpretation of this episode.)
135. *Le Jouvencel*, ii, pp. 100, 104: 'Premierement, ceulx qui le font vueillent oster le bien d'autruy, c'est assavoir leur honneur, pour se attribuer une vaine gloire qui est de petite valleur; et, en ce faisant, il ne fait service à nul, il despent son argent, il expose son corps pour tollir la vie ou l'onneur à cellui à qui il a à besongnier, qui lui vient à petit de profit; tant qu'il est occupé ad ce faire, il laisse à exploicter la guerre, le service de son Roy et de la chose publique; et nul ne doit exposer son corps, sinon en oeuvres meritoires ... Mais ces armes desplaisantes que voullez faire ne sont fondées sur aucune bonne querelle ne pour faire service à Dieu ne à homme, et l'envie que on y a ne vault riens; car elle procede d'orgueil ou d'autre vice ...'
136. Kilgour, op. cit., pp. 330-1.
137. See *supra*, pp. 65-8. The prohibitions of tournaments in the thirteenth and fourteenth centuries owed something to this view: see Denholm-Young, *The Country Gentry*, pp. 141-2; R. Harvey, *Moriz von Craûn and the Chivalric World* (Oxford 1961), pp. 113-28. The very fact that de Bueil argues against jousts and single combats of this kind may lend some support to the view that the tournament was still dangerous and could effectively simulate the conditions of war.

presiding over a judicial duel in a subsequent chapter, where the issue was one of ransom, and hence of honour.)[138]

His antipathy towards jousts and foot combats, however, was out of step with his contemporaries and immediate successors. The remarkable efflorescence of French chivalry associated with Bayart, Louis XII and Francis I demonstrated the enduring popularity of the chivalrous life-style adopted by Jacques de Lalaing and his contemporaries at the court of Burgundy.[139] Henry VIII was not unaffected by its attractions.[140] Such outward extravagances might be harnessed for the ends of the monarchy and a certain parallelism between service in war and tournament perpetuated, ensuring that the cult of chivalry still had a part to play in the nation-states of sixteenth-century Europe.

The continuation of some aspects of the cult of chivalry was also fostered by the character of warfare during the period from about 1450 to about 1530. Although, as we have seen, the final phases of the Hundred Years War consisted largely of siege-warfare, these years inaugurated a period of an exceptional number of pitched battles in European warfare. Philip the Good's well-documented desire for a decisive and exemplary victory in the field 'to avenge himself and cut short his war',[141] which led to the battle of Gavere and the defeat of the Ghenters in 1453 may have been influenced by financial exigencies. Certainly this course of action was to become increasingly common,[142] and Louis XI was out of tune with his contemporaries in this, as in other respects, when he tried to avoid battle at Montlhéry in July 1465.[143] From Caravaggio (1448) and Castillon (1453) to Marignano (1515) and Pavia (1525), the fight in the open field enabled noble leaders to apply the conventions of later medieval war to the full and exploit their cavalry forces on an unprecedented scale.[144] This development doubtless owed something to Charles the Bold's failure to make good use of artillery in battle, retarding for a little its devastating effects upon cavalry in the field. In the sixteenth century the cumulative effects of rapid changes in firearms effectively ruined the battle as a chivalric exercise: 'the balance which at the end of the fifteenth century seemed to have been tilted strongly in favour of the offensive, with the mobile pike phalanx, the great guns to blast away opposition, and the revival of cavalry shock action, had within twenty five years been sharply reversed by the development of fire power on the battlefield.'[145] War reverted to its earlier pattern of siege and counter-siege, and technological ingenuity was now applied on a massive scale to the science of

138. *Le Jouvencel*, ii, pp. 109-12.
139. See Keen, 'Huizinga, Kilgour and the decline of chivalry', pp. 12, 15.
140. Anglo, *Great Tournament Roll*, chs. 1, 3; *Spectacle, Pageantry and Early Tudor Politics*, ch.3.
141. La Marche, *Mémoires*, ii, p. 314; Vaughan, *Philip the Good*, pp. 328-31.
142. See Mallett, op. cit., p. 177.
143. See J. Dufournet, *La Destruction des Mythes dans les Mémoires de Philippe de Commynes* (Geneva 1966), pp. 62-4; *Rozier des Guerres*, pp. 64-5.
144. Oman, op. cit., ii, pp. 428-9; *The Art of War in the Sixteenth Century* (London 1937), pp. 35-6.
145. Howard, op. cit., p. 34.

Plate 28. A troop of cavalry on the march, from the *Mittelalterliches Hausbuch*, fo. 52r. Photo: Bodleian Library.

Plate 29. Military ordinances of Charles the Bold, duke of Burgundy (1473). This illuminated frontispiece shows the duke appointing his captains on New Year's Day. Each of them receives a bâton of office and a book containing the ordinances. London, British Library, Add. MS 36,619, fo. Ir.

ballistics and fortification.[146] This period (from *c.* 1450 to *c.*1530) was thus to some extent an aberration, where conditions of war offered an unusually fertile soil for some expressions of the cult of chivalry. After 1534 the battle went into rapid decline and with it chivalry entered a phase of decay from which it never recovered.[147]

Yet the cult of honour which replaced it had much in common with chivalric ideas. The behaviour of Renaissance nobles in war was informed by an emphasis upon personal honour and loyalty to a sovereign prince, motivated by the fear of dishonour. Ideas of honour and virtue, propounded in the didactic literature produced at the court of Burgundy during the fifteenth century, re-emerged in the humanistic writings of the Renaissance. Blaise de Monluc was drawing upon fifteenth-century precedents when he told his readers:

> Do not disdain, all those of you who wish to follow the practice of arms, to spend an hour or so acquainting yourselves with me in this book instead of reading *Amadis de Gaule* or *Lancelot du Lac*. You will begin to understand yourselves and train yourselves to be soldiers and captains, because one must first know how to obey in order to know how to command. This is not intended for sleek courtiers or men with soft hands, nor for those who love repose; but for those who, by the ways of virtue and at the risk of their lives, wish to render their name immortal just as I hope that I have, despite envy, made that of Monluc.[148]

His didactic tone, and his low opinion of Arthurian and other romances, carries with it two significant implications: first, that the reading of romances was still popular enough among his readers for him to urge them to spend their time otherwise; secondly, his emphasis upon obedience, and on the pursuit of virtue and renown, was quite consonant with the ideas which had circulated a century earlier at the Valois court of Burgundy. The Renaissance cult of honour and fame owed more than it was prepared to acknowledge to the medieval cult of chivalry.

146. Hale, 'The early development of the bastion', pp. 466-94.

147. Howard, op. cit., p. 34 for the 'virtual disappearance of major battles from European warfare during the century which separates the battle of Mühlberg in 1534 from that at Breitenfeld in 1631.'

148. Monluc, *Commentaires*, iii, p. 519: 'Ne desdaignés, vous qui désirés suivre le train des armes, au lieu de lire des Amadis ou Lancellots, d'employer quelque heure à me cognoistre dedans ce livre: vous apprendrés à vous cognoistre vous-mesmes, et à vous former pour estre soldats et cappitaines, car il fault sçavoir obéir pour sçavoir après bien commander. Cecy n'est pas pour les courtisans ou gens qui ont les mains polies, ny pour ceux qui ayment le repos; c'est pour ceux qui, par le chemin de la vertu, aux despens de leur vie, veulent éterniser leur nom comme, en despit de l'envie, j'espère que j'auray faict celuy de Monluc.'

Appendix

Clément Jannequin's 'La Guerre' (La Bataille de Marignan)

Jannequin wrote this choral piece to the following text in 1528, commemorating the battle which took place in 1515. See A. Spont, 'Marignan et l'organisation militaire sous François I', *Revue des Questions Historiques, nouv. sér.*, xxii (1899), 76-7.

Ecoutez tous, gentils Gallois,
La victoire du roi François,
Du noble roi François;
Et ores si bien ecoutez
Des coups ruez de tous costez.
Fifres soufflez, frappez tambours
Faites vos tours!
Aventuriers, bons compaignons,
Ensemble croisez vos tromblons;
Gardez soutien (?) gentils Gascons,
Nobles, sautez dans les arçons,
Frappez dedans, la lance au poing,
Donnez dedans, frappez dedans.
Soyez armé!
Chacun s'assaisonne:
Alarme! Alarme!
La fleur de lys, fleur de haut prix,
Le roi François
Y est en personne.
Sonnez, trompettes et clairons,
Pour resjouir les compaignons.

Fa fa li la li la lan fan,
Ta ri ra ri ra ri ra,
Boute-selle!
Gens d'armes à cheval,
Tôt à l'étendard.
Fa fa li la li la lan fan
Bruez, tournez,
Sonnez trompettes et clairons,

Gros courteaux et faucons,
Pour resjouir les compaignons.
Vom, pati, patoc, vom, vom.
Ta ri ra ri ra ri ra,
La, la, la
France!
Courage!
Donnez les horions
Chipe chope pa ta pan.
A mort! Avant!
Courage prenez.
Trique traque
Zin zin zin.
Ils sont perdus, ils sont confus
Victoire!
France! France!
Tout é ferlore, by Gotte!
Descampir!
Victoire au noble roi François!

War and Politics, 1400-1525:
a chronological summary

The following outline is intended as a summary guide to the major political and military events between 1400 and 1525 in England, France and Burgundy. Although no study of the political, social or economic history of the fifteenth and early sixteenth centuries can afford to neglect the far-reaching effects of continuous warfare upon the attitudes and behaviour of every social group, this in no way aims to provide such an account, and inevitably involves a measure of over-simplification.[1] However, a brief chronology may supply the reader unfamiliar with the details of the period with a broader framework in which to set the issues and events discussed in this book.

The Burgundian lands – that is, the duchy and *comté* of Burgundy and those lands inherited and otherwise acquired by the Valois dukes in the Low Countries – formed a highly significant political and strategic complex of power and wealth.[2] Their allegiance was sought by both France and England, who had been embroiled in the Hundred Years War since 1337. After the succession of the first Valois duke of Burgundy, Philip the Bold (1364-1404) to the *comté* of Flanders in 1384, Burgundy entered the conflict in an increasingly independent capacity. The influence of the dukes should not be underestimated: without Burgundian aid, Henry V would never have achieved his successes, nor would the Lancastrian dual monarchy of England and France have been established. The subsequent defection of Philip the Good of Burgundy (1419-1467) to Charles VII of France (1422-1461) deprived the English war effort of a vital prop. Although Burgundy never in fact gave active support to the Valois cause, his treaty with the French at Arras in 1435 was perhaps the real turning-point in English fortunes, and the Burgundian *volte-face* encouraged others to desert the Lancastrian cause. Nevertheless, the rulers of England, France and Burgundy remained preoccupied with the war and its consequences until at least 1475, even though active hostilities had more or less ceased after the English loss of Guyenne in 1453. No peace treaty was ever made and the English claims were intermittently revived by both Yorkists and Tudors.

After the recovery of Normandy (1450) and Guyenne (1451-3) from the English, the great principalities of Burgundy (1477), Provence (1481) and

---

1. For recent general surveys of the period see G.A. Holmes, *Europe: Hierarchy and Revolt, 1320-1450* (London 1975) and J.R. Hale, *Renaissance Europe, 1480-1520* (London 1971).

2. The most recent general account of the Valois house of Burgundy and its lands is R. Vaughan, *Valois Burgundy* (London, 1975).

Brittany (1492) came to the French crown through a combination of conquest, marriage and reversion. A similar principle lay behind the series of campaigns undertaken from 1494 onwards in Italy to enforce the claims of Charles VIII (1483-98) to the kingdom of Naples and Sicily. For most of the fifteenth century the claims of the French house of Anjou had been represented by René of Anjou, and on his death (1480) they reverted to the crown of France. In many ways Charles VIII's invasion was the culmination of fifty years of unsuccessful Angevin attempts to recover their Italian inheritance from the Aragonese monarchy.

To the North of the Alps, Habsburg-Valois succeeded Plantagenet-Valois conflict as the primary focus of European politics. The Burgundian lands in the Low Countries became Habsburg domains when the Emperor Maximilian I married Mary, only daughter of Charles the Bold, the last Valois duke of Burgundy (1467-77). Mary died in 1482, and the division of the Burgundian lands between the Empire and Louis XI of France (1461-83) which resulted was an inevitable cause of continuing tension. The Low Countries included some of the richest areas of Northern Europe, but also some of the most turbulent. Since 1435 much Burgundian energy and revenue had been expended on the suppression of Flemish revolts, and the origins of later sixteenth-century struggles for the possession of the Low Countries may be sought in the aftermath of the Burgundian period. Alongside this legacy of strife, however, there was a highly developed courtly and chivalric culture, and just as the Valois dukes had succeeded to the cultural legacy of the counts of Flanders and Artois in 1384, so the Austrian and Spanish Habsburgs assimilated and perpetuated many aspects of Burgundian art, literature and chivalry.

The Habsburg-Valois wars did not leave England isolated and uninvolved. After the effective end of civil strife in 1487, traditional enmity towards France re-asserted itself and the Tudors tended to ally with the Empire. Henry VIII invaded France in 1513, anxious for a second Agincourt: he was disappointed, but English forces continued to be used in alliance with the Empire. England had no standing army, but the other major powers employed permanent forces as well as foreign mercenaries in their wars. In the fifteenth century standing armies had been created in many European states (among them France, Burgundy, Venice and Milan) and the need to control and finance them became a major concern for governments. It is possible that their very existence tended to perpetuate warfare. Certainly there is little evidence that war was any less endemic in 1525 than it had been in 1400. The so-called 'Italian Wars', begun by Charles VIII in 1494, were not concluded until 1559, and France was then precipitated into violent civil and religious strife. Her experience in the sixteenth century was not entirely unlike that of fifteenth-century England: in both countries foreign war gave way to internal conflict in which the noble and military class with whom this book is concerned played a crucial and decisive rôle.

The chronological tables which follow list the major political and military events in the history of England, France and Burgundy during this period and fall under three headings: the Hundred Years War; Franco-Burgundian relations; and French intervention in Italy.

Tables of Events

1. THE HUNDRED YEARS WAR, 1415-1475

1415   Henry V of England invades France and wins the battle of Agincourt (25 Oct.).

1417   Invasion and occupation of Normandy by Henry V.

1419   Assassination of John the Fearless, duke of Burgundy, by partisans of the Dauphin Charles and the house of Orléans at Montéreau (10 Sept.). His son Philip the Good succeeds him and allies with Henry V against the Dauphin.

1420   Treaty of Troyes (21 May): Philip the Good swears to recognise Henry V and his successors as kings of France.

1422   Death of Henry V (31 Aug.) and Charles VI (21 Oct.) Henry VI succeeds as king of England and France, opposed by the Dauphin (Charles VII). John, duke of Bedford, is created Regent of France for Henry VI.

1424   Defeat of Dauphinist forces at Verneuil (17 Aug.) completes the English conquest of Normandy.

1428-9   An Anglo-Burgundian force besieges Orléans.

1429   Relief of Orléans by a Dauphinist army including Jeanne d'Arc (8 May).

1430   The Burgundians capture Jeanne d'Arc at Compiègne (23 May).

1431   Jeanne d'Arc burnt at the stake at Rouen (30 May). Henry VI crowned king of France at Paris (16 Dec.).

1435   Death of John, duke of Bedford (15 Sept.) Philip the Good and Charles VII are reconciled by the Treaty of Arras (20 Sept.). End of the Anglo-Burgundian alliance.

1436   Siege of Calais by Philip the Good. His army is depleted by desertion by Flemish contingents and routed by Humfrey, duke of Gloucester.

1437   Charles VII enters Paris (12 Nov.).

1439   First *ordonnance* of Charles VII on military reforms (Nov.). The
          crown claims a monopoly over the raising of troops in France.

1442   Expedition of Charles VII to Guyenne (June-Oct.).

1444   Truce of Tours between England and France (20 May). Henry VI
          is betrothed to Charles' niece, Margaret of Anjou, daughter of René
          of Anjou (23 May). The Dauphin Louis (later Louis XI) commands
          an expedition to Alsace and Lorraine in an attempt to rid France of
          the undisciplined companies of *Ecorcheurs.*

1445   Henry VI marries Margaret of Anjou (Mar.). Issue of Charles VII's
          ordonnances creating a permanent force of *compagnies d'ordonnance* (9
          Jan. and 26 May).

1448   Le Mans surrenders to Charles VII (16 Mar.). Occupation of the
          comté of Maine by the French. Renewal of the Anglo-French truce
          until 1 Apr. 1450.

1449   Sack of Fougères by François de Suriennes (24 Mar.) breaking the
          Anglo-French truce. Charles VII declares war on the English (31
          July). The French invade Normandy (Sept.-Dec.).

1450   Charles VII defeats the English at Formigny (15 Apr.). Reduction
          of Normandy by the French, using effective siege guns. Cherbourg
          surrenders on 12 Aug. and the English leave Normandy.

1451   First reconquest of Guyenne by Charles VII.

1452   Gascon revolt against French rule. A raid by John Talbot, earl of
          Shrewsbury (Oct.) recovers Bordeaux for the English.

1453   Guyenne is finally reconquered by the French (June-Oct.). Battle of
          Castillon (17 July) followed by the fall of Bordeaux (20 Oct.).
          Calais alone remains in English hands.

1475   Edward IV invades France in league with Charles the Bold of
          Burgundy. The French pay him a pension to withdraw.

                     2.   FRANCE AND BURGUNDY, 1430-1483

1430   Foundation of the Order of the *Toison d'Or* by Philip the Good (10
          Jan.).

1435   Treaty of Arras (20 Sept.).

1440   Philip the Good is implicated in the conspiracy known as the Praguerie against Charles VII (Feb.). Burgundian 'neutrality' in the Hundred Years War is established and relations with France worsen.

1447   Imposition of a *gabelle* (salt tax) upon the city of Ghent by Philip the Good's government (Jan.).

1451   Popular rebellion breaks out at Ghent (Dec.).

1452   Declaration of war by Philip the Good against the Ghent rebels (31 Mar.). Charles VII attempts to undermine Philip's authority by negotiating with the Ghenters.

1453   Battle of Gavere. Philip the Good defeats the Ghenters (23 July).

1456   Philip the Good harbours the exiled Dauphin Louis and supports him against his father Charles VII.

1458-61 State of hostility between France and Burgundy in which open war is averted by Charles VII's death.

1461   Death of Charles VII (22 July). Louis XI succeeds to the throne of France in alliance with Burgundy.

1465   War of the Public Weal against Louis XI by Charles, count of Charolais (the future Charles the Bold of Burgundy) and the dukes of Bourbon and Brittany. Louis' army is forced to withdraw after the battle of Montlhéry (15 July). Paris is besieged by the rebel magnates, but a peace treaty is concluded at Conflans (Oct.).

1466   Burgundian campaigns against the city of Liège.

1467   Death of Philip the Good (15 June). Charles the Bold succeeds as duke of Burgundy.

1468   Destruction of Liège by Charles the Bold. He marries Margaret of York, sister of Edward IV of England, at Bruges (3 July). The Anglo-Burgundian alliance against France is formally renewed.

1470-1 Henry VI, with aid from France, is restored to the English throne. In exile, Edward IV stays with Louis de Bruges, lord of la Gruthuyse, at Bruges. An Anglo-Burgundian expedition to England recovers the throne for the house of York.

1471   Burgundian invasion of France, successfully resisted by Louis XI.

1475   Charles the Bold annexes Lorraine (Nov.).

1476   Military defeats of Charles the Bold at Grandson (2 Mar.) and

Morat (22 June) by René II, duke of Lorraine, with Swiss and other allies.

1477   Defeat and death of Charles the Bold at Nancy by René II and the Swiss (5 Jan.). Louis XI annexes the duchy of Burgundy. Marriage of Maximilian of Austria and Mary of Burgundy (19 Aug.).

1482   Death of Mary of Burgundy (27 Mar.). Treaty of Arras divides the Burgundian lands between France and the Empire.

1483   Death of Louis XI (30 Aug.). Charles VIII succeeds as king of France.

3. ITALIAN WARFARE AND THE FRENCH INVASIONS, 1442-1525

1442   Victory of Alfonso V, king of Aragon, over René, duke of Anjou, count of Provence, titular king of Naples and Sicily (2 June). Aragonese rule is established in the kingdom of Naples.

1446   Alliance of Charles VII of France and Filippo Maria Visconti of Milan (29 Dec.). French claims to the Milanese succession are made through Charles, duke of Orléans.

1447   French intervention on behalf of the house of Orléans at Genoa fails (Jan.-Feb.). Death of Filippo Maria Visconti. The war of Milanese succession begins.

1448   Francesco Sforza, captain-general of the Milanese army, defeats the Venetians at the battle of Caravaggio. René of Anjou founds the Order of the *Croissant* (11 Aug.).

1450   Francesco Sforza becomes duke of Milan (25 Feb.).

1453   René of Anjou attempts armed intervention in Italy, and leads an expedition against Venice and the Aragonese in alliance with Milan and Florence (June).

1454   Peace treaty is made at Lodi by the five major Italian powers, ending the war of Milanese succession (9 Apr.). Francesco Sforza's title recognised.

1458   Death of Alfonso V of Aragon and Naples. Ferrante I succeeds to the kingdom of Naples.

1459-63   War to recover the kingdom of Naples for René of Anjou is undertaken by his son Jean, duke of Calabria.

1466 Death of Francesco Sforza (8 Mar.). Galeazzo Sforza succeeds as duke of Milan.

1476 Death of Galeazzo Sforza. Gian Galeazzo Sforza succeeds (1476-94).

1480 Death of René of Anjou.

1481 Death of Charles of Anjou, count of Maine. Provence is annexed to the crown of France.

1494 Invasion of Italy by Charles VIII of France. Fall of Naples to the French.

4. MAJOR BATTLES OF THE ITALIAN WARS

1495 Battle of Fornovo (6 July). Italian forces fail to cut off Charles VIII's march northwards from Naples.

1503 Battle of Cerignola (8 Apr.). The French and their Swiss mercenaries defeated by the Spanish.

1509 Italian army routed by the French at Agnadello (14 May).

1512 Battle of Ravenna (11 Apr.). The French and their Italian allies defeat the Spanish.

1513 Battle of Novara (6 June). French defeated with heavy losses.

1515 Francis I's victory at Marignano regains Milan for the French (15 Sept.).

1522 Battle of Bicocca (27 Apr.). Spanish victory over the French and Swiss.

1525 Siege and battle of Pavia (21 Feb.). Francis I defeated and imprisoned at Madrid by the Emperor Charles V.

Tables of Armour

Table I: **Comparative weights of complete armour and equipment.**

(i)   *Armour for man and horse*

	c. 1450	*c.* 1480	1875[*]	1909[*]
Weight of man	140 lb	140 lb		
Weight of armour	163 lb	126 lb 2 oz		
Arms, clothing, saddlery, etc.	30 lb	30 lb		
Total weight	333 lb[1]	296 lb 2 oz[2]		
British Household Cavalry (total weight of equipment)			308 lb	246 lb
British Heavy Cavalry (total weight of equipment)			280 lb	246 lb
German Cuirassier				334 lb

(ii)   *Armour for man alone*

	c. 1450	*c.* 1480	1875[*]	1909[*]
	57 lb[3]	46 lb 14½ oz[4]		
British infantryman			52 lb	59 lb 11 oz

1. Paris, Musee de L'Armee, G.I., *c.* 1450—60.
2. London, Wallace Collection, A.21, *c.* 1475—85.
3. Glasgow, City Museum, Scott Collection, *c.* 1440—50.
4. London, Wallace Collection, A.20, composite, *c.* 1470—1520.
* Figures derived from C.J. Ffoulkes, *The Armourer and his Craft from the xith to the* xvith *century* (London 1912), p. 119.

Table II: Comparative weights of pieces of armour.

		c. 1390	c. 1450	c. 1470	c. 1490	c. 1510
(i)	*Helmets*					
	Bascinet	6 lb 4 oz[1]				
	Barbute	3 lb 13 oz[2]				
	Sallet		6 lb 10 oz[3] 7 lb[5]		7 lb 15 oz[4]	
	Armet		7 lb 7 oz[6]	9 lb 10 oz[7]		16 lb 10 oz[9]
	Helm (for joust)			22 lb 4 oz[8]		19 lb 11 oz[10]
(ii)	Breast and back plates			16 lb 9½ oz[11]		10 lb 15 oz[12] 23 lb 4 oz[13] (for joust)
(iii)	Arm and shoulder defences			17 lb 13 oz[14]		22 lb 9 oz[15] (for joust)
(iv)	Leg and thigh defences			14 lb 5 oz[16]		11 lb 5½ oz[17]

Key: W.C.L. Wallace Collection, London. T.L.A. Tower of London Armouries.

1. Milanese, c. 1390–1410 (W.C.L., A.69).
2. N. Italian (W.C.L., A.74).
3. Italian, c. 1450 (Athens, Ethnological Museum).
4. Innsbruck, c. 1485 (Churburg Castle, no.62).
5. Milanese, c. 1450–70 (W.C.L., A.78).
6. Italian, c. 1450 (W.C.L., A.151).
7. Italian, c. 1450–80 (Athens, Ethnological Museum).
8. English (?), c. 1470 (T.L.A. IV/411).
9. English, c. 1515 (W.C.L., A.186).
10. German, c. 1500–20 (W.C.L., A.23).
11. S. German, c. 1475–85 (W.C.L., A.21).
12. German, c. 1500–20 (W.C.L., A.22).
13. German, c. 1500–20 (W.C.L., A.23).
14. S. German, c. 1475–85 (W.C.L., A.21).
15. German, c. 1500–20 (W.C.L., A.23).
16. S. German, c. 1475–85 (W.C.L., A.21).
17. German, c. 1510 (W.C.L., A.22).

Table III: Metallurgical analysis and strength of armour.

1. *Metallurgical composition* [1]

Sample	Carbon %
A Italian armour (wrought iron), *c.* 1400	0.10
B German armour (wrought iron with carburised surfaces), *c.* 1500	0.16
C Italian armour (wrought iron, carburised and quenched), *c.* 1480	0.23
D Italian armour (steel), *c.* 1490	0.47
E German armour (steel), *c.* 1520	0.62

1. Compiled from G.W. Henger, 'The metallography and chemical analysis of iron-base samples dating from antiquity to modern times', *Bulletin of the Historical Metallurgy Group,* iv (1970), p. 47.

2. *Strength of armour* [2]
   Properties of armour with 0.2% carbon content (as sample C above)

Mode of working	Tensile strength (=maximum load sustained in simple tension)	Elongation (=deformation required to produce fracture)
Cold worked (hammered)	44 tons per square inch	12%
Quenched	51 tons per square inch	14%
Slow cooled	30 tons per square inch	35%
Cold worked and then carburised	30 tons per square inch	35% [3]

2. Compiled from P. Jones, 'The Target', in R. Hardy, *Longbow: a Social and Military History* (Cambridge 1976), p. 204.
3. Based on the examination of an armour plate of *c.* 1520 in the Tower of London Armouries in A.R. Williams, 'Metallographic examination of sixteenth-century armour', *Bulletin of the Historical Metallurgy Group,* vi (1972), p. 17. The tensile strength of this sample is equivalent to that of 'typical mild steel' (p. 17).

Bibliography

1. PRIMARY SOURCES

i. Manuscript sources

BRUSSELS, Bibliothèque Royale
MSS 10238, 10976, 11047, 11124-6, 11205, 21551-69, II.1156, II.6288, II.7057

LILLE, Archives Départementales du Nord
MSS B.1933, 2010-12, 2055-8, 2068, 3417, 4065, 4089, 4103, 17668, 17674, 17698, 17700, 17707, 17721, 18842-3

LILLE, Archives Municipales (Archives Anciennes)
MSS 16.174, 16.194

LONDON, British Library
Additional Charter 4066
Additional MSS 15,469, 36,619
Harleian MS 4374-5
Landsdowne MS 285

LONDON, Public Record Office
C.61/127
E.101/189/12, 191/5, 191/7, 192/9, 193/15
E.101/404/6
E.101/650
E.364/84

OXFORD, Bodleian Library
MS Ashmole 1132
MS Ashmole 764
MS Rawlinson C.399

PARIS, Bibliothèque de l'Arsenal
MSS 33, 940, 2695

PARIS, Bibliothèque Nationale
MSS *français* 191, 387, 1216, 1278, 1280, 1957, 4736, 4985, 5867, 9087, 2692-3, 20492, 21809, 22297, 25204-5, 26092

MSS *français, nouvelles acquisitions* 10017
MSS *français, pièces originales* 1478, no.20, 3051, no.67943
MSS Clairambault 1241, 1309
MS Duchesne 108

VALENCIENNES, Bibliothèque Municipale
MS 776

VIENNA, Archiv des Ordens vom Goldenen Vliesse
Registers I, 2 (microfilm)

YORK, Borthwick Institute of Historical Research
Archbishops' Registers 10,20
Probate Register 1
Cause Papers G.290

ii. Printed sources

Analectes historiques, ed. M. Gachard (Brussels 1856).
Arbeau, Jean Thoinot *dit, Orchésographie* (Langres 1588).
Archives Historiques de la Gironde (Bordeaux 1859-1932, 58 vols).
Archives Municipales de Bordeaux, ed. H. Barckhausen, 5 vols, (Bordeaux 1867-90).
Banners, Standards & Badges from a Tudor MS in the College of Arms, ed. Lord Howard de Walden (London 1934).
Basin, Thomas, *Histoire de Charles VII*, ed. C. Samaran, 2 vols (Paris, 1933, 1944).
Bouchet, Jean, *Le Panégyric du Chevallier sans Reproche* (Paris 1527).
Bueil, Jean de, *Le Jouvencel*, ed. C. Favre & L. Lecestre, 2 vols (*SHF*, Paris, 1887-9).
Castiglione, Baldassare, *The Book of the Courtier*, tr. Sir Thomas Hoby (London 1974).
Charny, Geoffroi de, *Le Livre de Chevalerie* in Froissart, Jean, *Oeuvres*, ed. Kervyn de Lettenhove, 29 vols (Brussels 1870-7), i, part 2, pp. 463-533.
Chartier, Jean, *Chronique de Charles VII*, ed. Vallet de Viriville, 2 vols (Paris 1858).
— *Histoire de Charles VII*, ed. D. Godefroy (Paris 1661).
Chastellain, Georges, *Oeuvres*, ed. Kervyn de Lettenhove, 8 vols (Brussels 1863-6).
Choix de pièces inédites relatives au règne de Charles VI, ed. L. Douet d'Arcq, 2 vols (Paris 1863-4).
La Chronique du bon duc Loys de Bourbon, ed. A.M. Chazaud (*SHF*, Paris 1876).
Clercq, Jacques du, *Mémoires*, ed. F.A.T. de Reiffenberg, 2 vols (Brussels 1835).
A Collection of all the Wills ... of the Kings and Queens of England, ed. J. Nichols (London 1780).
A Collection of Ordinances and Regulations for the Government of the Royal Household (Society of Antiquaries, London 1790).

Commynes, Philippe de, *Mémoires*, ed. J. Calmette & G. Durville, 2 vols (Paris 1924).

'Compte du trésorier de la ville de Bordeaux pour 1442 (février-août)' *Bulletin philologique et historique*, 1961 (1963).

The Controversy between Sir Richard Scrope and Sir Robert Grosvenor, ed. N.H. Nicolas, 2 vols (London 1832).

Dynter, Edmond de, *Chronique des ducs de Brabant*, ed. P. de Ram, 3 vols (Brussels, 1854-7).

Escouchy, Mathieu d', *Chronique*, ed. G. du Fresne de Beaucourt, 3 vols (*SHF*, Paris 1863-4).

An Exhibition of Armour of Kings and Captains from the National Collections of Austria (Tower of London, London 1949).

Exposition des primitifs flamands et d'art ancien: Bruges, Ière section: Tableaux, ed. W.H.J. Weale (Bruges 1902).

Fourquevaux, Raymond de Beccarie de Pavie, sire de, *The 'Instructions sur le faict de la guerre'*, ed. G. Dickinson, (London 1954).

Fragmenta Sepulchralia, ed. M.H. Bloxam (Oxford 1840-50).

Haynin, Jean sire de, *Mémoires, 1465-77*, ed. D.D. Brouwers (Liège 1905-6).

The Heralds' Exhibition Catalogue, 1934, (London 1934, repr. 1970).

Hill, G.F. & Pollard, G., *Renaissance Medals from the Samuel H. Kress Collection* (London 1967).

L'Histoire du gentil seigneur de Bayart composée par le loyal serviteur, ed. M.J. Roman (*SHF*, Paris 1878).

Journal de Jehan Aubrion, Bourgeois de Metz, 1465-1512, ed. Lorédan Larchey (Metz 1857).

Knyghthode and Bataile, ed. R. Dyboski & Z.M. Arend (EETS, London 1935).

La Marche, Olivier de, *Mémoires*, ed. H. Beaune & J. d'Arbaumont, 4 vols (*SHF*, Paris, 1883-8).

— 'Le Livre de l'Advis de Gaige de Bataille' in *Traités du Duel Judiciaire: relations de Pas d'Armes et Tournois*, ed. B. Prost (Paris 1872).

Lannoy, Ghillebert de, *Oeuvres*, ed. C. Potvin, (Louvain 1878).

La Salle, Antoine de, *Le Petit Jehan de Saintré*, ed. J. Misrahi, C. Knudson (Geneva 1967).

Le Baker de Swynbroke, G., *Chronicon*, ed. E.M. Thompson, 2 vols (Oxford 1889).

Le Bouvier, Gilles, *Chronique* in *Histoire de Charles VII*, ed. D. Godefroy (Paris 1661).

— *Armorial de France*, ed. Vallet de Viriville (Paris 1866).

Lefèvre de St-Rémy, Jean, *Chronique*, ed. F. Morand (*SHF*, Paris 1876-81).

Leseur, Guillaume, *Histoire de Gaston IV, comte de Foix*, ed. H. Courteault, 2 vols (*SHF*, Paris 1893).

Letters and Papers illustrative of the Wars of the English in France during the reign of Henry VI, ed. J. Stevenson, 2 vols (RS, London 1861-4).

Lettres des Rois, Reines et autres Personnages des Cours de France et d'Angleterre, ed. J.J. Champollion-Figeac, 2 vols (Paris 1839-47).

Livre des Tournois – Traité de la Forme et Devis d'un Tournoi par le Roi René d'Anjou, ed. E. Pognon (Paris 1946).

Lull, Raimon, *The Book of the Ordre of Chyvalry*, tr. W. Caxton, ed. A.T.P. Byles (EETS, o.s., clxviii, London 1926).

N. Machiavelli, *The Art of War*, tr. P. Whitehorne, (London 1905).

Margny, Jean de, *L'Aventurier*, ed. J.R. de Chevannes (Paris 1938).

Mittelalterliches Hausbuch, ed. A. Essenwein (Frankfurt-am-Main 1887).

Monluc, Blaise seigneur de, *Commentaires*, ed. A. de Ruble, 3 vols (*SHF*, Paris, 1864-67).

Monstrelet, Enguerrand de, *Chroniques*, ed. J.A. Buchon, 12 vols (Paris 1826-7).

Montfaucon, B. de, *Monumens de la Monarchie françoise*, 3 vols (Paris 1731).

Oeuvres Complètes du Roi René, ed. H. de Quatrebarbes, 3 vols (Angers 1846).

Ordonnances des roys de France de la troisième race, 22 vols (Paris 1723-1846).

Parties inédites de l'oeuvre de Sicille, héraut d'Alphonse V, roi d'Aragon, ed. P. Roland (Mons 1867).

Pisan, Christine de, The *Livre de la Paix*, ed. C.C. Willard (The Hague 1958).

— The *Book of Fayttes of Armes and of Chyvalrye*, tr. W. Caxton, ed. A.T.P. Byles (EETS, os., clxxxix, London 1932, repr. 1937).

Queene Elizabethes Acadamy. A Boke of Precedence, ed. F.J. Furnival (EETS, London 1869).

La Règle du Temple, ed. H. de Curzon (*SHF*, Paris 1866).

'Rôles de l'armée rassemblée … par Gaston Phoebus, comte de Foix en 1376', ed. P. Raymond, *AHG*, xii (1870), pp. 133-71.

Le Rozier des Guerres, ed. A. d'Espagnet (Paris 1616).

Sallust, *The War with Catiline*, tr. J.C. Rolfe (London 1931).

Die Schweizerischen Bilderchroniken, ed. J. Zemp (Zurich 1897).

Testamenta Vetusta, ed. N.H. Nicolas, 2 vols (London 1836).

Traictié de la forme et devis dung tournoy par le Roi René, in F.H. Cripps-Day, *A History of the Tournament in England and France* (London 1918).

Traité sur l'art de guerre de Bérault Stuart, ed. E. de Comminges (The Hague 1976).

Traités du Duel Judiciaire: relations de Pas d'Armes et Tournois, ed. B. Prost (Paris 1872).

Vulson de la Colombière, Marc, *Le Vray Theâtre d'Honneur et de Chevalerie*, 2 vols (Paris 1648).

Upton, Nicholas, *De Studio Militari*, ed. F.P. Barnard (Oxford 1931).

A Visitation of the North of England, c. 1480-1500, ed. P. Hunter Blair, *Surtees Society*, cxliv (1930).

Le Voyage d'Outremer de Bertrandon de la Broquière, ed. C. Schefer (Paris, 1892).

Wallace Collection Catalogues. European Arms and Armour, ed. J.H. Mann (London 1962).

Wavrin, Jean de, *Recueil des cronicques*, 5 vols (RS, London 1864-91).

2. SECONDARY SOURCES

Adam-Even, P., 'Les fonctions militaires des hérauts d'armes', *Archives Héraldiques Suisses*, lxxi, (1957), pp. 2-33.

Allmand, C.T. (ed.), *War, Literature and Politics in the Late Middle Ages* (Liverpool 1976).

Anglo, Sidney, *The Great Tournament Roll of Westminster* (Oxford 1968).

— 'Anglo-Burgundian feats of arms: Smithfield, June 1467', *Guildhall Miscellany*, ii (1965), pp. 271-83.

— *Spectacle, Pageantry and Early Tudor Politics* (Oxford 1969).

— *Machiavelli: a Dissection* (London 1969).

— 'Financial and heraldic records of the English tournament', *Journal of the Society of Archivists*, ii (1960-4), pp. 183-95.

Armstrong, C.A.J., 'La Toison d'Or et la loi des armes', *PCEEBM*, v (1963), pp. 71-7.

— 'Had the Burgundian government a policy for the nobility?', *Britain and the Netherlands*, ed. J.S. Bromley & E.H. Kossman, ii (1962), pp. 9-32.

— 'The language question in the Low Countries', *Europe in the Late Middle Ages*, ed. J.R. Hale, J.R.L. Highfield & B. Smalley (London 1965), pp. 386-409.

— 'Sir John Fastolf & the law of arms', *War, Literature & Politics in the Late Middle Ages*, ed. C.T. Allmand (Liverpool 1976), pp. 45-56.

Armstrong, C.A.J., 'The court of Burgundy', *Courts of Europe, 1400-1700*, ed. A.G. Dickens (London 1977), pp. 55-75.

Ashmole, E., *The Institution, Laws and Ceremonies of the Order of the Garter* (London 1672).

Aston, Margaret, *The Fifteenth Century: the Prospect of Europe* (London 1968).

Baines, A. (ed.), *Musical Instruments through the Ages* (Harmondsworth 1961).

F. Bardon, *Diane de Poitiers et le Mythe de Diane* (Paris 1963).

Barnard, F.P., *Edward IV's French Expedition of 1475. The Leaders and their Badges* (London 1925).

Barnie, J., *War in Medieval Society: Social Values & the Hundred Years War 1337-99* (London 1974).

Baron, Hans, *The Crisis of the Early Italian Renaissance* (Princeton 1966).

Barroux, M., *Les Fêtes Royales de St-Denis en mai 1389* (Paris 1936).

Bartier, J., *Légistes et Gens de Finance au xve siècle. Les Conseillers des ducs de Bourgogne Philippe le Bon et Charles le Téméraire* (Brussels 1955).

Beaucourt, G. du Fresne de, *Histoire de Charles VII*, 6 vols. (Paris 1881-91).

Beltz, G.F., *Memorials of the most noble Order of the Garter* (London 1841).

Benson, L.D., *Malory's Morte Darthur* (Cambridge, Mass. 1976).

Berenson, B., *Italian Painters of the Renaissance. 2. Florentine and Central Italian Schools* (London 1968).

Blair, Claude, *European Armour* (London 1958).

Boinet, A., 'Un bibliophile du xve siècle: le grand Bâtard de Bourgogne', *BEC*, lxvii (1906), pp. 255-69.

Bossuat, A., 'Les prisonniers de guerre au xve siècle: la rançon de Guillaume de Chateauvillain', *AB*, xxiii (1951), 7-35.

— *Perrinet Gressart et François de Suriennes, agents d'Angleterre* (Paris 1936).

Bossuat, A., 'Le rétablissement de la paix sociale sous le règne de Charles VII', *MA*, lx (1954), pp. 137-62.

Bossuat, A., 'Le Parlement de Paris pendant l'occupation anglaise', *RH*, ccxxix (1963), pp. 19-40.

Bossuat, R., 'Vasque de Lucène, traducteur de Quinte-Curce, 1468', *BHR*, viii (1946), pp. 197-245.

— 'Jean Miélot, traducteur de Cicéron', *BEC* xcix (1938), pp. 108-33.

— 'Traductions françaises des "Commentaires" de César à la fin du xve siècle', *BHR*, iii (1943), pp. 253-73.

Boutruche, R., *La Crise d'une Société: Seigneurs et Paysans du Bordelais pendant la Guerre de Cent Ans* (2nd ed., Strasbourg 1963).

Brassart, F., *Le Pas du Perron Fée, tenu à Bruges en 1463* (Douai 1874).

Brusten, C., 'Les emblèmes de l'armée bourguignonne sous Charles le Téméraire', *Jahrbuch des Bernischen Historischen Museum in Bern*, xxxvii-xxxviii (1957-8), pp. 118-32.

— *L'Armée Bourguignonne de 1465 à 1468* (Brussels 1953).

Bryson, F.R., *The Point of Honour in Sixteenth-century Italy: an aspect of the life of the gentleman* (New York 1935).

Bullough, D.A., 'Games people played: drama and ritual as propaganda in medieval Europe', *TRHS*, 5th ser., xxiv (1974), pp. 92-122.

Buonaparte, Napoléon III & Favé, E., *Etudes sur le passé et l'avenir de l'artillerie*, 3 vols (Paris 1846-71).

Burne, A.H., *The Agincourt War* (London 1956).

Buttin, F., 'La Flèche des Juges de Camp', *Armes Anciennes*, iii (1954), pp. 57-64.

— 'La lance et l'arrêt de cuirasse', *Archaeologia*, xcix (1965), pp. 77-114.

Cazelles, R., *La Société Politique et la Crise de la Royauté sous Philippe de Valois* (Paris 1958).

Chomel, V., 'Chevaux de bataille et roncins en Dauphiné au xive siècle', *Cahiers d'Histoire*, vii (1962), pp. 5-23.

Cinq-Centième Anniversaire de la Bataille de Nancy (1477). Actes du colloque ... à l'Université de Nancy II (Nancy 1979).

Cipolla, C.M., *Guns and Sails* (London 1965).

Clephan, R.C., 'The ordnance of the fourteenth & fifteenth centuries', *Archaeological Journal*, lxviii (1911), pp. 49-64.

Cline, R., 'The influence of romances on the tournaments of the Middle Ages', *Speculum*, xx (1945), pp. 204-11.

Contamine, P., *Guerre, Etat et Société à la fin du Moyen Age: Etudes sur les Armées des Rois de France, 1337-1494* (Paris-The Hague 1972).

— 'The war literature of the late Middle Ages', *War, Literature & Politics in the Late Middle Ages*, ed. C.T. Allmand (Liverpool 1976), pp. 102-21.

— 'L'Artillerie Royale française à la vieille des guerres d'Italie', *Annales de Bretagne*, lxxi (1964), pp. 238-60.

— *Azincourt* (Paris 1964).

— 'Points de vue sur la chevalerie en France à la fin du Moyen Age', *Francia*, iv (1976), pp. 255-85.

— 'L'Histoire Militaire et l'Histoire de la Guerre dans la France médiévale depuis trente ans', *Actes du 100e Congrès National des Sociétés Savantes, Paris, 1975, Section de Philologie et d'Histoire jusqu'à 1610*, i (1977), pp. 71-93.

— 'Batailles, bannières, compagnies', *Actes du Colloque International de Cocherel* (Les Cahiers Vernonnais, 1964), pp. 19-32.

Contamine, P., (ed.), *La Noblesse au Moyen Age* (Paris 1976).

Coopland, G.W., 'Le Jouvencel (re-visited)', *Symposium*, v, I (1951), pp. 137-85.

Cripps-Day, F.H., *A History of the Tournament in England and France* (London 1918).

— 'On armour preserved in churches', *A Record of European Arms and Armour*, ed. G. Laking, v (London 1922), pp. 151-273.

— *Fragmentaria Armamentaria*, iv, *Church Armour (Addenda)* (Frome 1939).

Cruickshank, C.G., *Army Royal. Henry VIII's Invasion of France, 1513* (Oxford 1969).

— *Elizabeth's Army* (Oxford 1946).

Davies, M., *Rogier van der Weyden* (London 1972).

Delaissé, L.M.J. *A Century of Dutch Manuscript Illumination* (Berkeley & Los Angeles 1968).

— *La Miniature Flamande: le mécénat de Philippe le Bon* (Brussels 1959).

Delbrück, H., *A History of the Art of War within the Framework of Political History*, tr. W.J. Renfroe (Westport/London 1975).

Delisle, L., *Recherches sur la Librairie de Charles V*, 2 vols (Paris 1907).

Denholm-Young, N., 'The tournament in the thirteenth century', *Studies in Medieval History presented to F.M. Powicke*, ed. R.W. Hunt, W.A. Pantin, R.W. Southern (Oxford 1948).

— *The Country Gentry in the Fourteenth Century* (Oxford 1969).

— *History and Heraldry, 1254-1310* (Oxford 1965).

Dennis, Rodney, *The Heraldic Imagination* (London 1975).

Deuchler, F., (ed.), *Die Burgunderbeute und Werke Burgundischer Hofkunst* (Bernisches Historisches Museum, Bern, 1969).

Dillon, Viscount, 'Barriers and foot combats', *Archaeological Journal*, lxi (1904), pp. 276-308.

— 'On a MS collection of ordinances of chivalry of the fifteenth century, belonging to Lord Hastings', *Archaeologia*, lvii (1901), pp. 29-70.

— 'Ransom', *Archaeological Journal*, lxi (1904), pp. 102-19.

Dogaer, G. & Debae, F., *La Librairie de Philippe le Bon* (Brussels 1967).

Doutrepont, G., *La littérature française à la cour des ducs de Bourgogne* (Paris 1909).

— 'Jason et Gedéon, patrons de la Toison d'Or', *Mélanges Godefroid Kurth*, 2 vols (Liège-Paris 1908), ii, pp. 191-208.

Drouyn, L., *La Guienne Militaire* (Bordeaux-Paris 1865).

Dufournet, J., *La Destruction des Mythes dans les Mémoires de Philippe de Commynes* (Geneva 1966).

Durrieu, P., 'Les MSS à peinture de la bibliothèque … de Cheltenham', *BEC*, 1 (1889), pp. 386-404.

Durrieu, P., *La Miniature Flamande au temps de la cour de Bourgogne* (Brussels-Paris 1921).

Farmer, H.G., *Military Music* (New York 1950).

— *The Rise & Development of Military Music* (London 1912).

— 'Sixteenth & seventeenth-century military marches', *Journal of the Society for Army Historical Research*, xxviii (1950), pp. 49-53.

— 'The martial fife', ibid., xxiii (1945), pp. 66-71.

Ferguson, A.B., *The Indian Summer of English Chivalry* (Durham, North Carolina 1960).

Ffoulkes, C.J., *The Armourer and his Craft from the xith to the xvith century* (London 1912).

— 'Some aspects of the craft of the armourer', *Archaeologia*, lxxix (1929), pp. 13-28.

— 'On Italian armour from Chalcis in the Ethnological Museum at Athens', *Archaeologia*, lxii (1910), pp. 381-90.

— 'Armour from the Rotunda, Woolwich, transferred to the Armouries of the Tower, 1927', *Archaeologia*, lxxviii (1928), pp. 61-72.

Finò, J.F., *Forteresses de la France Médiévale* (Paris 1967).

Flutre, L., *Li Fais des Romans dans les littératures françaises et italiennes du xiiie au xve siècle* (Paris 1932).

Fuller, J.F.C., *Armament and History* (London 1946).

Gachard, P.L., 'Les livres du chancelier Hugonet', *Bulletin de la Commission Royale d'Histoire, ler sér.*, ii (1856), pp. 120-7.

Gaier, C., *L'Industrie et le Commerce des Armes dans les anciennes principautés belges du xiiie siècle à la fin du xve siècle* (Paris 1973).

— 'La cavalerie lourde en Europe occidentale du xiie au xvie siècle', *RIHM*, xxxi (1971), pp. 385-96.

— 'L'opinion des chefs de guerre français du xvie siècle sur les progrès de l'art militaire', ibid., xxix (1970), pp. 723-46.

Gailliard, J., *Inscriptions Funéraires et Monumentales de la Flandre Occidentale* 2 vols (Bruges 1861-3).

Genicot, L., 'La noblesse dans la société médiévale à propos des dernières études relatives aux terres d'Empire', *MA*, lxxi (1965), pp. 539-60.

Geyl, P., 'Huizinga as accuser of his age', *Encounters in History* (2nd ed., London 1967), pp. 188-237.

Gille, B., *Les Ingénieurs de la Renaissance* (Paris 1964).

Glénisson, J., 'Notes d'histoire militaire: quelques lettres de défi du xive siècle', *BEC*, cvii (1947-48), pp. 235-54.

Gombrich, E.H., *In Search of Cultural History* (Oxford 1969).

Guenée, B., 'La culture historique des nobles: le succés des *Faits des Romains* (xiiie-xve siècles)', *La Noblesse au Moyen Age*, ed. Contamine, P., (Paris 1976), pp. 261-88.

Guggisberg, H.R., 'Burckhardt und Huizinga', *Johan Huizinga, 1872-1945* (The Hague 1973), pp. 155-74.

Hale, J.R., 'War and public opinion in Renaissance Italy', *Italian Renaissance Studies*, ed. E.F. Jacob (London 1960).

— 'Fifteenth and sixteenth-century public opinion and war', *Past & Present*, xxii (1962), pp. 18-33.

— 'The early development of the Bastion: an Italian chronology', *Europe in the Late Middle Ages*, ed. J.R. Hale, J.R.L. Highfield & B. Smalley (London 1965), pp. 466-94.

— 'Gunpowder and the Renaissance', *From Renaissance to Counter-Reformation, Essays in Honour of Garret Mattingley*, ed. C.H. Carter (London 1966), pp. 113-44.

— 'Sixteenth-century explanations of war and violence', *Past & Present*, li (1971), pp. 3-26.

Hartshorne, A., 'Notes on collars of SS', *Archaeological Journal*, xxxix (1882), pp. 376-79.

Harvey, J., *The Black Prince* (London 1976).

Harvey, R., *Moriz von Craûn and the Chivalric World* (Oxford 1961).

Heers, J., *Fêtes, Jeux et Joûtes dans les sociétés d'Occident à la fin du Moyen Age* (Montreal/Paris 1971).

Hewitt, H.J., *The Organisation of War under Edward III, 1338-62* (Manchester 1966).

Henger, G.W., 'The metallography and chemical analysis of iron-base samples dating from Antiquity to modern times', *Bulletin of the Historical Metallurgy Group*, iv (1970), pp. 49-52.

Hexter, J.H., 'The education of the aristocracy in the Renaissance', *Reappraisals in History* (London 1961), pp. 45-70.

Hibbert, C., *Agincourt* (London 1964).

Hope, W. St. John, 'On a grant of arms under the great seal of Edward IV to Louis de Bruges, seigneur de la Gruthuyse and earl of Winchester, 1472', *Archaeologia*, lvi (1898), pp. 27-38.

— *The Stall-Plates of the Knights of the Order of the Garter, 1348-1485* (London 1901).

Howard, M., *War in European History* (Oxford 1976).

Hugenholtz, F.W.N., 'The fame of a masterwork', *Johan Huizinga, 1872-1945: Papers delivered to the Johan Huizinga Conference, Groningen, 11-15 Dec. 1972*, ed. W.R.H. Koops, E.H. Kossmann, G. van der Plaat (The Hague 1973), pp. 91-103.

Huizinga, J., *In the Shadow of Tomorrow* (London 1936).

— *The Waning of the Middle Ages*, tr. F. Hopman (Harmondsworth 1965).

— *Men and Ideas*, ed. J.S. Holmes, H. van Marle (London 1960).

— 'La valeur politique et militaire des idées de chevalerie à la fin du Moyen Age', *Revue d'histoire diplomatique*, xxv (1921), pp. 126-38.

— 'La physionomie morale de Philippe le Bon', *AB*, iv (1932), pp. 101-39.

— *Verzamelde Werken*, 8 vols (Haarlem 1948-53).

— *Homo Ludens* (London 1970).

— *Dutch Civilisation in the Seventeenth Century and other Essays*, ed. P. Geyl, F.W.N. Hugenholtz (London 1968).

Jacob, E.F., *Essays in Later Medieval History* (Manchester 1968).

Jacobsen, M.A., 'A Sforza miniature by Cristoforo da Preda', *Burlington Magazine*, cxvi (1974), pp. 91-6.

Jones, P., 'The target', in R. Hardy, *Longbow: a Social and Military History* (Cambridge 1976), pp. 204-8.

Kantorowicz, E.H., 'The Este portrait by Roger', *Selected Studies* (New York 1965), pp. 366-80.

— *The King's Two Bodies* (Princeton 1957).

Kauffman, C.M., 'The altar-piece of St George from Valencia', *Victoria and Albert Yearbook*, ii (1970), pp. 65-100.

Keegan, J., *The Face of Battle* (London 1976).

Keen, M.H., 'Chivalry, nobility and the man-at-arms', *War, Literature and Politics in the late Middle Ages*, ed. C.T. Allmand (Liverpool 1976), pp. 32-45.

— 'Huizinga, Kilgour and the decline of chivalry', *Medievalia et Humanistica*, vii (1977), pp. 1-20.

— *The Laws of War in the Late Middle Ages* (London 1965).

— & Daniel, M., 'English diplomacy and the sack of Fougères in 1449', *History*, lix (1974), pp. 375-91.

Kiernan, V.G., 'Foreign mercenaries and absolute monarchy', *Crisis in Europe, 1560-1660*, ed. T.H. Aston (London 1965), pp. 117-40.

Kilgour, R.L., *The Decline of Chivalry as shown in the French Literature of the late Middle Ages* (Cambridge, Mass. 1937).

Kipling, G., *The Triumph of Honour: Burgundian Origins of the Elizabethan Renaissance* (Leiden 1977).

Knecht, R.J., *Francis I and Absolute Monarchy* (London 1969).

Kohler, C., *Les Suisses dans les Guerres d'Italie, 1506-12* (Paris 1897).

Koops, W.R.H., Kossmann, E.H., Van der Plaat, G., (eds) *Johan Huizinga, 1872-1945: papers delivered to the Johan Huizinga conference, Groningen 11-15 Dec. 1972* (The Hague 1973).

Lacaze, Y., 'Le rôle des traditions dans la genèse d'un sentiment national au xve siècle: la Bourgogne de Philippe le Bon', *BEC*, cxxix (1971), pp. 303-85.

Laking, G., *A Record of European Arms and Armour through Seven Centuries*, 2 vols (London 1920).

La Marche, A. Leçoy de la, *Le Roi René*, 2 vols (Paris 1875).

Lannoy, Baudouin de, *Jean de Lannoy le Bâtisseur, 1410-1492* (Paris 1937).

Lathuillière, R., *Guiron le Courtois* (Geneva 1966).

Lebey, A., *Le Connétable de Bourbon, 1490-1527* (Paris 1904).

Lehrs, M., *Der Meister 'W.A.'* (Dresden 1895).

Lemarignier, J.F., *Recherches sur l'hommage en marche et les frontières féodales* (Lille 1945).

Lemoisne, P.A., *Les Xylographies du xive et xve siècles*, 2 vols (Paris/Brussels 1930).

Lewis, P.S., 'Une devise de chevalerie inconnue, créée par un comte de Foix? Le Dragon', *AM*, lxxvi (1964), pp. 77-84.

— *Later Medieval France: the Polity* (London 1968).

— 'Decayed and non-feudalism in later medieval France', *BIHR*, xxxvii (1964), pp. 161-74.

Lindner, A., *Der Breslauer Froissart* (Berlin 1912).

Lodge, E.C. *Gascony under English Rule, 1152-1453* (London 1926).

London, H. Stanford, *The Life of William Bruges, first Garter King of Arms* (Harleian Society, London 1970).

Lot, F., *L'art militaire et les armées au Moyen Age*, 2 vols (Paris 1946).

— *Recherches sur les effectifs des armées françaises des Guerres d'Italie aux Guerres de Religion, 1494-1562* (Paris 1962).

Mallett, M.E., *Mercenaries and their Masters: Warfare in Renaissance Italy* (London 1974).

Mandrot, B. de, *Les relations de Charles VII et de Louis XI avec les cantons suisses* (Zurich 1881).

Mann, J.G., *The Tomb and Funeral Achievements of Edward the Black Prince* (Canterbury 1972).

— 'Notes on armour of the Maximilian period and the Italian wars', *Archaeologia*, lxxix (1929), pp. 217-44.

— 'Notes on the armour worn in Spain from the 10th to the 15th century', *Archaeologia*, lxxxiii (1933), pp. 285-305.

— 'Notes on the evolution of plate armour in Germany in the 14th and 15th centuries', *Archaeologia*, lxxxvii (1934), pp. 69-97.

— 'The Sanctuary of the Madonna della Grazie, with notes on the evolution of Italian armour during the 15th century', *Archaeologia*, lxxx (1930), pp. 117-42.

— 'A further account of armour preserved in the Sanctuary of the Madonna della Grazie near Mantua', *Archaeologia*, lxxxvii (1937), pp. 311-52.

Marix, J., *Histoire de la Musique et des Musiciens de la cour de Bourgogne sous le règne de Philippe le Bon* (Strasbourg 1939).

Mathew, G., *The Court of Richard II* (London 1968).

— 'Ideals of knighthood in late fourteenth-century England', *Studies in Medieval History presented to F.M. Powicke*, ed. R.W. Hunt, W.A. Pantin, R.W. Southern (Oxford 1948), pp. 354-62.

McFarlane, K.B., 'The Wars of the Roses', *Proceedings of the British Academy*, 1 (1964), pp. 87-119.

McFarlane, K.B., *The Nobility of Later Medieval England* (Oxford 1973).

Meiss, M., *French Painting at the Time of John, duke of Berry: the Boucicaut Master* (London 1968).

— *Andrea Mantegna as Illuminator: an episode in Renaissance art, humanism and diplomacy* (New York/Hamburg 1957).

— 'A lost portrait of Jean de Berry by the Limburgs', *Burlington Magazine*, cv (1963), pp. 51-3.

Menestrier, C.F., *Origine des Armoiries* (Paris 1680).

— *Traité des Tournois, Joustes, Carrousels et autres spectacles publiques* (Lyon 1669).

Michaud, H., 'Les institutions militaires des guerres d'Italie aux guerres de religion', *RH*, cccccxiii (1971), pp. 29-43.

Mirot, L., 'La Messe du "Requiem" de Du Guesclin (1389)', *Revue des Questions Historiques*, xxvi (1903), pp. 228-33.

Mitchell, J.H., *The Court of the Connétable* (New Haven 1947).

Monfrin, J., 'Les Traducteurs et leur public en France au Moyen Age', *L'Humanisme Médiéval dans les littératures romanes du xiie au xive siècle*, (Paris 1964), pp. 247-64.

— 'Le goût des lettres antiques à la cour de Bourgogne au xve siècle', *Bulletin de la Société Nationale des Antiquaires de France*, (1967), pp. 285-9.

Morel, H., 'La fin du duel judiciaire en France et la naissance du point d'honneur', *Revue historique de droit français et étranger*, ive sér., xlii (1964), pp. 579-614.

— 'Une association de seigneurs gascons au quatorzième siècle', *Mélanges Halphen*, ed. F. Lot *et al.* (Paris 1951), pp. 523-6.

Morris, J.E., 'The archers at Crécy', *EHR*, xii (1897), pp. 427-36.

Nef, J.U., *War and Human Progress, c. 1494-c. 1640* (London 1950).

Nève, J., *Antoine de la Salle: sa vie et ses ouvrages* (Paris/Brussels 1903).

New Cambridge Modern History, i, ed. J.R. Hale (Cambridge 1957); ii, ed. G.R. Elton (Cambridge 1958).

Nicholas, D.M., *Town and Countryside: social, Economic and Political Tensions in Fourteenth-Century Flanders* (Bruges 1971).

Oman, C.W.C., *A History of the Art of War in the Middle Ages*, 2 vols (London 1924).

— *The Art of War in the Sixteenth Century* (London 1937).

O'Neill, B.J. St John, *Castles and Cannon* (Oxford 1960).

Pannier, L., *La noble maison de St-Ouen ... et l'Ordre de l'Etoile d'après les documents originaux* (Paris 1872).

Peine, S., *St Barbara, die Schutzheiliger der Bergleute und der Artillerie, und ihr Darstellung in der Kunst* (Freiberg 1896).

Perrett, P.M., *Histoire des relations de la France avec la Venise*, 2 vols (Paris 1896).

Piaget, A., 'Le Livre Messire Geoffroi de Charny', *Romania*, xxvi (1897), pp. 394-411.

Pickford, C.E., *L'Evolution du Roman Arthurien en Prose vers la fin du Moyen Age* (Paris 1960).

Pieri, P., 'Sur les dimensions de l'histoire militaire', *Annales*, xviii (1963), pp. 625-38.

Pitt-Rivers, J., 'Honour and social status', *Honour and Shame: the Values of Mediterranean Society*, ed. J.G. Peristiany (London 1965), pp. 19-77.

Planche, A., 'Du tournoi au theâtre en Bourgogne. Le Pas de la Fontaine des Pleurs à Châlon-sur-Saône, 1449-50', *MA*, lxxxi (1975), pp. 97-128.

Pope-Hennessy, J., *The Portrait in the Renaissance* (London/New York 1966).

Reiffenberg, F.A.T., Baron de, *Histoire de l'Ordre de la Toison d'Or* (Brussels 1830).

Ring, G., *A Century of French Painting, 1400-1500* (London 1949).

Ritter, R., *Châteaux, donjons et places fortes* (Paris 1953).

Robertson, G., *Giovanni Bellini* (Oxford 1968).

Roman, J., 'Le grand sceau de l'Ordre du Croissant', *Bulletin de la Société Nationale des Antiquaires de France*, lix (1897), pp. 183-6.

Rosenthal, E., 'The invention of the columnar device of the Emperor Charles V at the court of Burgundy in Flanders in 1516', *JWCI*, xxxvi (1973), pp. 198-230.

Ross, C.D., *Edward IV* (London 1974).

Runciman, S., *The Fall of Constantinople, 1453* (Cambridge 1965).

Russell, J.G., *The Field of the Cloth of Gold* (London 1969).

Ryder, A.J., 'The evolution of imperial government in Naples under Alfonso V', *Europe in the Late Middle Ages*, ed. J.R. Hale, J.R.L. Highfield & B. Smalley (London 1965), pp. 332-67.

Seward, D., *Prince of the Renaissance* (London 1974).

Smail, R.C., *Crusading Warfare (1097-1193)* (Cambridge, 2nd ed. 1976).

Southern, R.W., *The Making of the Middle Ages* (London 1959).

Spont, A., 'Marignan et l'organisation militaire sous François I', *Revue des questions historiques, nouv. sér.* xxii (1899), pp. 58-77.

Squibb, G.D., *The High Court of Chivalry* (London 1959).

Stein, H., *Charles de France* (Paris 1909).

Terlinden, le Vicomte, 'Les origines religieuses et politiques de la Toison d'Or' *PCEEBM*, v (1963), pp. 35-46.

Thomas, P., 'Mépris des nobles à l'égard de leurs inférieurs au xve siècle', *Revue du Nord*, xix (1933), pp. 230-2.

Thordeman, B., *Armour from the Battle of Wisby, 1361*, 2 vols (Stockholm, 1939).

Tomasi, G.L., *Ritratto del Condottiero* (Turin 1967).

Tourneur, V., 'Les origines de la Toison d'Or et la symbolique des insignes de celui-ci', *Bulletin de l'Académie Royale de Belgique. Lettres, 5e sér,* xlii (1956), pp. 300-23.

Tout, T.F., 'Firearms in England in the fourteenth century', *EHR,* xxvi (1911), pp. 666-88.

Trapp, Oswald Graf, & Mann, J.G., *The Armoury of the Castle of Churburg* (London 1929).

Trease, G., *The Condottieri* (London 1970).

Trevor-Roper, H.R., *The Rise of Christian Europe* (London 1965).

Vaivre, J.B. de, & Jequier, L., 'Elements d'héraldique médiévale: orientations pour l'étude et l'utilisation des armoriaux du Moyen Age', *Cahiers d'Héraldique,* i (Paris, 1974), pp. i-xxxiv.

Vale, M.G.A., 'A fourteenth-century order of chivalry: the *Tiercelet*', *EHR,* lxxxii (1967), pp. 332-41.

— 'The last years of English Gascony, 1451-1453', *TRHS,* 5th ser. xix (1969), pp. 119-38.

— *English Gascony, 1399-1453* (Oxford 1970).

— 'Sir John Fastolf's "report" of 1435', *Nottingham Medieval Studies,* xvii (1973), pp. 78-84.

— *Charles VII* (London 1974).

— *Piety, Charity and Literacy among the Yorkshire Gentry, 1370-1480* (Borthwick Papers No.50, York 1976).

Van Camp, G., 'Portraits de chevaliers de la Toison d'Or', *Bulletin des Musées royaux des Beaux-Arts de Belgique,* ii (1953), pp. 87-9.

Van Praet, L., *Recherches sur Louis de Bruges* (Paris 1831).

Vaughan, R., *Philip the Bold. The Formation of the Burgundian State* (London 1962).

— *John the Fearless* (London 1966).

— *Philip the Good* (London 1970).

— *Charles the Bold* (London 1973).

— *Valois Burgundy* (London 1975).

Verbruggen, J.F., 'La tactique militaire des armées de chevaliers', *Revue du Nord,* xxix (1946), pp. 164-8.

— 'L'art militaire en Europe occidentale du ixe au xive siècle,' *RIHM,* iv (1955), pp. 488-502.

— *The Art of Warfare in Western Europe during the Middle Ages,* tr. S. Willard & S.C.M. Southern (Amsterdam 1977).

Vinaver, E., *The Rise of Romance* (Oxford 1971).

Vindry, Fleury, *Dictionnaire de l'Etat Major français au xvie siècle,* 2 vols (Paris 1901).

Von Radowitz, J., *Die Devisen und Motto des späteren Mittelalters* (Stuttgart 1850).

Wagner, A.R., *Heralds and Heraldry in the Middle Ages* (2nd ed., Oxford 1964).

— *Heralds of England* (London 1967).

— 'Heraldry', in *Medieval England,* ed. A.L. Poole, 2 vols (Oxford 1958), i, pp. 338-81.

Warner, G.F., *Valerius Maximus. Miniatures of the School of Jean Fouquet* (London 1907).

Warner, P., *British Battlefields: the South* (London 1975).

— *British Battlefields: the North* (London 1975).

Weever, J., *Ancient Funeral Monuments* (London 1631).

Wiley, W.L., *The Gentleman of Renaissance France* (Harvard 1954).

Willard, C.C., 'Isabel of Portugal and the French translation of the "Triunfo de las Doñas" ', *Revue Belge de Philologie et d'Histoire*, xliii, II (1965), pp. 961-9.

— 'Isabel of Portugal: patroness of humanism?', *Miscellanea di studi e ricerche sul Quattrocento francese a cura di Franco Simone* (Turin 1966), pp. 532-45.

— 'The concept of true nobility at the Burgundian court', *Studies in the Renaissance*, xiv (1967), pp. 33-48.

Williams, A.R., 'Metallographic examination of 16th-century armour', *Bulletin of the Historical Metallurgy Group*, vi (1972), pp. 15-23.

— 'Medieval metalworking: armour plate and the advance of metallurgy', *The Chartered Mechanical Engineer*, Sept. 1978, pp. 109-14.

— 'Some firing tests with simulated 15th-century handguns', *Journal of the Arms and Armour Society*, viii (1974), pp. 114-20.

Wind, E., *Pagan Mysteries in the Renaissance* (London 1967).

Wright, N.A.R., 'The "Tree of Battles" of Honoré Bouvet', *War, Literature and Politics in the Later Middle Ages*, ed. C.T. Allmand, (Liverpool 1976), pp. 12-31.

Wys, R.L., 'Die neun Helden', *Zeitschrift für schweizerische Archaeologie und Kunstgeschichte*, xvii (1957), pp. 73-106.

Yates, F.A., 'Elizabethan chivalry: the romance of the Accession Day Tilts', *JWCI*, xx (1957), pp. 4-25.

— *Astraea. The Imperial Theme in the Sixteenth Century* (Harmondsworth 1977).

Index